RICE, RUPEES, AND RITUAL

RICE, RUPEES, AND RITUAL

Economy and Society Among the Samosir Batak of Sumatra

D. George Sherman

with the assistance of Hedy Bruyns Sherman

STANFORD UNIVERSITY PRESS 1990

Stanford, California

Stanford University Press

Stanford, California

Printed in the United States of America

CIP data appear at the end of the book

To Hedy

without whose nurturing and hard work
I would have been unable to do the research,
winnow the findings, and write this interpretation

Unang lupa ho ahu, ito.

Acknowledgments

I could not have written this book if it were not for the aid and long devotion of Hedy Bruyns Sherman. Her visible contributions—the accompanying drawings, figures, map designs, compiled statistics, botanical references, and many photographs—evidence only a small fraction of all her care and assistance.

I was also fortunate in receiving the aid and encouragement of many others. James T. Siegel introduced me to the ethnology of Island Southeast Asia and guided my study of culture and meaning. He and Davydd J. Greenwood, Bernd Lambert, and Benedict R. Anderson contributed many useful observations on earlier drafts (as did the anonymous reviewers). Along with Michael Meeker, A. Thomas Kirsch, O. W. Wolters, and Donald S. Pitkin, they were instrumental in forming my point of view. I of course take full responsibility for the uses to which I have put their teachings or suggestions.

Susan Rodgers, R. Griffin Coleman, P. Voorhoeve, D. van der Meulen, Michael R. Dove, Bruce Koppel, Tsuyoshi Kato, Neil Jamieson, and the late David H. Penny were generous with their knowledge. I am indebted to the Indonesian Council of Scientific Research (LIPI) and to my Indonesian sponsor, Dr. Taufik Abdullah, of the National Institute of Social and Economic Research (LEKNAS), who funded a field assistantship for a year of this study. Sue Rowe, Alan W. Smith, Frans and Julie Leenders, Janneka Frankena, Daniel and Nina Keller, and Margaret Bruyns provided shelter and other help.

Field research was made possible by a grant from the U.S. Department of Health, Education and Welfare under Title VI of the Fulbright-Hays Act, supplemented by the Cornell Southeast Asia Program and my parents. The East-West Center's postdoctoral fellowship program, administered by Glenn Shive, and the Resource Systems Institute, under director Seiji Naya, provided encouragement as well as financial and secretarial support and facilities for further research during the first rewriting, as did the Department of Anthropology of Dartmouth College during the final copyediting. Audrey Kahin and Benedict Anderson, who coedited the April 1980 issue of *Indonesia* in which most of Chapter 7 first appeared, helped greatly in clarifying the prose. Much credit for editing is also due to my editors at Stanford Press, William W. Carver and John Feneron, to their dedicated proofreader, Louise Herndon, and to Deborah Hodges.

The staffs of the School of Agriculture of the University of North Sumatra (USU), the Medan Teacher's Institute (IKIP), the Koninklijk Institut voor de Tropen (Amsterdam), the Rijksherbarium (Leiden), and the libraries of Cornell University, Amherst College, and the Universities of Singapore, Massachusetts, Hawaii at Manoa, and of Dartmouth College, were gracious and very helpful.

The text was laid out in Microsoft® Word 3.02 on a Macintosh™ SE. Thanks are due to Robert Brenstein, Jane Evans of the Personal Computer Center at Dartmouth College, Anton Anderson, for Figures 3.1 and 6.1, and Helen Mango, for Kroy lettering and map drawing.

In transcribing tape recordings of ritual oratory, I had the help of a very special informant, a drummer, who had been blind from early childhood. Drummers must listen to absolutely everything that is declaimed during dance-dedications at a feast, since they play punctuative tattoos (called 'reports to God') at significant pauses. This man had honed his power of hearing, to catch the words of feast orations amid the din, for seven years before he agreed to do the same with those I had recorded. My thanks to Pargonsi, the drummer, to the three young men who took on the demanding duties of field assistant, and to the many other villagers and the residents of the surrounding area, who were generous with their time, hospitable with their food and drink, and patient with their explanations.

D.G.S.

Contents

Maps and Figures

Maps

Figures

Tables

A Note on Pronunciation and Orthography

The best guide to pronunciation of Toba Batak words is that given by J. C. Vergouwen:

> The stress on a Batak word falls on the penultimate syllable whatever the length of the word, for example *dábu, dabu-dábu, dabu-dabúan, pardabu-dabuánon.* [Thus Samosir is pronounced "Samósir."] The 'e' in words such as *bere, dege, lehan,* etc., is pronounced as the vowel in break or eight. (1964:4)

In the contemporary spelling, "j" is pronounced "dj," as in jump.

The following convention has been adopted in citations of spoken Batak words or phrases that I recorded in writing or on tape: whether or not the original is cited parenthetically in the text, I have used double quotation marks (" ") to indicate a usage of my own in English that is not to be taken as a direct translation of Batak usage. Contrariwise, single quotation marks (' ') in my own expository text indicate my best efforts to give as direct a translation as possible of Batak usage, however much it may strain the English.

Quotation marks in reference to the statements of other writers are double when their words are cited directly. Single quotes are used for a close gloss of others' words and intention. Theoretical terms under discussion may also be in double or single quotes. In some cases the quotes are compounded simply to highlight a usage we tend to take for granted.

Further information on the Samosir dialect of Toba Batak may be found in Sarumpaet (1986).

RICE, RUPEES, AND RITUAL

Introduction

The area of northern Sumatra, Indonesia, called Samosir is a large 'island' in Lake Toba and the west coast of the lake crater, including a volcanic cone, Pusuk Buhit, whence the Toba Batak claim to have originated (see Map 1). The Bataks of Samosir had terraced much of the land for rice fields by the time they were colonized by the Dutch in 1906.

Among the most overt effects of colonial penetration are: the cessation of feuding; the conversion of many, though not the majority, of the villagers to one or another Christian denomination; the availability and attraction of education; outmigration; the vastly increased flow of goods (both import of manufactures and export of newly introduced crops and other goods); and the adoption of cash, not only for market transactions but also for many ritual prestations.[1]

This book addresses the questions of whether the set of values that largely shapes the local economy has been fundamentally changed by the widespread adoption of cash or, indeed, by any of the major, overt, social effects of colonial penetration, missionization, and subsequent Japanese and Indonesian administrations.

The Bataklands comprise one of the peripheral hinterlands that characterize the interiors of the islands of Sumatra, Borneo, and Sulawesi, as well as the mountain ranges—home of the so-called *montagnard* hill tribes—that divide the lowland rice plains of the mainland of Southeast Asia from one another. As Sahlins put it, "they are hinter-

[1]Prestation, as Mauss (1967 [1925]) used it, means, somewhat contradictorily, 'an obligatory gift.'

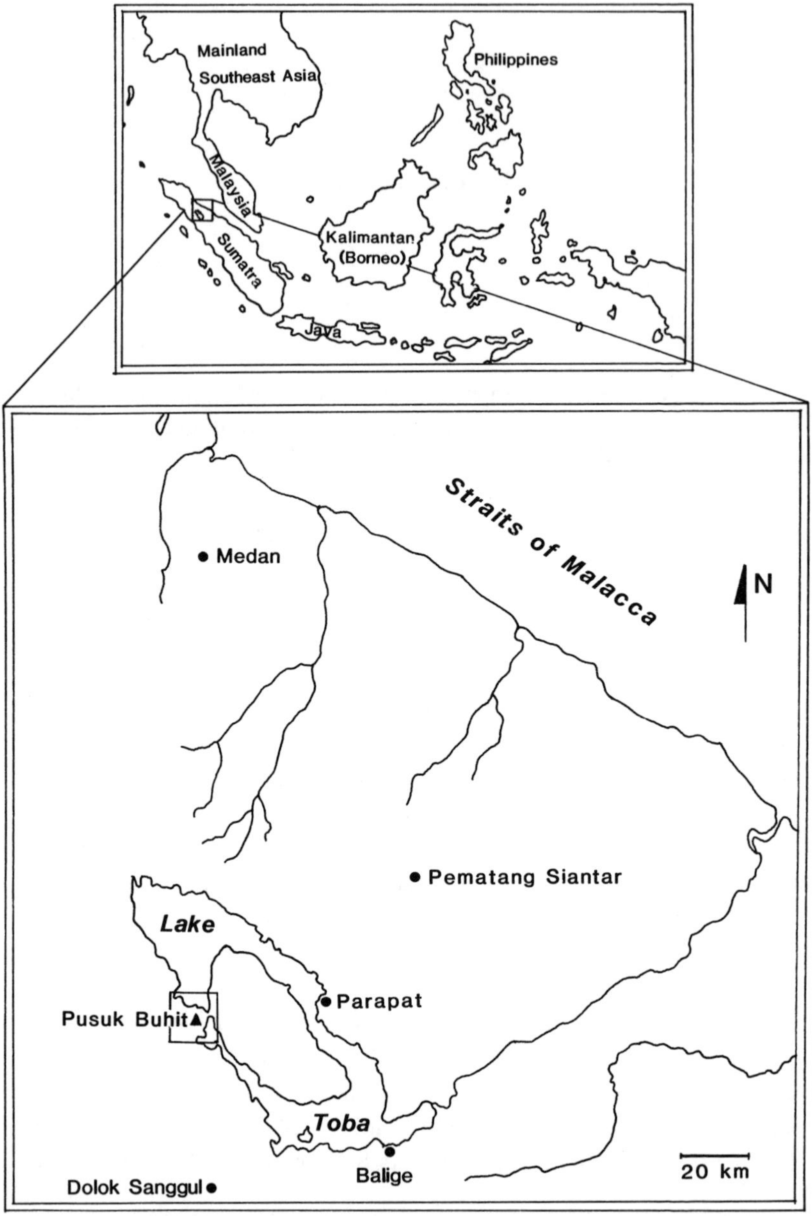

Map 1. The location of Samosir in Southeast Asia and the position of Pusuk Buhit.

lands engaged by petty market trade . . . to more sophisticated cultural centers" (1972:224). Historical evidence suggests that, for what are now Batak-speaking areas, this engagement may date back to the fifth century A.D. But where people once haggled in volumes of rice or bartered goods for goods, they now pay for things in bills and coins. In the earliest administrative report I found on the area, written in 1913, W. Middendorp noted that "trade is frequently barter for which rice is the medium of exchange, desired by the market women. As a result, the officials often complain that they can get no merchandise for their money." By contrast, women and men now accept nothing but money in markets. A complete changeover seems to have occurred. But what has happened is not as simple as it seems.

Money was, in fact, already being used by Samosir Batak. In the same report, the writer gives the 1913 prices, in guilders, for buffalo, cattle, pigs, and other livestock, and for woven cloaks or "blessing shawls." The question of why market women would refuse to take money for merchandise from Dutch officials cannot be answered out of hand.

One of the major frames of reference raised by considering the case at hand is the theory that in the changeover from barter of goods for goods or for rice to the barter of goods for cash, we are confronting a more momentous shift of the spread of the phenomenon of what Polanyi called "gain and profit made on exchange" (1944:43)—in a sense, of "capitalism." Putting the issue somewhat differently, there is a question here of whether "the profit motive," with its supposed corrosive individualism, has altered Batak society (or had it indeed already been altered when Bataks began exporting products in exchange for imports, which, even in precolonial times, included coins?). And, since money is now the only medium of marketplace exchange, has this or other aspects of its use affected social organization and values? In *The Great Transformation*, Polanyi implied that monetization did not necessarily entail a definitive shift to an economy based on such a "market principle" of "gain and profit made on exchange." He praises Aristotle for having maintained

> that gain was a motive peculiar to production for the market, and that the money factor introduced a new element into the situation, yet nevertheless, as long as markets and money were mere accessories to an otherwise self-sufficient household, the principle of production for use [dominating "production for exchange" in a "householding economy"] could operate. (1944:54)

J. H. Boeke, who coined the term "dual economy," on the other hand, believed that monetization did, in and of itself, have drastic effects:

> [W]e can no longer imagine the natural ties of the precapitalistic village. . . . Such a vigorous communal sense . . . was bound up with a type of village self-sufficiency which irrevocably came to its end with the penetration of a money economy. (Boeke 1966:308; cited in Keyes 1983)

It is significant that money in Samosir did not come to be used solely in place of barter of goods for goods. It came to be substituted for a pre-existing medium of exchange—namely, rice. What alterations of social organization and values can be attributed to this case of monetization?

An answer entails an interpretive ethnography based on a study of a unique but, one hopes, representative village. Of course, the ethnographic enterprise has many precedents, and any detailed micro-study of a single small village will reflect both the strengths and weaknesses of this traditional approach. It is useful to list the major weaknesses, eloquently described by Appadurai as "infirmities of [anthropological] practice":

> [1] the limits of human observation and scientific objectivism [including, as his discussion makes clear, the conceptual apparatus], [2] the hazards of the non-representativeness of our small objects of study, [3] the fiction of units of analysis that are isolable from one another, [4] the myth of complete and uniform culture-sharing within communities, [5] the illusion of the transparency of ethnography. (Appadurai 1986:759)

I proceed with these inevitable drawbacks very much in mind but held in abeyance (see Appendix A).

It is first necessary to establish a multifaceted baseline from which to assess social and cultural change, as will be done in Parts I and II.

Social forms can be viewed from a number of traditional anthropological perspectives, such as "kinship" and "class," and, perhaps most usefully, in terms of "the nature of Batak social hierarchy." A study of aspects of Batak cultural ecology and political economy perforce involves ethnological comparisons. As Donham puts it more generally, it is

> methodologically important to be aware of the family of possibilities contained in any congery of institutional arrangements [so as to] train attention . . . on distinctly local matters and conditions rather than *the* structure of [a given] political economy. (1985:271)

Clans, lineages, feuds, feasting, the "peace of the market," and other institutions were never unique to the Samosir Batak. They are, indeed, comparable with institutions of other hinterland peoples, and they often make use of trappings and vocabulary associated with lowland civilizations. (There are, according to J. Gonda [1952:62-66], some 175 Batak words, such as *raja* and *marga*, derived from Sanskrit. Others are from the Arabic lexicon, the Dutch, and, more recently, the English.)

Perhaps most prominent among the "family of possibilities" we need to raise are the Batak-Kachin analogies drawn by E. R. Leach (1966a). Leach was the first to point out that "matrilateral rotating connubia," marriage patterns in which men tend to marry women of their mothers' clans, are as characteristic of the Batak as of the Kachin. Leach claimed that in Kachin society, with its patrilineal clans, those who are wife-givers tend to essentially become feudal overlords of their "vassal," "tenant" wife-receivers (1965:78, 257). If so, of course, this would affect our understanding of the traditional shape of Samosir society, and also the implicit contrast with its present shape. One of my concerns is to test the feudal analogy, at least in the ethnographic present. Does inequality—the ritual superiority of wife-givers, who are also often those 'of the land'—entail class division?[2] Friedman (1975) maintains that class stratification is characteristic of

[2]See Kipp (1983) for a fine critique of Leach's position.

similar societies. Other, related views in the substantivist tradition associated with the work of Karl Polanyi hold that such stratification has come about with the commoditization of land and labor, as a result of the adoption of money.[3]

In Part IV, I will compare differential access to resources or factors of production—land, labor, livestock, and others—on the basis of clan membership with access based on age and available household labor.

Before reconstructing the process of monetization, in Parts I, II, and III, it is necessary to expand on three interpretive frameworks that will be used in the analysis. The first two bring the discussion quite emphatically into the formalist-substantivist debate (Dalton 1961; Cook 1966):

the role of rice in the Batak economy,
the role and political economy of feasting in such societies, and
the cultural ecology of dry- and flooded-field rice-growing.

The role of rice in the Batak economy. While rice has a ubiquitous and sometimes central place in any Asian society, one would not expect its role to be identical, or to be given identical expression, from one society to the next.

In spite of any differences, Marshall Sahlins (1965) proposed that the export of rice by the Iban and Dayak of Borneo, the Lamet of Indochina, and, by implication, the Batak of Sumatra made them "distinctive" from ancient times "for unusual external relations—unusual, that is, in a strictly primitive milieu." The gist of his argument is that these societies are of a "type in which balanced exchange, if not exactly dominant, acquires unusual prominence." They lack the purportedly typical progression from "generalized exchange" (free give-and-take) among closely related people, "balanced" among those not related, and "negative" (i.e., stealing, cheating, raiding) among those from distant areas. Sahlins maintains that such Southeast Asian societies

> are hinterlands engaged by petty market trade . . . to more sophisticated cultural

[3]See, e.g., Polanyi (1957, chap. 6); Bohannan (1955, 1967); Sahlins (1960); Wolf (1963); Scott (1976).

> centers. From the perspective of the advanced centers, they are backwaters serving as secondary sources of rice and other goods. . . . From the hinterlands view, the critical aspect of the intercultural relation is that the subsistence staple, rice, is exported for cash, iron tools, and prestige goods, many of the last quite expensive. . . . (Sahlins 1972:224; 1965:178f.)

This is unexceptionable, but what strikes Sahlins as "critical" is that they export rice. He reasons that, therefore,

> the engagement with the market makes a key minimal demand: that internal community relations permit household accumulation of rice. . . . The fortunate households cannot be responsible for the unfortunate [or] the external trade relations are simply not sustained. (loc. cit.)

Sahlins draws six "consequences" from the lack of sharing, which is "decreed by export" of rice:

> (1) Different households, by virtue of variations in ratio and number of effective producers, amass different amounts of the subsistence-export staple. . . . These differences, however, are not liquidated in favor of need [i.e., there is no "generalized exchange"]. Instead (2) the intensity of sharing within the village . . . is low, and (3) the principal reciprocal relation between households is a closely balanced exchange of labor service. . . . Balanced labor-exchange . . . maintains the productive advantage . . . of the family with more adult workers. The only goods that customarily move in generalized reciprocity are game and perhaps . . . animals sacrificed. . . . (4) Even household commensality may be rigidly supervised, subjected to accounting . . . in the interest of developing an exchange reserve, hence less sociable than ordinary primitive commensality. . . . (5) Restricted sharing . . . finds its social complement in an atomization and fragmentation of community structure. . . . Large local descent groups are absent or inconsequential. . . . (6) Prestige apparently hinges on obtaining exotic items—Chinese pottery, brass gongs, etc.—from the outside in exchange for rice or work. Prestige does not, obviously cannot, rest on generous assistance to one's fellows in the manner of a tribal big-man. . . . As a result, there are no strong leaders. . . . (Sahlins 1972:225-226)

Sahlins prefaced these suggestions with the caution that he offered them "with all the deference of one who has had no field experience in the area." This was laudable, since his analysis departs significantly from several commonly accepted viewpoints.

Take the last of these, consequence number 6. The first thing that might occur to many readers is the contrary example of Leach's depiction of the Kachin *gumsa*, "autocratic chiefs," trying to imitate Shan princes. Their positions are no more nor less heritable than the positions of Melanesian big men, but they nevertheless rose to power and were "strong leaders" for longer or shorter periods.

Or, take number 5, "restricted sharing . . . [with] large local descent groups . . . absent or inconsequential." One can argue that in hinterland societies made up of 'clans' (groups whose members cannot marry each other), "large local descent groups" are neither "absent" nor "inconsequential." There are, for example, in the tree-like patrilineal Batak genealogy a few hundred clans, but with total membership of over a million.

There is, however, something that seems to capture Batak, as well as non-unilineal Ifugao, social reality in Sahlins' characterization, "atomization and fragmentation of community structure." In later chapters, I will speak to this and to each of the presumed consequences of rice export in turn.

The merit of Sahlins' analysis of rice's role in hinterland political economies is that he appraises what might be termed "the cultural-ecological nature" of rice as one key to understanding the "distinctive" character of hinterland societies and, it might be argued, in some ways, of all Asian societies. Each ethnic group, presumably, has a distinct figuration of the value of this preferred staple, but they tend to share a common lexicon out of which the figures of speech are drawn. Hence, we can say that there is a distinct, millennia-old, civilization-wide, cultural ecology of rice-growing. How else explain Georges Condominas' assertion that rice "remains unchallenged as the principal food of almost all Southeast Asian populations, to whom *a shortage of it is tantamount to famine*, even if other food plants are available" (1980:246, emphasis added)? How else explain that for the Ifugao of northern Luzon, the Philippines, it is "a shameful matter . . . not to eat rice. . . . [A man] lowers himself if he plants a sweet-potatoe garden"? Yet, as Brosius, who cites this observation (from Villaverde

1909), points out, over half the Ifugao diet is of sweet potatoes (1983:2-3). An analogous situation is found among the Batak, with respect to both tubers and corn, and much the same could be documented in many ethnographies. One would have to search far to find a society in this area where any starch but rice is thought fit to serve at a feast. Ecologist Otto Soemarwoto (1983) has even argued that the promotion of "green revolution," high-yielding varieties of rice in Indonesia reinforces what he calls "the strong and enduring social value placed on rice."

The role and political economy of feasting. This brings me to the second major interpretive framework I wish to discuss here: the role of feasting in economic analyses of such societies. Sahlins' claim that there is "restricted sharing" must be related to the role of feasting or, more accurately, to whatever model we employ of feasting. Series of feasts are described in the literature on numerous hinterland Southeast Asian peoples. They are clearly of a type that has many exemplars, across the world, from nearby Melanesia to the northwest coast of America and the Amazon Basin. Indeed, there is a commonly argued viewpoint that, for Southeast Asian societies, "feasts of merit" or "feasts of honor" serve as mechanisms of redistribution, leveling wealth differences (Stevenson 1943; Leach 1965) and guaranteeing subsistence (Scott 1976). I will later explain why Sahlins was wise to avoid subscribing to that view—which of course was precluded by his considering the export potential of rice to encourage hoarding.

I will devote a good part of the presentation in later chapters to feasts. Much that is done in them involves what are to some degree calculated, economic transactions, and similar feast systems have been referred to by a number of theorists, including Sahlins, as driving production, as incentives for producing surplus—and hence, as serving political-economic functions. An assessment of the extent and significance of monetization depends in part on one's model of the nature of "traditional" feasting. It will determine one's assessment of the degree of change in feasting and thus of the effects of monetization.

In my view, a salient similarity between the organizations of highland Southeast Asian communities and those of the lowland plains communities of the major river systems of Southeast Asia is that, as Popkin writes of Vietnam,

> the system of feasts, far from leveling inequality or exhausting all the wealthy, barred many peasants from high positions. . . . It was common for a man to go heavily into debt in order to finance the feasts required of those hoping to rise in the village ranking system. (1979:99)

I also agree that "village procedures were not progressively redistributive" (Popkin 1979:61) and that the redistribution view of feasting, along with other related theories, leads to "a view of commercialization and market development as the peasant's fall from grace" (ibid.:63-64). In the views of James Scott, Eric Wolf, and others, commercialization of village agriculture has been by nature detrimental to indigenous, non-Western cultures. I would prefer to take each case as it comes. Among the principles of the universalistic, "moral economy" school of thought that Popkin enumerates (1979:7-12) are the following: (1) capitalism turns land, labor, and wealth into commodities (a proposition that is difficult but not impossible to maintain for the Batak case); (2) the peasant keeps the market at arm's length (a proposition that, with caveats, could be applied to Batak villagers); (3) there is a guarantee of minimal subsistence in village society (one that I will argue never could have applied); and (4) following C. Geertz's idea of "agricultural involution," there is a minimization of socioeconomic contrasts, of economic inequality, through work sharing (which again for the Batak could only have applied with difficulty and not at all by comparison to Java—if indeed it ever applied there).[4]

Popkin argues that village institutions "work less well than [moral economists] maintain . . . because of conflicts between individual and group interests" and that "more attention must be paid to motivations for personal gain" (ibid.:17). This last point is reminiscent of Foster's view of universal peasant "extreme individualism" (1967), which, in putting perceptions entirely in our terms, leads to ethnocentric judg-

[4]Cf. Alexander and Alexander 1982; Dove 1985a.

ments. One is then at a loss to understand how, for instance, "propaganda" drawing on "legends and nationalist feelings" could have "spread through the country [of Vietnam]" (Popkin 1979:218) and have served to help rally the National Liberation Front against the French and later the Americans.

Popkin may overstate the case as involving a drive for individual status as opposed to a kind of group prosperity and well-being—what Kirsch (1973) called "ritual efficacy." A further argument of his, however, does pinpoint a serious weakness of "moral economy" views—namely, that the "extensive use of credit and interest rates in precapitalist village society contradicts moral economy predictions" (1979:53). Indeed, some of the key facts Sahlins overlooked are that rice is often borrowed and repaid, both with interest and without. The relevance of these facts to the political economy of feasting will be brought out in due course. Here, I turn to the third area of theoretical outlook and analysis that is tied to a concern with the changing relations of rice and cash.

The cultural ecology of dry- and flooded-field rice. The agricultures practiced in Southeast Asia are usually grouped under two headings: swidden (shifting, slash-and-burn) cultivation of dry fields and *sawah* (wet-rice cultivation on irrigated terraces). Geertz's *Agricultural Involution* (1963) gives one of the best general descriptions of the pure forms of these types. He points out that wet rice in Indonesia is found mainly on the "inner" islands of Java and Bali and swidden agriculture mainly on "outer" islands such as Borneo, Sumatra, and Sulawesi. Yet the dichotomy is difficult to apply to three major ethnic groups of the northern half of Sumatra—the Minangkabau, the Achehnese, and the Batak—who all cultivate flooded-field rice. In addition, it ignores dry-field grassland farming, which is widely practiced by Toba and other Bataks.

I came to more fully appreciate the role of rice in the village and regional economies of Samosir as the result of my own findings and with the help of archival materials. While in the village, I devoted much effort to studying rice production as a major facet of the agricultural economy, in part because of the unusual methods of cultivation in supposedly unfarmable *Imperata* grassland, to be described in Part III.

Another aspect of the cultural ecology of rice that will be brought out is its role in the frequent rituals, as food, as gift, and as blessing medium. Since I found land, livestock, other prestige goods, and cash used as gifts in rituals and since on many occasions rice was also given in that way, I argue that the "social value of rice" is far more central to Batak culture than Sahlins' outlook could possibly manage to convey—that focusing on the traditional potential of exporting it does not go nearly far enough.

Some of the pertinent views of historical materialists are also relevant to the cultural ecology. It is probably impossible to refute claims that the system of beliefs and values (or more accurately, the amalgam of such systems), the "culture" of any given "society," is mere "ideology," "false consciousness." Theorists who hold this view claim that, although ideology may motivate action, it cannot explain the determined political and economic relationships—master and slave, merchant and market-goer, tax collector and peasant—through which the members of a historically specific society are constrained to act (see Bloch 1975:211). Meillassoux, for example, writes that the political authority in a "domestic community"

> must, to be preserved, devise and develop a coercive and authoritarian ideology. Religion, magic ritual, and a terrorism based on superstition is inflicted upon dependents, young people and above all on pubescent women. (Meillassoux 1981:45)

Indeed, as Meillassoux argues, women and "juniors" can be viewed as oppressed in domestic agricultural communities, and, as he also argues, such communities can be considered snared in the toils of a worldwide class system, in the service of which they provide sources of cheap export commodities or wage migrants, whose cost of reproduction is borne by their genitors to the profit of the system that employs their "cheap labour." But if the widespread and idiosyncratic features of a given community and their internal consistency as a cultural system are ignored, then we are at a loss to explain that, although it is "oppressed, divided, counted, taxed, [and] recruited, the domestic community totters but still resists . . . under the crushing weight of imperialism" (ibid.:87). Yet Meillassoux is forced to admit that "domestic relations of production have not disappeared completely. They still support millions of productive units integrated to a greater or lesser degree in the capitalist economy" (loc. cit.).

Meillassoux would not consider the Batak community described herein to exemplify his ideal "domestic community." In his view, such communities exist only when they interact solely with other similar communities, and a great deal to the contrary will be described. In fact, it appears that the minted currencies of Western states and trading corporations were used in ceremonial exchange even before the Dutch colonized Samosir. And at present, as in many other societies, cash is a prime component of bridewealth. But for Meillassoux,

> When money . . . replaces local matrimonial goods in marriage transactions, then for their keepers, women become equivalent to livestock, and marriage to the lease of livestock by which women's reproductive abilities are loaned out. (1981:74)

My rejection of such views will be presented in due course. I will, however, have recourse to a number of components of Meillassoux's model of the "domestic community," to such cultural ecological features as sedentism, primary reliance on cereal agriculture, social positions based on "the juridical-ideological relations of kinship," age, and gender, which closely parallel aspects of Batak society. Yet it seems pointless to conclude, as he does, that through contact with the capitalist mode of production, the domestic mode "is simultaneously maintained and destroyed . . . both exists and does not exist" (ibid.:97).

It exists, period. And this book chronicles the life of one such community. The work also seeks to develop an alternative viewpoint that will help form a better understanding of the continuing bases of that life, an understanding that lies in appreciating the bases for the integrity and resilience of Batak culture.

Although the village on which the study focuses is unique, it is the basis for generalizations on the agricultural system and economy of the

Samosir area (which is part of a larger region of about one million Toba-Batak language speakers). The reader should bear in mind that when I write of "the Batak" or "the Toba" or "Samosir Batak," without specific reference to sources other than my field notes, I am generalizing from the activities, life histories, and expressive speech and ritual of a sample village population. The book is in five parts:

I. Environment and history.
II. Sociocultural effects of colonial penetration.
III. Agriculture and trade.
IV. Access to resources: labor and land in interpreting the economy.
V. Modeling Samosir Batak economy.

Throughout, I will refer to the extent and significance of monetization and of class and hierarchy that have been raised in this Introduction. In the concluding chapters, I will readdress these issues directly and examine the persistence of Samosirese values from the standpoint of the role of rice in the economy, with the groundwork of the cultural and agricultural systems as a point of departure.

PART I

ENVIRONMENT AND HISTORY

As is true anywhere in the world, there is much about the human ecology of Samosir, north Sumatra, that does not meet the eye. As soon as one attempts to describe what does, one is forced to refer to that which does not. The first chapter concerns deceptive appearances. I describe the place of the village of Huta Ginjang, the environment, and the area's demography. I then give an account of Dutch-induced agricultural change, the first of several indictments of colonial policies for the Samosir microcosm of the larger Dutch experiment in what is now Indonesia.

The second chapter expands on the historical background of the area and on the changes imposed by the Dutch and those resulting from their influence, particularly regarding monetization.

Chapter 1

Deceptive Appearances: Environment, Demography, and Agricultural Change

The hamlet cluster on which this study is based is called Huta Ginjang, 'top village.' It lies some 3 degrees north of the Equator, perched about two miles up the north side of Pusuk Buhit, 'Mount Navel,' a dormant volcano that connects Samosir 'island' (actually a vast peninsula in Lake Toba) to the body of Sumatra (see Map 2). The nearly 600 inhabitants of the village share a single spring for all water they use domestically.

Generally the climate of Sumatra is characterized as being of "equatorial monsoon" type. Samosir has the most pronounced dry season of all Sumatra, since it lies in a highland crater, from which the surrounding landmass slopes down to the encircling seas (see Map 1). In the dry season, the winds blow in, often with incredible and repeated gusts, from the southwest and from the west. They may start as early as April and continue well into October. Beginning in July, the wind often blows constantly, day and night, at some 50 miles an hour, with gusts up to 80 miles an hour.

At times one gazes out over the parched expanse of the northern half of Samosir 'island' and imagines that if only its clayey whiteness were a dark tree-green, the misty clouds that hover around the lake at the edges of the crater would somehow yield a bounteous wet rain rather than the mistlike drizzle that never penetrates the ground more than an eighth of an inch. After a three-week blow, the wind lets up and gives way to scorching hot, clear days with only a rare puff of cloud in sight. Then, just as it seems that enough of these rare puffs are appearing

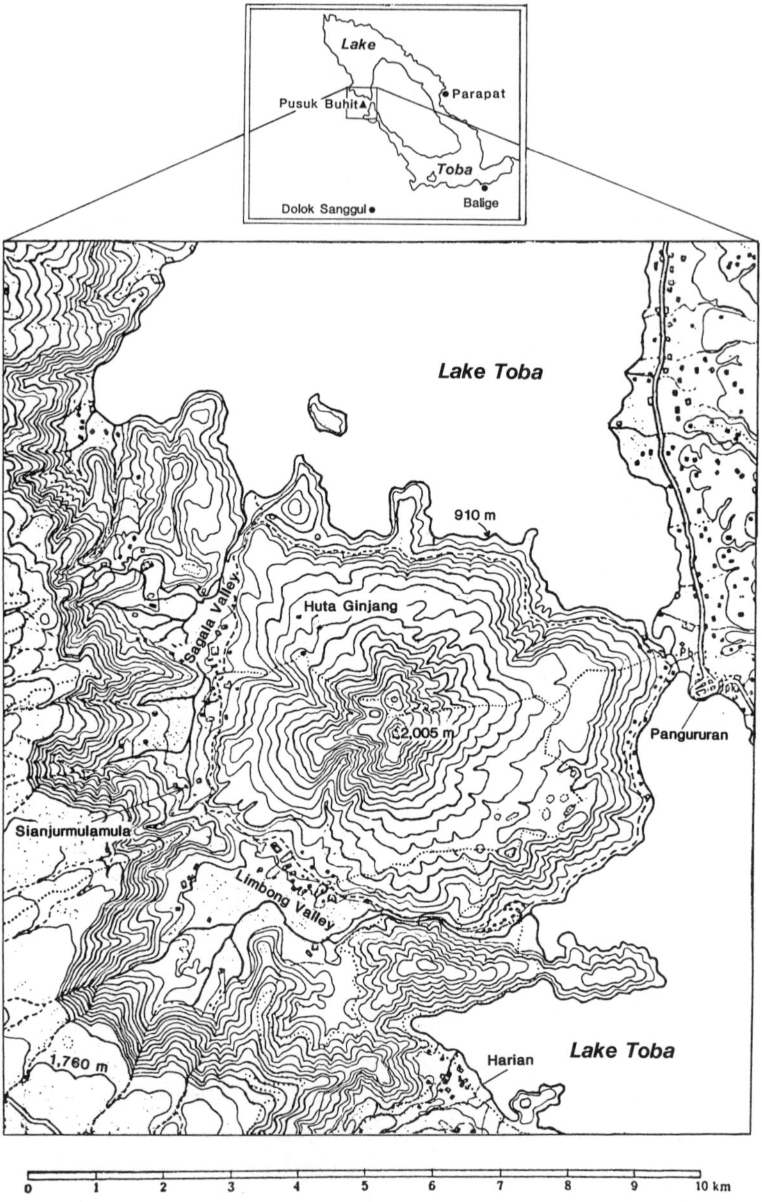

Map 2. Mount Pusuk Buhit, with Sagala and Limbong Valleys and Huta Ginjang.

TABLE 1.1
Monthly Variation of Rainfall (mm)

Jan.	Feb.	Mar.	Apr.	May	June	July	Aug.	Sept.	Oct.	Nov.	Dec.
215	162	178	162	120	57	45	40	155	172	195	180

SOURCE: Oerlemans 1937.

to give rise to a real thunderhead or two, the wind starts up again, and what had seemed to be clouds reveal themselves to have been apparitions dissipating into the mist-bearing collar that sits, apparently immobile, hugging the upper edges of the lake crater in uncanny defiance of the wind. The sky turns white, and another three-week blow begins. So it goes, alternately, from May through September, primarily between June and August.

The seasonal oscillation of rainfall recorded between 1922 and 1928 by the Dutch administrators at Pangururan, the town at the point where the mountain and island are joined, can be seen in Table 1.1.

Mt. Pusuk Buhit in the early dry season, from the north. Huta Ginjang lies half-way up on the right. Farmers' fields extend beyond far upper left puff of smoke.

Whereas in the dry season, during the stretches of overcast gale winds, the sun often does not break through the cloud cover, much of the "rainy season" is actually sunny for most of the morning and afternoon, except for an hour's downpour toward the evening. Parts of the rainy season are, then, much hotter than parts of the dry season.

From its vantage point halfway up the mountain, Huta Ginjang overlooks the north end of Samosir and, to the west, the raised, stream-fed bowl of Sagala Valley (invisible from the lake or from Samosir Peninsula), that has one bottleneck egress lying between the mountain and the lake-crater wall that encircles both. In 1933, J. C. Vergouwen referred to this area as the "out-of-the-way mountain territory of Sagala."[1] Numerous other isolated, well-watered valleys nestle in the crevices of the vast crater enclosing the lake. What makes for Sagala's apparent isolation is that it is not a thoroughfare and is divided from the lake by a long-solidified shoulder of the mountain. To the south, it is cut off from its proper extension, Limbong Valley, by another shoulder of Pusuk Buhit. (Two of the grandsons of the first man, Si Raja Batak, were named Limbong Mulana and Sagala Raja.)

Sagala Valley from the north. A school roof visible at right, below concrete tombs.

[1]Vergouwen (1964:255). A discussion of his remarks on what he thought extraordinary marriage practices in Sagala is found in Sherman (1982:324-325).

Pusuk Buhit seen from the northwest, in the early dry season, June 1978.

Hundreds of tourists each year pass within 5 kilometers of the village on "round-the-island" diesel steamer tours and do not see it. Its existence is signaled by what appears to be a tiny clump of trees in the vast, seemingly barren and uninhabitable expanse of brush and savannah that cloaks the mountain. A keen eye may note the darker brown of cultivated areas of level stone terraces, an occasional puff of smoke from some distant shoulder (the sign of a raging savannah fire), or the deeper green that sets off ripening rice in scattered, minimally terraced patches high on the mountain. But even the ubiquitous terraces of the mountain's middle and lower reaches are normally hidden from sight by brush and *Imperata* grass cover, at least until a boat reaches the canal at Pangururan and passes through the land bridge that connects the mountain to the Samosir peninsula. There, the terraces covering the lower half (as high as the eye can see) are in almost constant use, and at seasons when most are planted, the mountainside resembles a wall of stone.

Water and Settlement Patterns

Sianjurmula-mula, the purported site of the original Batak hamlet and home of the first man, Si Raja Batak, is at the southern end of

Sagala Valley, at the foot of the spur connecting the mountain to the high plateau that extends west from the lip of the crater. It was on our way to visit it that my wife, Hedy, and I happened on the village of Huta Ginjang.

Ultimately, the existence of this village may be attributed to the fortuitous occurrence of a spring on the northwest flank of the mountain. Water is carried to the houses throughout the year by women and girls, who imitate the carrying of buckets from the time they learn to walk. Villagers bathe, wash clothes, and get water for household use at a divided bathing place with three pipes below a small holding tank. Two pipes go into the women's compartment and one into the men's, since some women and girls need water for domestic purposes while others are bathing or washing clothes. No water is piped for household use to any of the hamlets because many are afraid that the flow would not be sufficient to meet the needs of washing, etc., and they therefore refuse to invest in pipe. In the dry season the downstream bed of the brook is parched for months, because all the "excess" water is diverted for irrigation.

The area on the southern flank of the mountain contrasts with Huta Ginjang on its north. It was never even settled in the traditional walled-hamlet pattern, because of the lack of year-round springs. Some 200 scattered houses built there in the recent past have rectangular concrete water tanks with a capacity of 2,000 to 3,000 gallons of water fed by gutters that run around the edge of the roofs.

Until this century, Sumatra's coastal lowlands had much lower population densities than the interior highlands. In 1824, on a journey to what is now the site of the regional capital, Tarutung, the missionaries Burton and Ward, after scaling the escarpment on the Indian Ocean side of Sumatra, were astounded to find a long, broad valley of wet-rice terraces between grass-covered hills.

Why were population densities greater in the highlands? In addition to Batak fear that the spirits thought to cause tropical diseases are more prevalent in the lowland areas and to their dislike of the heat and humidity of those areas, it may be that over the course of many centuries the denizens of the coastal areas grew averse to their exposure to the levying of taxes and demands of fealty by coastal/riverine patrols emanating from Śrivijaya and other maritime powers that controlled the sea-lanes. A trend to move upland, away from the coast, may have developed. Lower temperatures and less rain in the mountains would also have favored the deforestation so necessary to high population densities, because forest would not retake clearings as quickly as under moister conditions. In particular, the pronounced dry season of the Samosir region would have inhibited regrowth of secondary forest, and lake fish would have helped assure settlers a reliable source of protein. At the same time, the perennial springs could be exploited for irrigating rice.

Dutch data on Samosir population, based on the counts of village headmen who were expected to collect and pay taxes for those under their jurisdiction, might be underreported. In 1913 there were 78,169 Samosirese (40,187 males and 37,982 females) in 2,236 hamlets (Middendorp 1913:13). By 1931, the number had risen to 96,267. The chief administrator (Dutch, *Controleur*) at the time remarked that "emigration is hardly taking place" (van Bemmelen 1931:13-14). Although much out-migration has since occurred, the Indonesian government reported the 1980 population as 126,696. These and other data are shown in terms of density in Table 1.2.[2]

The density of over 500 persons per square mile far exceeds the densities reported for forest shifting cultivators (Conklin [1957:10] reports a range of 65-91 for the Hanunóo; Freeman [1970:133], a range of 52-65 for the Iban; Dove [1985:381], 30 persons per square mile for the Kantu'; Hanks [1972:57], an average of 31 persons per

[2]See Biro Pusat Statistik (1957:18) and Biro Pusat Statistik (1971:18). I am using the data for the *kecamatan* (subdistricts) of Simanindo, Pangururan, Harian, Onan Runggu, Palipi. Calculating the population density depends on which figure one accepts for the area of the Samosir region (see Sherman 1980, note 1; 1982, map 2.5). According to Joustra (1910:8), the 'island' is 766 km^2 and the west lake coast areas some 400 km^2. However, Oerlemans (1937:1) takes exception to these figures, reporting that the forester of Tarutung records the total area of Samosir as 644 km^2. I am using this latter figure, which includes both peninsular and west coast Samosir. According to a recent article by Sarumpaet (1986:73), the "island" is 520 km^2.

TABLE 1.2
Density of Samosir's Population and Increments per Year

Year	Persons per km²	Persons per mile²	Percent increase/year
1907	110	285	-
1913	121	313	1.8%
1926	134	347	0.8
1931	149	386	2.3
1956	182	471	0.9
1970	186	482	0.2
1980	196	507	0.5

square mile based on six cases). However, from the area of fallow terraces one sees in Samosir, the population may have been even higher at times in the precolonial past. This would explain the exaggerated claim, often made by educated, city Batak, that Samosir, or their lake-region homeland generally, has been deserted by all but the very old and the very young. The notion of near-total abandonment of the Toba homeland has a strong and pernicious hold, perhaps because quite a number of young men become emigrants for varying lengths of time. Yet, as will be shown, in spite of adverse climatic and other environmental factors, the people maintain a firm foothold and finance a variety of means of more or less successful outmigration in agriculture, trade, and education.

Illusions of Timelessness in the Landscape

Most accounts of Batak agriculture highlight the feats of engineering of their irrigation systems, but mention of the equally impressive, rain-dependent, dry-field terracing, so much in evidence in the Samosir area, is rare. All around Mount Pusuk Buhit and in the valleys on the west, north, and east sides of the lake, as on the east side of Samosir, the earth on which terraces were built appears to be more

A farmer (bent over, 6 terraces up from the bottom), his son (to the right, 7 up), and daughter (center, 9 up) prepare an irrigable field for dry-season bulb planting.

Five-foot-high terraces in a non-irrigable mulched garlic field. Cassava is growing on the edges of the walls. Man and wife visible in lower left corner. Proximity to the hamlets inhibits burning in this area, hence the brush. Foreground: Imperata.

than half stone, much of it boulders. A tremendous amount of effort and skill was required to transform the terrain into the humanized landscape it now presents to the eye.

Contemporary villagers remain expert rock-wall builders. Steepness of slope never appears to prevent terracing, either for irrigated fields or for dry. In long-fallow areas, walls are completely dismantled when a field is reworked. They are also built around some fields next to cattle paths, and in the past walls were built between certain clan areas. Running up the western side of Mount Pusuk Buhit, from the point at which the Sagala and Limbong Valleys come closest to joining, is a wall of boulders, surrounded on both sides by deep drainage ditches. Its purpose was said to have been not to keep cattle in but to prevent attacks by horse-mounted riders!

It is easy to imagine that, except for terracing, walls, and irrigation ditches, the landscape of the Toba Lake crater is the product of traditional agriculture in conjunction with natural causes and to assume that where the earth appears scarred by erosion, the terrain has been exploited in a prodigal manner because it is "so deforested." But the appearance of parts of the area has other causes, including mining of sulfur, of stone for road-building, and even of earth for production of china.

Another example of the difficulties of taking the landscape of this area to be comprehensible to the naked eye involves what may be termed "reclamation." D. van der Meulen writes that in 1915 or so, when he was an administrator in the area, Dutch engineers undertook to create additional lakeside fields: "The Batu Bongbong [Hindering Stone], the threshold in the Asahan River, just at its outlet from the lake [of which it is the sole drain], was flattened with dynamite, by which the lake surface was substantially lowered" (van der Meulen 1977:57).

> For administration this meant . . . a sudden aggravation of civil law. Wholesale quarrels over land rights [in newly exposed lakeside fields] arose and if the administrators delayed with their decisions then men fought it out. Bataks . . . stood there generally up to their knees in the thick mud. We were carried out on crude sedan-chairs to a higher spot. (ibid.:55-56)

A further instance of introduced change was the Dutch program of reforestation, which has been continued by the Indonesian government. The reports of Dutch Controleurs invariably refer to the fact that very little of the primary forest is left on Samosir and discuss the measures taken to reforest the upper reaches of the peninsula. Middendorp (1913:8-9) noted that the "*alang-alang* [*Imperata*] fields which are set ablaze every year" are usually so treated "for obtaining pasture for livestock which find fodder in the new-fired grass, whereas the Bataks also have the conviction that many fires are beneficial . . . keeping [animal pests] and insects in a standoff." But these just observations had little effect on later policy. Large areas of the upper reaches of the Samosir peninsula and the east side of the lake were planted in forest, and the burning of pastures was banned, to their long-term detriment. There was a purported need for forest cover to induce more rain. Apparently unheeded was a report by J. van Breda de Haan on rainfall in plantation areas of the East Coast of Sumatra (1898), "largely devoted to the presentation of data showing that there is no demonstrable correlation between deforestation and rainfall" (Bartlett 1957:191).[3] Further justification for forest planting was that it would increase the supply of wood for construction of dwellings (Haibach 1927:11), but the forests that were planted were not of locally used hardwood trees. Instead of providing a local source of lumber, they have become government reserves by default, reducing the available pasture area without benefitting the inhabitants, since only those with government contracts are permitted to cut the trees.

Dutch Agricultural Initiatives

The broadly conceived Dutch plans for altering the landscape essentially arose because agriculture was a central concern of administration. Middendorp listed rice, corn, and sweet potatoes in decreasing order of importance for subsistence. Rice was grown in "dry fields on

[3]For recent attacks on the persistent notion that forest cover induces rain, see Daubenmire (1974:88-89) and Hamilton (1983).

an incline," rainfed terraces, and irrigable fields. According to him, at that time, "agriculture, the main means of livelihood," was "not sufficient to provide the subsistence needs of the people" (Middendorp 1913:19). We can trace the vagaries of the supply and demand for staples in several other Controleurs' reports. The next one available noted that in 1927 it was "no longer possible to speak of a shortage of food during the past years. If the weather conditions do not bring on a bad harvest people have enough for their daily sustenance":

> In 1922 rice worth 13,000 guilders was still imported. This amount got smaller with the years and in the past year [1927] was still a little above 5000 guilders. But a similar amount was exported from the neighboring areas of rice surplus, Limbong and Sagala, to the East Coast. (Haibach 1927:21)

A few years later, van Bemmelen claimed that the rice crop had to be supplemented by a large import from Porsea (at the south end of the lake) and that "due to lack of rice, a great part of the population subsists on corn and sweet potatoes" (1931:15).

I will come back to the point regarding people "subsisting on corn and sweet potatoes" below and in Chapter 6, where we examine contemporary self-sufficiency in rice in Huta Ginjang. Here I want to make the point that even before they had a clear grasp of the agricultural system and its vicissitudes, the Dutch were actively trying to alter that system as a complement to their concern with subsistence by introducing commercial export crops, as well as by other means to be described in the next section. Seven years after the outset of their regime, Middendorp noted:

> *Peanuts*, first introduced by Controleur Stap in 1907 or 1908 grow very well in Samosir, so that [already] a small export goes on from Onan Runggu to Balige. . . .
>
> *Coffee* is much planted . . . and in 1911-1913 the amount rose to 200,961. . . . I bid coffee *adat* ['custom'] to be complied with by the [appointed area heads] . . . namely that each household have in the ground 100 trees, all hamlet headmen 150, all village headmen 250, all *raja padua* 300, and all *Djaihutan* 500. The upland fallow suitable lands were then taken and divided up with generally mutual agreement. (Middendorp 1913:22)

This passage shows both indigenous aptitudes and the character that Dutch administration often assumed. So-called coffee *adat* was pure invention, as were all the ranks except "hamlet headman."

The report for 1931 refers to what turned out to be the most pervasive cropping change of all. The growing of several species of shallots and garlic was demonstrated in 1930 by an extension officer of the agricultural service to the "area heads" assembled at Pangururan (van Bemmelen 1931:15-16).

The Evolution of Women's Work

Commercialization of agriculture came to have profound effects on patterns of subsistence and livelihood. These can best be appreciated from the point of view of the evolution of women's work.

The sexual division of labor depicted in much of the literature on the Toba Batak does not apply to the traditional pattern in Samosir. In a passage cited by E. M. Loeb, Junghuhn (1847) maintained that

> in Toba . . . the women do almost all the work, in the house as well as in the fields. . . . The men smoke tobacco out of their big copper pipes, watch the children . . . hold councils . . . and—conduct war. The building of houses and the cutting down of trees for the houses are about the only varieties of work which the men perform in times of peace. (Loeb 1935:29-30; see also Marsden 1811:382)

The missionaries Burton and Ward received a similar impression on their two-week tour of Silindung in 1824:

> With so few luxuries or refinements, and with so much assistance from the opposite sex and the liberal hand of nature, it will be readily inferred that the men lead a life of extreme inactivity. It seemed to us, indeed, a matter of some astonishment, that such an appearance of civil order should be maintained, with so much leisure for the operation of the evil propensities of human nature. (Burton and Ward 1827:512)

One wonders whether these impressions were not caused by the unprecedented appearances of the explorers themselves—whether their very presence brought about the effects that they observed by drawing crowds of men to their retinues, while modesty, which remains a social imperative for women, kept the latter busy at their work.

In Samosir, however, the situation that greeted the Dutch was the inverse of that which purportedly existed in other Batak areas. To their consternation, the Dutch discovered that women were not the productive agricultural workers they had found them to be elsewhere. In fact, probably as a result of the environmental and climatic factors described above—the prolonged, windy, dry season—a characteristically Samosirese sexual division of labor had developed prior to the coming of the Dutch. As Middendorp put it, in 1913:

> The women of the division of Samosir do not work on the land as in Silindung, in Toba and in the Karolands. They do the cooking and almost all women weave *ulos* [blessing shawls]. The finished cloths are traded in the markets and a great many are exported to all the surrounding areas, Barus, Dairi, Sumatra's East Coast, Uluan, Toba, Muara, and the Toba Plateau. The products of this craft are worth from 1 to 20 and sometimes as much as 25 guilders apiece. (Middendorp 1913:34)

Haibach, whose figures show that woven shawls brought in 12.6 percent of export income, noted that "in no other division of the Bataklands is so much value attached to this cottage industry," and he added the striking observation:

> So it happened that for a few years one met no women in the fields, a man worked in the field, carried water and firewood [in Samosir]. Herein a change is coming. In my opinion, the shortage of food in earlier years is partly due to the fact that women did not help out in farming. (1927:21-22)

He enjoined his successors to give encouragement, "to pay a compliment to those women one meets in fields on inspection tours" (loc. cit.).

Not surprisingly, a change in the traditional Samosirese division of labor occurred. With the introduction of cash crops that were in demand in the cities and on plantations of the East Coast, with conscription of men for corvée in lieu of taxes, and with (mostly male) wage migration, women were forced to take on a greater role in preparing the fields and in planting and tending the crops.

While *ulos* (blessing shawls) were traditionally prestige items and among the most important articles of ceremonial exchange, they also served practical uses such as swaddling for babies carried on women's backs, ceremonial skirts, and dress shawls (everyday clothing was of bark-cloth). Hence, two further factors may have come to influence the change in the sexual division of labor. The first was the Dutch ban on large-scale feasts, at which as many as 100 shawls were bestowed by guests in just one of numerous half-hour-long dances. Then, probably in the 1950s, machine-made *ulos* began to be produced in large quantities. As a result, the demand for handmade shawls of lower grades must have declined precipitously. Since these were customarily woven by unskilled beginners, the incentive for girls to learn to weave would thereby have been undermined, in spite of the esteem that Haibach (1927:21) notes was ascribed to the skill.

Weaving is still a seasonal occupation of women in areas of peninsular Samosir that do not have a source of irrigation water or loamy soils. But in the rainy season, there and in the better-watered valleys on the western shores of the lake, women put away their weaving. As Penny wrote of a Toba Batak village at the south end of the lake, "The

Weaving with a backstrap loom (peninsular Samosir).

characteristic work-group is a man and his wife" (Penny 1964:93). Only four women did any weaving in Huta Ginjang during the period of this study.

Of Dutch Contempt: Water Resources and Time of Planting

Finally, let us take an example of colonial agricultural policy formulation that further demonstrates its nature and provides an opportunity for a recapitulation of the themes of the chapter—environment, demography, and agricultural change.

Several end-of-term reports (*Memories van Overgave*) by Dutch administrators of Samosir refer to the fact that early dry-season winds may destroy a substantial part of the rice crop. They enjoin their successors to impress on the leaders of the people that the danger could be averted by planting earlier. In 1913, Middendorp wrote:

> In the dry months, July and August, heavy gale winds come up, sometimes beginning in June and ending in September. They are often accompanied by whirlwinds which in June do a great deal of damage to the ripening wet-rice. By planting earlier, men could avoid [the danger]. (1913:9-10)

Writing in 1927, Haibach agreed, but took exception to part of the above:

> [In 1923 the gusts of wind] came up with unusual fierceness as early as April 15 and kept blowing three days and nights. A great deal of damage was thereby caused to the ripening rice, wherefore the resident administrator must be careful to *call attention so that the rice fields be planted on time* in the Negeri which lie in valleys on the mainland. If the cultivation of the rice fields be completed by the end of the calendar year, the fields have no trouble from the winds, so that the harvest can be done when the rice is fully ripe. (Haibach 1927:13-14, emphasis added)

Of course, as several remarks already cited might suggest, the Batak probably complained to the Controleur, and to any Dutchman who would listen, of not having enough rice, of having to eat corn and tubers. But it is clear that localized and even regional disasters were not uncommon. One must wonder at the Dutch assumption that people could have consistently miscalculated the time of planting their preferred crop. How was that possible?

The villagers I lived with always feared being caught out by fluctuations in the pattern of weather from year to year. They have a basic scheme of expectations for the seasonal cycle, to which the lunar months are adjusted, but they are typically faced with a dilemma in choosing the appropriate time to plant dry rice and rain-fed wet rice. The first heavy rain of the season may be followed by a month of drought. If a crop of dry rice is killed as a result, their remedy is re-hoeing and replanting when the rains come again. In the valley the difficulties are, if anything, greater. Wet-rice seedlings are raised in seedbeds and transplanted about 40 days after sowing. If a drought occurs and the seedbeds dry out after planting, the loss is total, for it is too late to replant. Moreover, if the dry season lasts longer than normal, most of the streams that water the Samosir rice plains and the Sagala Valley run low just at the time when large amounts of water are needed to flood and soften the terraces. For these reasons, planting of seedbeds is postponed until well into the rainy season. But this entails risk of later winds.

The decision of when to plant was certainly not made haphazardly in Dutch times. Astrologer-priests, using a lunar calendar adjusted to the solar year by attention to constellations (Parkin 1978:220f.), still determine the date of planting seedbeds for wet rice. The choices of planting times are, however, governed to a large extent by vagaries of the climatic cycle and by the length of the growing season. The ritual purification of seeds before planting in 1977 took place in Sagala Valley, at Lumban Suha, on October 20, several weeks after the rains had begun in earnest. But when the rains do not come until November, as was said to have happened in 1975, the planting of both wet and dry rice is delayed. Even without such a delay in initial planting, there is always a risk of windstorms during the final stages of ripening. Between May 12 and 14, 1978, winds of great force ruined portions of the crop of 23 households in Huta Ginjang, amounting to some nine tons of rice, as well as large amounts of corn and coffee beans. Half a dozen households had, in fact, taken a chance and planted dry-field rice when the first rains came the preceding September but had lost their plantings because no more rain fell for several weeks.

The "double bind" of late rains and early winds was lost upon even the best-intentioned Dutch civil servants. The fact that many Samosirese could not grow enough rice to supply their wants was viewed as resulting from a failure to time the planting correctly, rather than from environmental constraints. It was thought that the problem could be solved by issuing timely directives from the office of the Controleur.

The failure to view the problem of planting time in relation to water resources is, of course, tied to the overall task of enlightenment and raising living standards to which many of the "Ethical School" administrators were devoted. Similar license to interfere is exemplified in their ban on stabling livestock under houses, their ban on pasture burning (Sherman 1982:699), and policies of planting forest and lowering the lake level. More than evincing an annoying paternalism and penchant for bureaucratic meddling, the case at hand is another instance of what Castles calls the "unlimited contempt" of Dutch officials for Batak agriculture:

> Thus Vorstman could write that a great advantage of awarding land to plantations [in the Toba Batak area of Pangaribuan] was that the people would be forced to use land more economically and 'learn the meaning of intensive cultivation.' . . . [The Controleur of Silindung] told Marcks that plantations would bring more welfare to the Bataks than their own '*Misswirtschaft*' [mismanagement] in the forests. (Castles 1972:132-133 and n. 27)

This contempt was prone to exacerbation in the area of Samosir by the severity of the dry season, the denuded aspect of the landscape (in spite of ubiquitous terracing), and, perhaps, by the pagan loyalties of the inhabitants.

Examining environment, demography, and Dutch-induced agricultural change from the perspective of the difficulties of apprehending reality—of deceptive appearances—has raised a number of salient points. The most important is this: the Samosir population, supporting itself through agriculture, livestock-raising, fishing, and weaving, was quite high relative to the population of many other regions of the equatorial monsoon belt. If we take into account the pronounced and often prolonged dry season and the untoward winds that arise even in the rainy season, Dutch contempt of Batak agriculture was unwarranted and precluded its just appreciation.

Unfortunately, the first few generations of Western-educated Batak were taught Dutch views and adopted Dutch attitudes toward the indigenous agriculture (Penny 1964:230), and most positions of power in government bureaucracies have been held by this elite. The same attitudes were undoubtedly communicated by Dutch administrators to appointed Batak leaders and may have "filtered out" to the population at large. The clearest residue of this kind of attitude was in government attitudes to grassland, which I will treat in a separate chapter. What needs to be emphasized in the overall context of this study is that, by dint of great effort and by disposition and desire, Samosir Batak became part-time producers of goods for exchange, not just for use. Although it is perhaps unanswerable, it is worth raising the question, Were there ever "Batak" communities that did not produce for outside trade? Or is such production part of what it means to be Batak? This is a question to which we will return.

Under Dutch prodding, some increased commercialization of agriculture took place. And women have become cultivators. Yet it appears that there was already substantial trade in locally woven shawls in 1913. In other words, women were already producers of a key export. The fact that agricultural production for exchange (as opposed to for use) is now so prominent is thus by no means an indication of fundamental disruption of traditional cultural patterns.

Chapter 2

History and Change

This chapter describes the historical background of the Samosir area in its regional setting and more of the specific changes imposed on the Batak by the Dutch, including abolition of debt-bondage and introduction of taxes. Developing a focus on the effects of monetization, it provides a general treatment of how the people have adapted to and interact with the larger world.

The Historical Geography of Trade

Sumatra forms the western side of Asia's most heavily plied trade route, the Straits of Malacca, which was traditionally the preferred route between India and China. In *Early Indonesian Commerce*, O. W. Wolters shows that there is a good likelihood that (among other commodities) both the preservative camphor and the incense benzoin, gathered by tapping certain trees, were introduced to China as early as the fifth century A.D. "as a backwash of western Asian trade with China, which resulted in China's accidental interest in certain Indonesian trade products resembling those of western Asia" (Wolters 1967:118). He reasons that, given the traditional habitat of the trees in question, these products probably originated in what are now the Batak highlands and were exported through Barus, a small sheltered port on the west coast of Sumatra.

The Batak highlands had the contradictory attributes of being close to the center of, but peripheral to, the historical geography of mercantile trade in Southeast Asia. The tension between their centrality and their isolation is exemplified in their reputation "as far back as Marco Polo . . . as a fierce, cannibalistic people to be avoided by all outsiders" (Pederson 1970:17-18). Aside from a few questionable exceptions, there are no eyewitness accounts to bear out this reputation, but it certainly would not have attracted traders inland.

Pederson (1970:18) notes that "the Dutch East India Company secured a trade agreement with several Batak *radjas* . . . as early as 1694, but . . . they succeeded in penetrating only the coastal fringe of Batakland." In fact, however, 1694 was not early for Dutch activity on the Indian Ocean side of Sumatra. Farther south, according to Dobbin (1977:4),

> gold was first acquired officially on behalf of [the Dutch East India Company] at Pariaman in 1651 . . . [and] in 1663 a factory [trading post/bulking center] was established [at Padang] with the intention of cultivating an already existing gold route from the [Minangkabau] uplands.

The Dutch, having come in search of pepper, soon established a rule that cloth could be sold to the Minangkabau only for gold. Cotton goods acquired in India were apparently in great demand, for by the late 1660s, the Dutch were receiving over 100,000 guilders' worth of gold for them from Minangkabau traders every year.

The Batak may also have exported gold. In 1515, Tomé Pires (1944:161-163) noted that the ports of Barus and Singkel were both sources. In addition to wanting cloth for highland products, the inhabitants (whether coastal residents or itinerant uplanders) likely would have been impelled to seek metals such as bronze and iron for hunting, agricultural, and even tree-tapping implements. The relative rarity of local iron is signaled by the observation of the early-nineteenth-century missionaries Burton and Ward, among the first Europeans to visit the Toba Batak highlands, that "[t]he implements of husbandry of the Bataks are principally made of wood" (1827:511).

Their reference to "an extraordinary consumption of salt amongst the Bataks" (Burton and Ward 1827:498) suggests another motivation for trade. Whether produced on the coast or imported from abroad, salt was probably a valued upland import. Marsden (1811:380) notes that salt was the most common medium of exchange near the coast "for small payments." Highlanders probably traded benzoin and other goods for it, since, according to contemporary villagers, people in pre-Dutch times most often entered debt-bondage for a few liters of salt! Perhaps the early missionary-explorers' impression of its excessive consumption may be read as evidence of its use as a status symbol in the highlands.

Markets and Ports of Trade

According to a secondhand report cited by Marsden, much of the trade between the highland plains and the coastal bays was effected by intermediaries:

> For the convenience of carrying on the inland-trade, there are established at the back of Tappanuli, which is their great mart, four stages, at which successively they hold public fairs or markets on every fourth day throughout the year; each fair, of course, lasting one day. The people in the district of the fourth stage assemble with their goods at the appointed place, to which those of the third resort in order to purchase them. The people of the third, in like manner, supply the wants of the second, and the second of the first, who dispose, on the day the

Contemporary market scene. The corner where pandanus mats are sold.

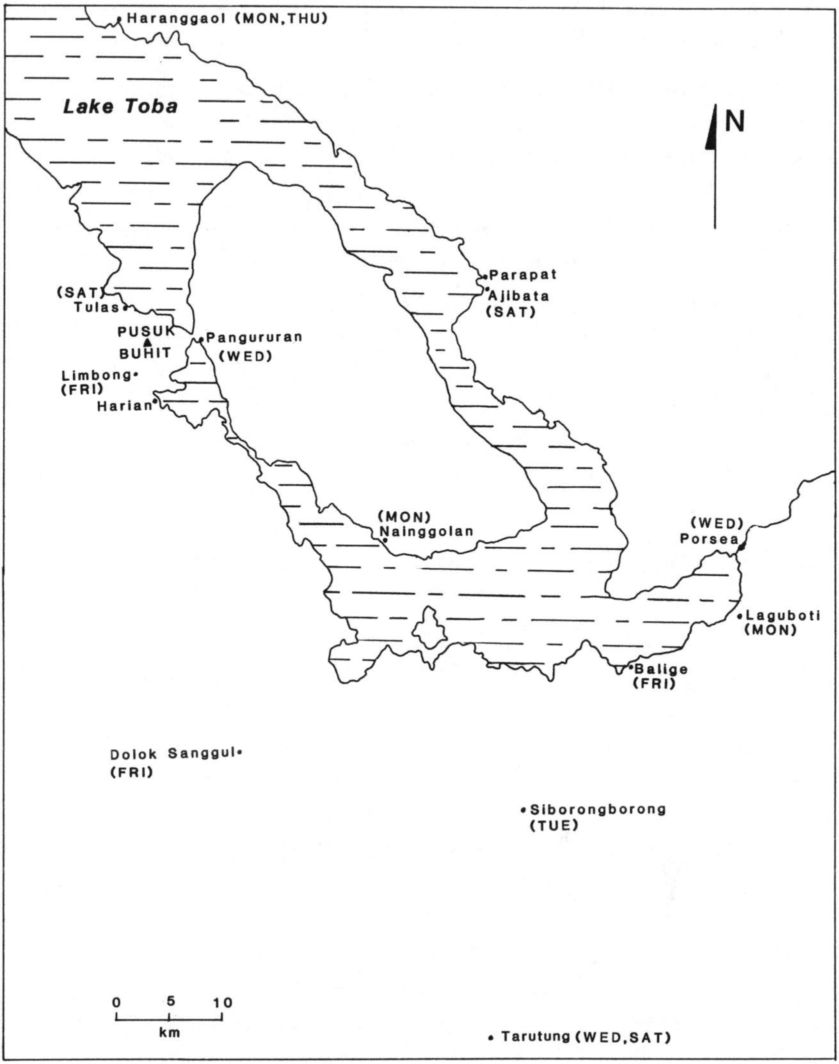

Map 3. Alternation of market days on the Toba circuit.

> market is held, of the merchandise for which they have trafficked with the Europeans and Malays. (1811:379-380)

We can also infer that in 1824, and probably much earlier, there was a system of markets in the highland Silindung Valley, for the village of Burton and Ward's host "happened to be the seat of the market on the day" of their arrival (1827:489), implying that a number of villages served in that capacity on a rotating basis. This picture of periodic markets in which some overlapping of traders' circuits occurred is not unlike that first pointed out by G. W. Skinner (1964) for China and by Chayanov (1964) for Russia.[1] The present alternation of days for a selection of regional markets can be seen in Map 3.

Presumably, trading ventures were based on established alliances and were subject to some level of tolls by those in a position to demand them. Burton and Ward were told that a year before, twenty persons had been executed,

> inhabitants of a village situated near the path leading to the coast, whom our host represented as having so often plundered the passengers that their conduct became at length intolerable. (1827:507)

Although benzoin is still widely grown and tapped today in the Dairilands and in the Toba Batak areas south of Lake Toba, neither camphor nor benzoin grows well in the Samosir region (the Dutch did try to establish the latter there). It is impossible to say precisely how and to what degree Samosir was linked to the precolonial export trade, yet when the Dutch took over, they confiscated some 7,000 firearms (Middendorp 1913:16), which could not have come there in such quantities without substantial trade. A further observation by Burton and Ward, referring specifically to the Silindung area, suggests that rice was a regional export and raises the possibility that the Samosir export of rice observed by later Controleurs was as traditional as the export of shawls.

> Rice and sweet potatoes constitute the principal articles of food, and cultivation

[1]Cf. Hill (1986:56) for an African instance in which markets so linked did not comprise a hierarchy centered on city markets.

> is confined almost exclusively to them. The former is produced both on the hills and in the vallies in great abundance, *and forms a principal article of their barter with the bay.* On the hills it is grown by the dry process . . . in the vallies irrigation is employed with some ingenuity. (1827:510; emphasis added)

The coastal demand for rice evidenced by this statement suggests that a similar situation obtained for other surplus-producing areas. This, indeed, puts the Batak highlands squarely into the category of Southeast Asian hinterland societies that Sahlins (1965:179f.) considered to be "unusual" in the prominence of their balanced exchange. Other possible traditional exports from Samosir, including shawls and livestock, may be inferred from W. Middendorp's 1913 end-of-term report, to which I will return in due course.

The Legacy of Supralocal Colonial Government

Only one old man and one old woman in Huta Ginjang remembered the coming of the Dutch in 1906, from Dairi in the west, led by '*Tuan* Stap,' who became the first Controleur of Samosir. Asked what she thought about the invasion, the woman responded to the effect that "only when the Dutch came did it get peaceful. Before, feuding (*marmusu*) prevailed." The administration imposed its own settlements on unresolved disputes and established a statute of limitations in that "legal claims could no longer be made in respect of contracts concluded before the sensational battle of Tangga Batu in 1883" (Vergouwen 1964:143). Other changes were also imposed, and two will be treated here—the abolition of debt-bondage and the advent of taxes.

Abolition of debt-bondage and slavery. Slavery "in any form was forbidden after the establishment of the Netherlands Indies Government and all traces of its having existed have now been expunged, except in South Tapanuli," wrote Vergouwen in 1933 (Vergouwen 1964:327). Two questions we need to consider are: What made it possible for the former institution of debt-bondage to have been readily expunged among the Toba Batak, and what kind of social dislocation did this abolition of a "traditional Batak social institution" cause?

Although Vergouwen specifically noted the lack of a class system among the Toba (1964:110), some writers have claimed that precolonial Batak society consisted of "three ranks, the nobles, the commoners, and the slaves" (Loeb 1935:40). To say that the traditional social system was characterized by such classes conjures up a demographic hierarchy—the familiar pyramid, with nobility at the apex, resting on the backs of the masses, who form the base. But when the Dutch took a count in 1909, they found only 1,533 male and 698 female bond-slaves in Samosir, 3 percent of the population (Middendorp 1913:12). There was, then, no pyramid. The term "nobility" and the concept of class stratification thus may well be inappropriate for describing Toba Batak society.

Vergouwen distinguished three levels of peonage among the Toba, analogous to those found among the Kachin (Green, cited in Leach 1965:299f.). The least onerous involved a man living in the creditor's village who

> had to assist [the creditor] in important works, such as cultivating land, repairing the village wall, and so on. In his spare time he could try to scrape enough together towards discharging his debt. . . . [Secondly,] a dweller in the house of his creditor . . . had to place all his working force at his creditor's disposal without in any way thereby diminishing his debt. Kinsmen and affines could buy such a man out . . . which fact distinguished a peon from a slave proper. (Vergouwen 1964:327)

Leach also remarks that "the status of the male . . . was that of a 'semi-permanent debtor' rather than a chattel," and similar statements were made by Stevenson (1943:176f.) about the Chin and by Mills (1922:111) about the Lhota Naga.

Distinctions between the rich and poor in everyday dress, shelter, and labor were not obvious at the time of Dutch penetration, nor are they now, except in towns, and, to some degree, at feasts.

> One early Dutch visitor tells us that except on ceremonial occasions it was hard to tell chiefs and their sons from the rest of the population: the owner of vast herds might go around in only a dirty pair of shorts. The chiefs were marked off by the deference they commanded, the size of the bride price they demanded

> for their daughters and the costly magnificence of their wedding and funerals. They had a face-to-face relationship with their subjects . . . people bound to them by strongly-held mutual . . . obligations. (Castles 1972:118)

Writing of *gumsa* ("autocratic") Kachin society, Leach made a similar observation (though it somehow vitiates its own terms):

> Within any one domain there is no substantial difference in standard of living between the aristocrats and the commoners—members of both classes eat the same food, wear the same clothes, practise the same skills. Master and slave live in the same house under almost the same conditions. (Leach 1965:162)

Controleur Middendorp thought that if the slaves were "set free all at once," it would "put too many men in a position of having no work or position, so that, among other things, the number of thieves . . . would of necessity increase." Hence the institution was abolished with delicacy:

> It was decided that all slaves were to be considered debt slaves, and that each was worth fifty guilders, and that each, beginning January 1, 1910, would earn one guilder a month, so that by March 1, 1914, slavery would thus be officially over and done with. (Middendorp 1913:12)

Once they had been freed, many Samosir debt-bondsmen may have elected to maintain both their places and their relationships of mutual obligations.

Taxes and compulsory labor. Though apparently accomplishing its purpose, the edict must also have helped the Dutch inculcate their view that (discrete periods of labor) time is money. Before long, the people of Samosir were further enlightened on Western ethics: corvée labor became the predominant mode of paying government taxes. By assessing taxes in cash, the Dutch, like colonial administrators in Africa and elsewhere, were probably trying to force their subjects to seek wage labor on plantations or to grow cash crops, with "the deliberate object of provoking a transition from pure subsistence to a cash economy" (Clark and Haswell 1964:65; see also Scott 1976:97-98). While emancipating the debt-bondsmen, they proceeded to universalize indebtedness to an all-knowing higher authority and probably did so with equally strong moral conviction. The Dutch notion of Batak men as lazy, by no means unique in Western views of "natives" (Sahlins 1972:85-86), was undoubtedly a convenient ethical warrant.

Taxes were much higher (and money much scarcer) under the Dutch than at present. According to a former headman, the tax per household was 6 Rupiah at a time when Rp. 1 bought 36 liters, or the equivalent of 216 liters of unhusked rice (about 120 kilos). For richer members of the community, the tax was Rp. 10 per household, which represents a rate about six times the levy in 1978 (16 liters of husked rice per household to the headman for his own disposition), when most villagers were in arrears. Even young unmarried men (*doli-doli*) had to pay a head tax of 72 liters of unhusked rice per year or perform corvée labor. For the headmen to fulfill the administration's expectations would have been no mean feat.

Not all Bataks submitted with equanimity. A millenarian movement began in 1915 after "a certain Djaman in sickness had a vision of the High God. . . . He was to set up a sect. . . . A Batak holy state would arise under Si Singamangaradja with no taxes or compulsory labor" (Castles 1972:82-83). But the Dutch managed to put down such brief flare-ups and enforce the peace in Samosir for some thirty-five years with only a small garrison, governing through so-called *adat* chiefs, termed *kepala negeri* or "territorial heads," one for each of the territories. Vergouwen noted that

> in the course of the last few decades there has been a tremendous amount of Government activity in the Toba Batak Country and a corps of Batak civil servants have been introduced between the European administration and the chiefs. . . . [The latter] became no more than the mouthpieces of government. (1964:129-130)

But, as Castles points out, the Dutch also adopted a policy of drawing civil-service recruits from the chiefs' families (1974:74). And, while they had few problems in maintaining control and exacting taxes and corvée labor, the Dutch were distressed by the ceaseless complaints of the people, none of whom seemed willing to submit to any other's authority. Even with elected "chiefs" or headmen of villages, the Dutch were unable to quell the stream of complaints because the field of candidates was never limited to two, and clear majorities were rare or nonexistent (Castles 1972:203-214).

Steps in the Partial Transition to a Cash Economy

In his end-of-term report of 1913, W. Middendorp reported that horses in the Pangururan market sold for 30 to 200 guilders (depending on health, size, and age), and about 600 horses, at an average price of 60 guilders, were sold to other regions. Buffalo sold for 100 guilders, cattle ("which are small") for 30 to 40 guilders, pigs for 5 to 35, sheep and goats for about 4 guilders, and a certain rare fish (probably the large-scaled black *ihan*, still used for special offerings) from 5 to 60 guilders apiece (Middendorp 1913:27-33). Blessing shawls woven by Samosir women ranged in price from 1 up to 25 guilders (Middendorp 1913:34).

Livestock prices may have resulted from Dutch-influenced demand in the lowlands. Yet the fact that guilder prices were given at such an early date of Dutch occupation of this literal backwater suggests that the demand was indigenous and "traditional." Even if this were not so for livestock, prices for blessing shawls indicate a regional and indigenous demand unaffected by the Dutch. Indeed, such prices could have been only partly, if at all, due to expenditures of a small garrison of Dutch consumers stationed at Pangururan because, as I noted, Middendorp also wrote that "trade is frequently barter, for which hulled rice is used as the medium of payment, desired by the market women. *The officials often complain that as a result they can get no merchandise for their money*" (Middendorp 1913:32, emphasis added). I will return to this apparent paradox.

Vergouwen depicted the significance of cash in precolonial Batak society in a vivid historical reconstruction. It helps to amplify the picture of precolonial economy derived from sources already cited.

> Before Dutch administration extended over the Toba country, intercourse with the outside world was mainly limited to the export of benzoin and the import of

> salt and tobacco. The amount of money in the country was small and . . . consisted of Spanish dollars and small coins introduced by the (Dutch) East India Company. Among the Batak themselves, money was not the usual medium of exchange. . . . There was too little of it for that. In the village and in the market goods were still exchanged in the main on a goods-for-goods basis. . . . In the main, money had other functions and served other purposes than just as a medium with which to buy goods. . . . It could be used to denote a girl who was destined to become the bride of one's son. . . . Men gambled with money. It secured the protracted use of a plot of land belonging to another man who needed ready cash and when he claimed the land back he paid back the money he had received. Copper money was exchanged against tobacco, weight for weight; money was loaned out at interest. (Vergouwen 1964:294-295)

But, he adds, "it was not only money to which interest could accrue; if rice were loaned because of a rice shortage, *morlali eme*, it had to be returned augmented."

A number of important inferences can be drawn from this. Coinage was scarce but widespread in the Bataklands before the establishment of Dutch authority. The specie traditionally used for taking land in pledge and for bridewealth—perhaps also for paying indemnities ("blood money")—was minted in the outside world. Specie itself was thus an imported valuable. It was rice, not money, that served as a general medium of exchange, not only in the market but in ritual as well: "The *guguan* = contribution to a joint ceremony was reckoned in measures of rice" (loc. cit.). "One could get practically anything for rice" (ibid.:319). Cash had been integrated into the Batak economy, not as a medium of exchange, but, "in common with many other things [land, livestock, shawls, and perhaps even weapons or tools as] a valuable item," and, further, "it could not be acquired to the same degree" (ibid.:295).

The term *manuhor*, 'to buy' (a cognate of Malay *menukar* = exchange), had come to be applied to transactions of goods for cash, but it was not "exclusively applied to the conversion of money into goods required" (loc. cit.). It is still not exclusively so applied, and the example that Vergouwen gave in the 1930s is still applicable—bridewealth:

> That the term *tuhor* was not only used to denote an exchange of goods against rice is clear from the expression *tuhor ni boru* [*ni* = of, *boru* = woman/daughter] and the composition of the marriage payment [which may include cattle, cash and other items]. (ibid.:319)

Now let us briefly consider how things have changed from the apparent precolonial situation. Although ceremonial payments of bridewealth, usually in the wake of an elopement, are still the norm, cash has taken over as the medium of exchange in the market and is as frequently used in ritual as rice. Contributions to a joint ceremony by participating principals and their wife-giving affines are no longer reckoned in rice but in cash, though they may be made in rice—and that is often done. On the other hand, few Bataks in Sagala today would take a field in pawn in return for a loan of cash, as Vergouwen claimed was done, unless its value were phrased in terms of the rice-in-the-husk equivalent at the time of the loan. Even before the devaluations to which the rupiah has been subjected since 1978, the Batak had apparently grown accustomed to the inflation of money.

Those who loan cash insist on phrasing the loan in terms of rice, which indicates that their economy has become tied to the world economy, where inflation has been endemic; but it does not indicate that their economy has become entirely monetized. In fact, rice is still a prominent means of both ritual and secular exchange. Many town and city schools and hostels require partial payment of board in rice. It remains a medium of credit in village life, as well as the premier means of subsistence—and not just for those in the village. Rice is often carried or sent to feed emigrants engaged in trade and pioneering.

One may, therefore, refer to this society's having taken certain "steps in a partial transition to a cash economy." The paradox of a market in which rice was a medium of exchange and livestock and shawls had guilder prices—but women would not accept guilders for their goods—has been posed. It can only be explained when in due course the appropriate background and analytical framework have been established.

Increased Mobility, the Colonial World Market, and Schooling

Dutch-imposed peace made it possible for Bataks to travel in relative safety over large areas where most would have been loathe to venture. For the purpose of marketing, the lake was traditionally traversed by large canoes made from hollowed logs, powered by 50 or more paddlers. But out-migration of Samosirese and of Toba Bataks occurred only in limited fashion prior to World War II. Most disdained becoming full-time plantation workers, and owners were forced to bring in Chinese and Javanese "coolies." Geertz reports:

> In 1913 about 48,000 Chinese and 27,000 Javanese coolies worked on east Sumatra tobacco estates, and of the total work force of more than 85,000, less than 1,000 were natives of the area itself. . . . More than 95 percent of the over-all total were contract coolies but of the small local group 95 percent were free. (Geertz 1963:110 and n. 47)

Dutch policy worked to limit the pioneering of land on the East Coast, leaving the way clear for plantation expansion and seasonal

Truck-engine-powered lake steamer, laden with goods and marketers.

wage-migration. With the exception of Toba Batak from the Silindung and Balige areas, who were granted newly created wet-rice lands (served by a Dutch-financed irrigation system) to provide a local source of rice for the plantations, out-migration was limited by people's dispositions and the need for identity papers, which could be had only by paying a tax of 10 guilders (Oerlemans 1937:50). As was noted, this was the yearly tax on a rich household, so it inhibited emigration.

Vergouwen's assessment that the flow of cash into the Toba Batak area prior to 1930 "in the form of the wages earned on Sumatra's East coast by labourers . . . amounts to only a few thousand guilders" (1964:295) is probably greatly underestimated. Haibach reported that 1926 exports from Samosir alone totaled 215,800 guilders, of which 119,408 were received for livestock, 42,000 for corn, peanuts, pots, fish, chickens, and other small articles, and 27,300 for shawls (Haibach 1927:23). He listed the following amounts spent on imports: 80,000 for yarn, 52,000 for salt, 47,400 for cloth, and 15,500 for tobacco. Even before the Great Depression, then, Samosir's connection to the colonial world economy was not entirely by means of a pool of seasonal wage migrants.

The Depression occurred at about the same time that the Dutch Agricultural Extension Service introduced shallots and demonstrated manuring. It cut heavily into the income of the tobacco and rubber plantations of the East Coast, and the need for wage migrants declined. By 1931, the number of coolies working in the plantations had in any case risen from 85,000 some twenty years earlier to 350,000, half of whom were "free" (Geertz 1963:110, n. 47).

As the Controleur who left in 1935 wrote, "Export crops filled a strongly felt need [for money], and the economic condition of [Samosir] has stood up quite well" (Welter 1935:12). Samosir's export of shallots in 1934 amounted to 16,035 guilders' worth, and cabbage worth 17,786 guilders was also exported. There was even "a large import of European and Japanese yarn, cloth, glassware, etc." Welter also noted that unemployment had not yet arisen: "Almost everyone has their own parcel of land so as to provide their livelihood" (1935:26).

Given the sources of cash in and around the plantations, most trade in this century flowed between Samosir and the East Coast. It continues to go from North Samosir to the ports of Ajibata, Tiga Ras, and Haranggaol (by diesel-powered steamers rather than canoes) and thence to the Karo highland market of Kabanjahe or the administrative center of the Simalungun district, Pematang Siantar, and by either route to Medan. These are also the routes taken by most Samosirese who travel—be it in search of schooling, employment, or experience.

In 1934, peninsular Samosir had one government-run and 37 mission-run schools with 2,670 students taught by 52 teachers (Welter 1935). At present, almost all children attend grade school, and some 80 percent of village offspring under eighteen were in school. Even the *bius* priests expend funds on schooling and forgo other amenities if they have boys or girls who show promise and desire to continue.

Villagers often said that they farmed to live, and if they could work in an office and 'eat wages,' they would do so. They view education as the only way other than trade to ameliorate the positions of their children. Having children in school is perhaps the most promising means, for themselves or their descendants, to tap or connect to the power and wealth that vitalize the world beyond the borders of the lake. (And, indeed, they often denigrate village life as 'too quiet' in contrast to the 'bustling activity' and noise of town and city.) Some think that 'if you work in an office (*karejo di kantor*), you just sit down and sign paper and you get money,' but most are not entirely naive, realizing both the limits of their means—many school fees are "unofficial" in North Sumatra—or their children's aptitudes. During the speaking of 'last will and testaments' (*tona*), elders called upon children to 'be diligent in working the land, so that you may live, so that you may eat'; only select descendants were exhorted to get ahead by studying hard. (To be sure, some parents are overly sanguine: at least two young men were said to have run away to avoid continued schooling.)

Several factors explain the attraction that education came to exercise on the Toba Batak and the position it has come to occupy in their

The port of Haranggaol. Irrigable and dry terraces are dotted with fruit and other useful trees. Note burned areas in the steep pasture. Decades of government-mandated and funded "reforestation" have resulted in some blocks of Pinus merkusii *(upper right), which can be tapped by contractors for sap for turpentine.*

The main means of transport from lakeside to distant markets: Chevys.

worldly aims since first offered by missionaries. In the first place, there was a predisposition to literacy, in that "formerly only a chosen few were instructed in the wisdom of the *datu* [shaman/augurer] and learning [the Batak alphabet] was associated with magical science as a venerated source of power" (Pederson 1970:88). Striving for positions of wealth and power also underlay the desire for education.

> Ignorance was associated with weakness. . . . [M]issionaries reported with dismay the materialistic enthusiasm for advancement among the Batak. . . . To emulate European education and material wealth and attain higher social prestige became an expression of *hamadjuon* [progress] for the modern Batak. (ibid.:88-93; see also Keuning 1958:19)

With the exception of some grade-school teachers, those who have earned an academic title have no way to fit back into the village other than when attending rituals. (This is basically because they are expected, and themselves expect, to make most of their living by means other than manual labor.) Nonetheless, this quandary seems to reinforce both the feasting system and the urge to provide education. Many of the educated who have reached positions of prominence or relative financial security have demonstrated a desire to sponsor feasts or construct tombs to honor the spirits of their forebears. Thus, it may be said, education holds a traditional hope for the average household: that children may better carry on the line and more lavishly honor the spirits of their ancestors.

Many of those who do not leave the area for schooling are eager to seek alternate means of earning their livelihoods or better farming situations. Young men and, increasingly, young women often long to get out and gain experience beyond the confines of their home area. But this may not be entirely new. Pioneering outside the home region was probably a traditional means of alleviating population pressure (or escaping irreconcilable conflicts), judging by the Toba Batak genealogy, which, superimposed on a map, would appear as an outward spiral of new clans mixed with radiating lineages of old ones.

Post-World War II Developments

The lessons of the Dutch period went beyond the introduction of a notion of supralocal governmental enforcement of order and suppression of feuding. The experience of much of the male populace outside their home area tended to unify them in their shared ethnic identity in opposition to other Batak groups. During the struggle to prevent the Dutch from reimposing their rule after World War II, Samosir was the scene of battles for jurisdiction between different factions:

> [A]rmed bands from Karo and Aceh overran Dairi and Samosir at the end of April 1946 in collaboration with disaffected elements in those districts, and made many arrests. When army and police from [the Toba area] counterattacked a bloody interethnic conflict ensued. The Toba settlers fled from the Tiga Lingga area [in Karoland]. After casualties had run into many hundreds, a government commission succeeded in restoring peace in mid-June 1946. (Castles 1974:76)

This was one of three occasions cited by Castles to show that "when internecine fighting reached a peak . . . the lines were drawn, crudely speaking, Toba versus non-Toba" (ibid.:80; see also Liddle 1972, *passim*).

The 'Social Revolution,' in which many former Dutch-supported local rulers in East Sumatra were executed, did not occur in the Batak areas of Northern Tapanuli. "[T]he Tapanuli chiefs, whose position had been far less grand and who were bound to their peoples by kinship ties, were able to give up their positions without bloodshed. Elected councils took their place" (Castles 1974:75-76). The lines of conflict that developed during the secessionist movements that occurred in several areas of Indonesia, including the Bataklands, from 1956 to 1958 again pitted Karo against Toba, and again, local intervillage peace did not break down.

As Benedict R. Anderson has described the postwar situation generally, the state "had very little ability to tax or to administer heavily until the late 1960s. Since then, it has largely relied on income from multinational [oil and other resource-extracting] corporations, and," he cautions, "this needs to be kept in mind in explaining the current strength of indigenous socio-cultural forms at the village level" (personal communication 1982). There is, indeed, little direct state presence in the village (mainly the school and occasional election rituals), but the appropriation of communal pasturelands for tree plantings by the Forestry Department has recently caused problems in many areas of North Tapanuli. Those in Sagala did not get reported in the newspaper as did a number of others (see Chapter 7, n. 6). Yet, given government policy of claiming eminent domain over fallow grasslands in the Dutch pattern of classifying them as "waste land" or "empty land" (Geertz 1963:83-84), conflicts can be expected to escalate and resources to be squandered in tree plantings consumed in fires set by herdboys. One of the tactics used by the Forestry Department is to get a headman to sign over the rights to a parcel without consulting neighboring headmen. Those propositioned have difficulty resisting the temptation for gain because often the very headmen who have signed over such rights are granted the planting contract (*borongan*) and receive an honorarium for each sapling planted.

One of the village elders said that when he married, he borrowed '100, stone money' (i.e., in coin) at a monthly interest charge of a volume of rice, 'five *solup* and a quarter *tangkar*' (the *solup* is a now-defunct measuring container made of a section of bamboo). Interest on cash loans in measures of rice is found elsewhere in hinterland Southeast Asia (Kunstadter 1978:117). In Samosir it represents a "development" from a system in which rice served as the major medium of exchange and in which interest in kind was traditionally charged for loans of rice. And now cash is the medium of loans phrased in volumes of rice.

Again, the question that arises, noted at the outset of our discussion, is whether this and other changes have occasioned fundamental social and cultural dislocations. Or, putting it differently: given the seemingly major changes that have taken place, how could an essential core of Batak values have been maintained?

PART II

SOCIOCULTURAL EFFECTS OF COLONIAL PENETRATION

The preceding chapter described the overt political and economic effects of the Dutch on Samosir Batak society. The following three chapters treat the effects of colonial penetration on Batak political and religious organization. This will provide perspective on the matrix of values in which rice and money have come to serve complementary and sometimes overlapping roles.

To assess the degree to which change has affected Batak culture and society, one must keep in mind their resistance to what could not be adapted, such as attempts by the Dutch to introduce "chiefs" (territorial rulers) with real, though circumscribed, authority, where there had only fitfully been any in "traditional" society. As part of the project of establishing a baseline from which to assess change, Chapter 3 takes up the bases of traditional Batak polities. We also begin to examine other areas of Batak cultural resistance, which are developed further in Chapters 4 and 5 and later: resistance to the church ideal of equal inheritance for women, to church opposition to elopement, ancestral tomb shrines, or playing of the gondang *feast-orchestra.*

In spite of overt changes in many aspects of Batak life and in spite of the additional "cognitive dissonance" these changes may have occasioned for modern Bataks beyond what their ancestors may have suffered, there has not been a disintegration of traditional Toba Batak social institutions. Some institutions, like feud and debt-bondage were abolished, and people found they could live without their most overt forms. But they did not disintegrate of their own accord, and their abolition did not cause others to do so. If traditional social institutions had disintegrated, people would not still argue about their position in a line of dancers at a feast—they would no longer care about such manifestations of who they are. But they do, just as they argue about the order in which they receive their portion of bridewealth. Relations to kin and to the supernatural, mediated by household and communal social ritual, are still the moorings of Batak social life, both ideologically and empirically. This will be borne out, here and in the following chapters, by a description and analysis of the political, religious, and social relations among villagers.

Because our attempt to grasp the web of relationships that make up Batak society and the meaningful tissue of language and action by which Batak culture is re-created and transmitted is based in part on socioeconomic comparisons of the resources of indigenously defined "descent groups," it is necessary, first, to describe how those groupings are constituted and what defines them. In doing so in Chapter 3, I will also bring out, in preliminary fashion, aspects of inequality and hierarchy, particularly with respect to control of resources in land, and the role of women in relationships between men.

Chapter 3

Ethnohistory, Inequality, and Contemporary Village Politics

Among Samosir Batak, the only concept resembling sovereignty over territory is derived from the act of pioneering. This can best be understood in terms of ethnohistory and the role it plays in contemporary village politics. Accounts of the past are also useful in describing the lineage system of the village.

One way to conceptualize Samosir Batak social ideals is in terms of what Meillassoux (1981) has called "the juridical-ideological principles of kinship." It is justified because putting these matters into our terms is a way to effect "cultural translation." The Batak categories of *marga* ("moiety"/"clan"/"sub-clan") and *suhi* ("minimal" or "localized lineage") unite some households and differentiate them from others. It is a patrilineal society in that, among other things, while women do not join their husband's clans or take their clan names, their children do. A second principle is that of exogamy: people may not marry others of their own clan. A third is that the "direction" of a marriage between two lineages of different clans may not be reversed for five generations: one cannot marry a woman from a lineage to which one's patriline has "given" a sister or daughter as a wife. As a result of marriage with women from lineages of other clans, some men within a given lineage come to establish alliances with some men of other clans. Eventually, such alliances tend to overshadow the unity of members of a given line of descent.

An account of some village disputes will demonstrate the principles of Batak kinship in operation on a general level. This is a necessary preliminary to the later discussion of access to "factors of production," such as land, livestock, and labor. I here describe Batak society in terms of a lineage model because I later discuss exchange and access to the factors of production on the parts of lineages and clans.

To explain the terms in which villagers think about their social world and its place in the cosmos and on which their social institutions and notions of sovereignty, as we imagine them, are constructed, it is useful to begin with a brief account of the settling of the Sagala Valley and the foundation and expansion of its topmost hamlet cluster, Huta Ginjang. These accounts contain what Malinowski referred to as "mythical charters" of pioneering, the foundation of hamlets by patrilineal ancestors, and the formation of alliances sealed by marriages.

Original Settlement of Sagala and Huta Ginjang

I was told that Si Raja Batak, the first man, was born by a large boulder called Batu Hobon, "Rice-bin Stone," which lies in the top of the ridge separating the Sagala and Limbong Valleys and connecting the mountain to the high tableland on the west side of the Toba crater. Sagala Raja, the first Sagala, was a grandson of Si Raja Batak. He remained in the first hamlet, Huta Urat (*urat* = root). For twelve years his first wife bore no children, and he decided to take a second. Both wives then got pregnant and, it is sometimes claimed, the second wife gave birth at sunrise and the first at sunset on the same day, both to boys. One son founded "Inner Village" (Huta Bagas) and his brother "Outer Village" (Huta Ruar). A later son remained at the dwelling place of his parents. Except for clearings, the entire valley was at that time covered with forest.

A double calamity then struck: a ferocious wild boar clad in chain and a seven-headed eagle made it impossible for people to go outside their houses. They were saved by a man of the Purba clan, out canoeing, who noticed rice husks floating into the lake at the mouth of the river that drains the valley through its bottleneck on the north side. He followed the banks of the river to find the people who had pounded the rice and thus arrived at the village where Sagala Raja lived with his wives and children. Purba offered to shoot the boar and eagle with his magical blowpipe on the condition that he be given a wife if he succeeded. Although he was severely injured when part of the eagle fell on him, he recovered and was given a bride. He then requested land from his father-in-law, Sagala Raja, and was told that if he shot toward the north, the land between his dart and the lake would henceforth be his *golat* to bequeath to his descendants. In this manner his descendants became the *boru tano* ('wife-receivers-of-the-earth') of the Sagalas.

Many hamlets were founded by the descendants of Sagala Raja and his son-in-law, who became *marga* (clan) Siboro. Subsequent local history consists of the founding of branch hamlets and rather truncated accounts of past inter-village feuding (*marmusu*). That of Huta Ginjang is not atypical. Si Raja Huta Ruar, the son of Sagala Raja's first wife, had four sons. The second of the four, Si Ruma Pintu, founded a hamlet of that name next to Huta Ruar. The fourth son of one of his descendants abducted the daughter of Raja Situmorang of Harian, the valley to the immediate south of Limbong, an especially serious crime, since the girl was already promised in marriage. The man's older brothers feared the wrath of the girl's father and refused admittance to the couple, who fled up the mountain to a small spring, thus becoming the first to 'pioneer the land' of Huta Ginjang (*manombang tano Huta Ginjang*).[1]

This account is often cited in matters of ritual precedence among lineages of the Sagala clan in Huta Ginjang. While the "mother village," Ruma Pintu, has only four houses left, there are 54 households of the descendants of Sagala Ruma Pintu in Huta Ginjang (and many others in the hamlet clusters of Si Hudon and Janji Matogu in the northern half of the valley). Some say that the older brothers of the village founder followed him within a few years because they had heard of the bounteously yielding land he had found. Others say that their hamlet was burned by enemies, the older brothers lost their

[1]Vergouwen (1964:118) gives *manombang* as 'being the first to utilize an area,' although Warneck (1977) translates it as "to mine." The use I heard is also in Ypes (1932:355), however, for Laguboti and the Toba Plateau (ibid.:383; 390) (Dr. P. Voorhoeve, personal communication 1981).

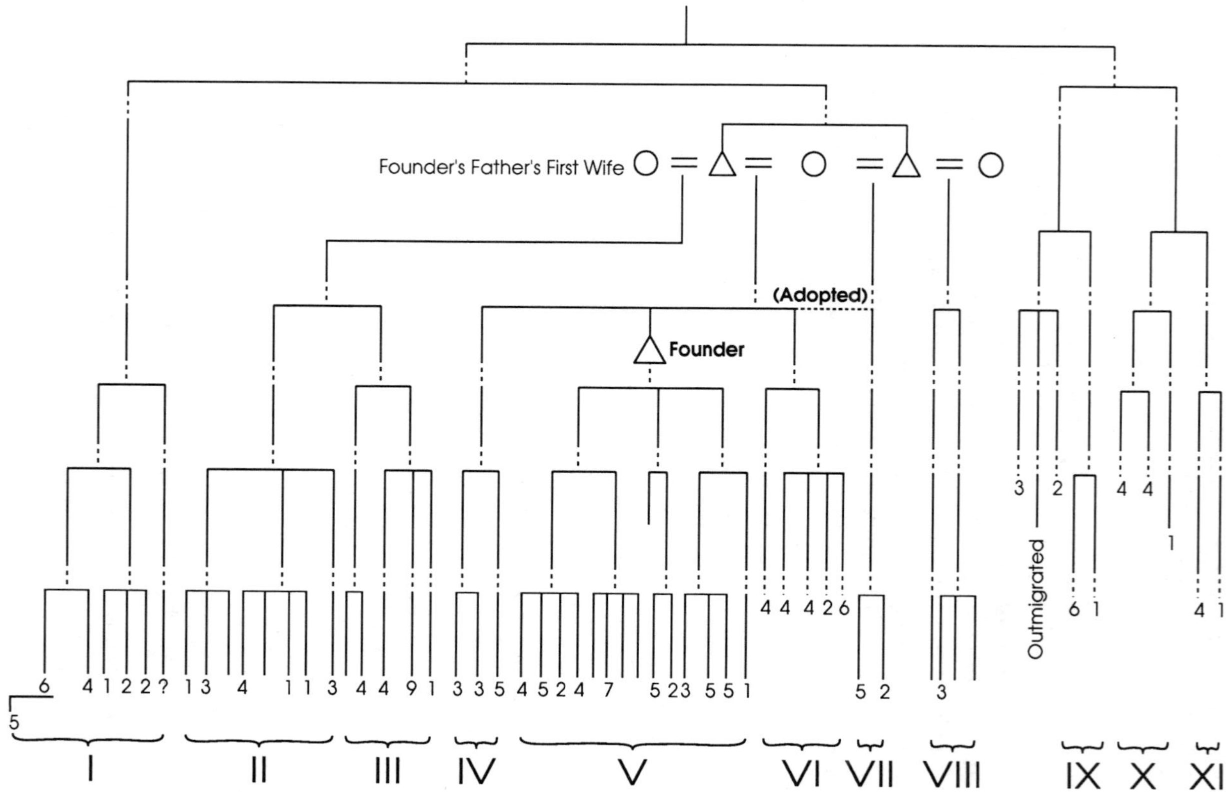

Figure 3.1. Schematic genealogy of Huta Ginjang Sagala men.

stores of rice, were driven out, and went up the mountain to seek shelter. Whatever the case, some of their descendants have maintained or reestablished a modicum of wet-rice holdings in the valley.

Localized Lineages in the Hamlet Cluster

The genealogy (*tarombo*) of the Sagalas of the Ruma Pintu subclan in Huta Ginjang can be shown schematically—as they sometimes do with matchsticks arranged in upside-down Vs in more pyramidal form when conversing among themselves (without encouragement on the part of an inquiring anthropologist). The most compact diagram appears in Figure 3.1.

For the groups indicated where Roman numerals have been used, villagers speak of *suhi* (literally, corners), which I translate as "lineage" or "minimal, localized lineage." The lineages are never mentioned as such in other than ritual contexts. Indeed, it is only in ritual contexts that contemporary villagers actually 'line up according to the genealogy.' Lineages are not referred to by the names of ancestors but by those of contemporary representatives, often with nicknames, personal names, or teknonyms ('Father of So-and-so'), depending on the speaker.

Table 3.1 shows the number of household heads of each lineage of the Sagala clan in the hamlets shown in Map 4. It can be seen that there is a tendency toward dispersal of residence on the part of close agnatic kin of the larger descent groups, though lineage I is an exception.

A topographical map made by the Dutch during the late 1920s and early 1930s shows only three hamlets where now there are eight distinguishable. It bears out the accounts of villagers that all but three hamlets had been founded by their fathers or, in half the cases, by themselves. Two pre-Dutch hamlets and all the rest were founded by men of Sagala lineages (III, V, VII, VIII, and X). The proliferation of hamlets was undoubtedly made possible by the *pax nederlandica*, the prolonged, imposed, intervillage peace of the colonial period.

The other half of village household heads were members of eleven clans. The first to join the Sagalas was a man of the Sigiro clan, who

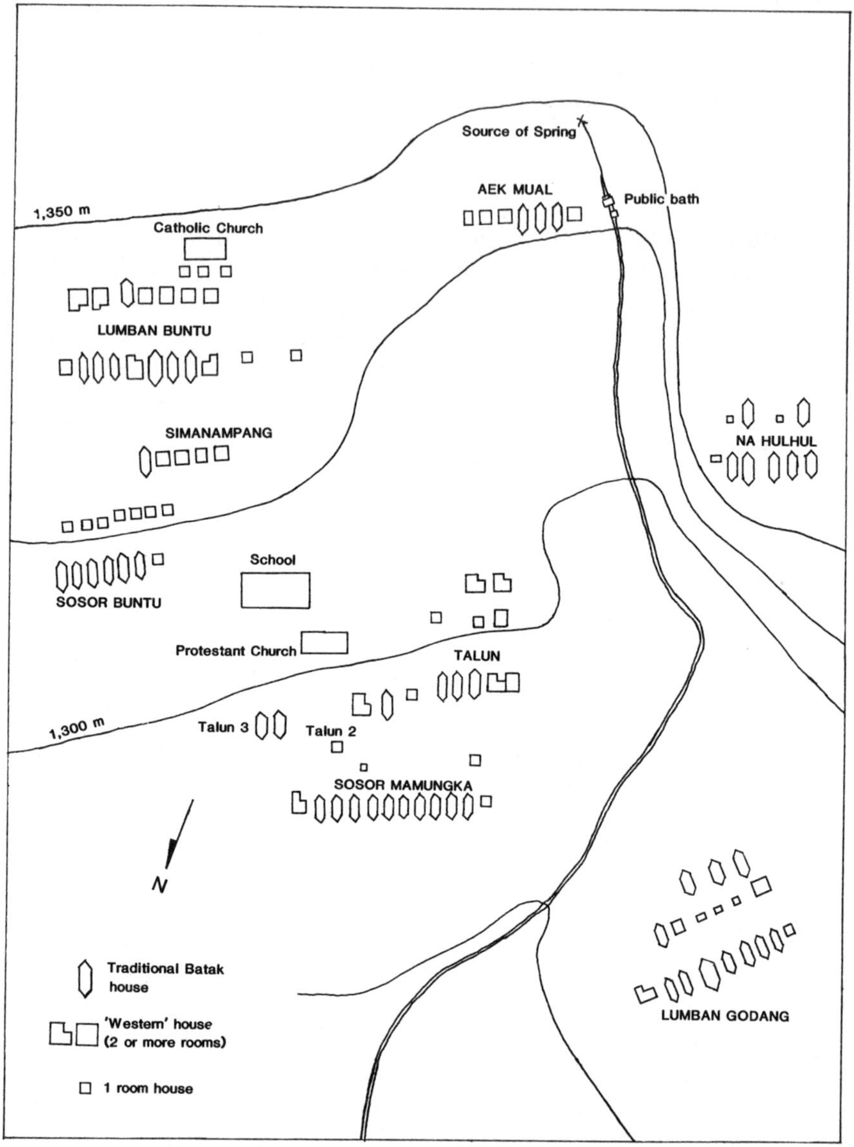

Map 4. Layout of the hamlets of Huta Ginjang (not to scale).

TABLE 3.1
Households of Sagala Ruma Pintu Lineages by Hamlet

Hamlets	Lineages (*suhi*)										
	I	II	III	IV	V	VI	VII	VIII	IX	X	XI
Lumban Godang				1	6	3					
Sosor Mamungka		6	3	1							
Talun		1	2		1	2	2				
Talun-2					1						
Talun-3					1						
Sosor Buntu									3	3	2
Simanampang				1				2			
Lumban Buntu	8										
Aek Mual				1	3	1					
Na Hul Hul	(no Sagalas)										

NOTE: Two Sagala households of another subclan are not included.

was given a bride and *golat* rights to land as a reward for heroic feats, as was the Siboro man who saved Sagala Raja. They are hence referred to as 'daughters' or 'wife-receivers of the land' (*boru tano*). The story of how this came about is intertwined with that of the founder's descendants. The founder's mother, his father's second wife, bore three sons (the founder being the third) and then a girl and a boy after the death of his father, when she had been taken in leviratic marriage by his father's younger brother (see the genealogy, Fig. 3.1, above). Her daughter's marriage to the heroic Sigiro was in return for his protecting the flank of the hillside, below Na Hul Hul, under which his brothers-in-law resided (see Map 4).[2] But a debate arose over whether the girl had been conceived by the founder's father or by the latter's younger brother. In spite of claims that the founder had adopted his younger half-sister and half-brother (to establish their

[2]Wife-receiving groups of the Kachin village that Leach studied are also said to have been "allocated village sites in the conquered territory of Hpalang" as a reward for military aid (Leach 1965:93).

sibling status), the latter's descendants claim to be of a different line (Sherman 1982:705-711).

Other alliances were established by additional Sagala lineages with members of other wife-receiving clans who came to live in the hamlets already built. In addition, the ancestors of a number of men who were wife-givers of Sagalas had 'followed their sisters' to the village after the latter married Sagala men. Three men of the present generation have done so. (Ways in which in-dwelling wife-receivers and wife-givers are found interspersed with Sagalas in the hamlets are indicated in Table 3.2 and in the sample hamlet maps and genealogical diagrams, Figures 3.3 and 3.4.)

Batak Categories and the Segmentary Lineage Model

The Batak conceive of a key aspect of their social organization in terms that correspond to "segmentary lineage structure." A few examples of their thinking on these matters support this assertion and illustrate aspects of village hierarchies that take shape and dissolve with the passage of time.

On one occasion, a group of descendants of the village founder drew up the guest list for a marriage ceremony and expressed the thought that the 'order of call' for their party's receipt of plates of food and, later, of bridewealth payments 'shows the genealogy' (*pataridahon tarombo*). They wrote out a list to insure that no one was left out. First they debated their own relative order, using such expressions as, 'It has to go by stairs [from those closest to the bride's father in the genealogy to those whose precedence is the result of seniority]' (*ingkon martangga-tangga*); 'in a line' (*marjejer*); 'everyone has to be classified' (*ingkon na margoli-goli be do*); 'it is here that the classifications of people are visible' (*ison do tarida goli-goli ni angka jolma*).[3] There was virtually no debate on the order of members of other lineages.

[3]The word *goli-goli* indicates a small terrace or a raised bed in a field. Warneck (1977), however, does not give that meaning. According to him, *goli* means "*Zeichen der Einteilung*" (German, mark of an arrangement, a classification) and "*definitives oder vorläufiges Ende an einer Sache*" (a definite or provisional end of a matter); he gives *margoli* as 'settled, agreed, all right.'

TABLE 3.2
Clan and Hamlet Residence of Household Heads

Name of hamlet (number of households)	Sagala	Wife-receivers of Sagala	Wife-givers of Sagala
Lumban Godang (18)	10	3 Sigiro 1 Limbong 1 Simalango 1 Situngkir	1 Simalango 1 Simbolon
Sosor Mamungka (15)	10	1 Sigiro 1 Simanjorang 1 Simaibang	
Talun-1 (13)	10	2 Simanjorang	1 Sitanggang
Talun-2 (2)	1	1 Limbong	
Talun-3 (1)	1		
Sosor Buntu (17)	8	1 Sigiro 1 Simanjorang 1 Limbong 1 Saragi 1 Tamba	2 Sigiro 2 Simbolon
Simanampang (5)	3	2 Simanjorang	
Lumban Buntu (20)	8	2 Simanjorang 1 Limbong 2 Saragi 1 Sinaga	1 Sigiro 3 Naibaho 2 Simbolon
Aek Mual (8)	5	2 Sigiro 1 Limbong	
Na Hul Hul (13)	-	8 Sigiro 1 Simanjorang	4 Simarmata

Figure 3.2. Wide-angle view of part of a row of houses, showing houses 4-9 in Figure 3.3. The houses face on a raised terrace courtyard. The gondang orchestra sits in the balcony at a feast of the owner of such a house. (All doors face to this side. Those with visible doors are not in traditional style. Those whose doors are not visible have recessed stairs, by which to enter. It is said the doors were formerly hidden in this way to force an observer to duck in front of the doorway to see if the door was open or barred.)

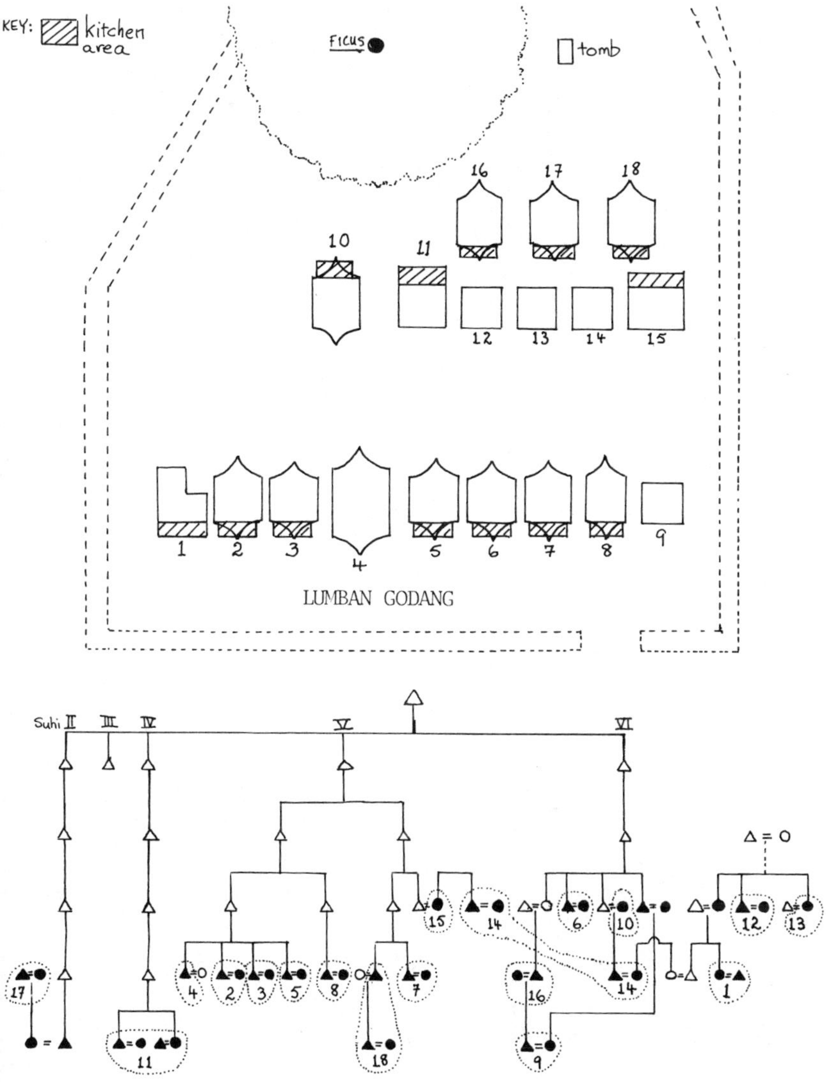

Figure 3.3. Genealogy and residence (Lumban Godang).

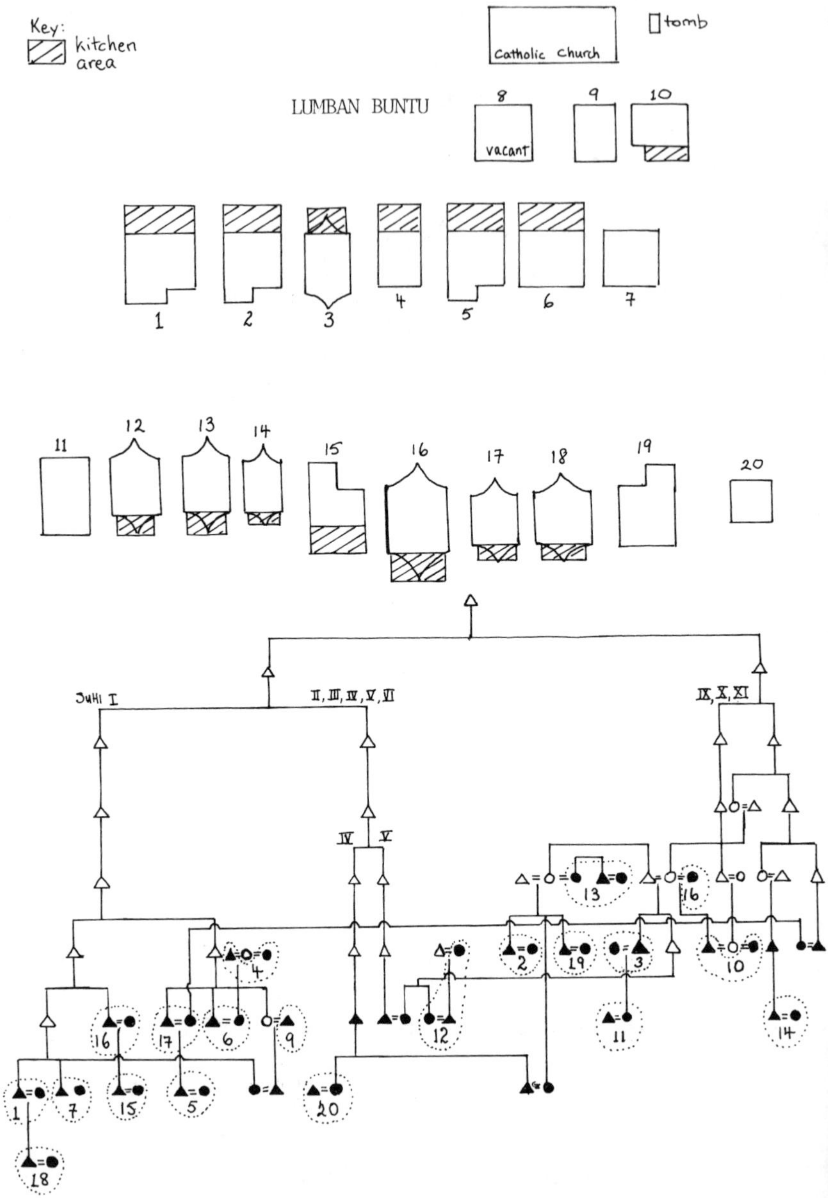

Figure 3.4. Genealogy and residence (Lumban Buntu).

And there is a good degree of correlation between the list they compiled and genealogical data gathered separately, so the above metaphors can be taken as evidence of an indigenous conceptual scheme of the patrilineal genealogy of Sagalas.[4]

Their first concern in setting up the order of call was to make all the lineages stemming ('dispersing,' *na marserak*) from a mutual great-great grandfather 'visible.' Thus, they first listed one person from the eldest line of each lineage (II-VI) descended from the founder's father. When asked why, the answer was, 'So they will show, those of one ancestor' (*Asa tarida nasida saompu*). But when they were forced to choose between the desire to please by giving precedence and the necessity of making individual sublineages 'visible,' they listed IIa2, IIa3, IIb1—Roman numerals indicate lineage, lowercase letters indicate the birth order of the sublineage, and Arabic numbers indicate the person's order of birth. They skipped IIb2, in order to first list IIc, 'So that his father be visible' (*asa tarida amangna*). Yet for reasons having to do with relative age and even perhaps with shared relationships through women who were sisters, they had listed IIa3 before IIb1. The rest of the Sagalas were listed in order of increasing distance starting with the descendants of the founder's younger brother. Wife-receivers (twelve "father's sisters" and eleven "sisters") and the remaining classificatory wife-receivers in the village, the 16 wife-givers (less a barren couple), the mother's father and bride's mother's brother. All except the last two were listed according to the order of increasing genealogical 'distance' of their Sagala in-laws from the principals.

The use of metaphors such as 'by nodes' (*na margoli-goli*) indicates

[4]If we use Roman numerals to indicate lineage, lowercase letters to indicate the birth order of the sublineage, asterisks to indicate that the person in question is one generation grade below the bulk of household heads within his lineage, and Arabic numbers to indicate men's order of birth relative to other members of the sublineage, then the order that they set up for those following the members of the bride's father's lineage (V) can be shown thus: IIa*1, IIIa1, IVb1, VIa1, IIa2, IIa3, IIb1, IIc, IIb2, IIb4, IIb*2, IIIb1, IIIb (widowed step-mother of IIIbl), IIIb2, IIIb3, IIIa2, IIIb5, IVc, IVa*1, IVa2, VIb*1, VIc*2, VIc*3, VIc*4, VIe*2, VIIIa, VIIIb1, VIIIb2, VIIIb3, VIIIb*1, VIIa, VIIb, Ia1, Ib, Ic2, Ic3, Ib*1, Ia6, Ic*1, Ib*2, Ib*3, Ib*4, Ia*1, Xa1, Xa2, XIa, IXb, IXc, Xb, Xa*1, Xa*2, Xa*3, XIa*1, IXa. (For a fuller account, see Sherman 1982:175-176, 712-718.)

that the genealogy is a cognitive map. But while they know the relative "positions" of the various lineages and the names of four or five generations of their own lineage ancestors, they often do not know, or are only imperfectly aware of, ancestors of men of other lineages. One man claimed that in former times no one except the descendants of Ompu Niermas, grandfather of the founder of the village, had known the genealogy and that when people from Huta Ginjang made the trip to the market at Pangururan, 6 kilometers away on the east side of the mountain, they claimed to be descended from the founder's grandfather, even if they were not. Some members of lineages I and X admitted that this might have been true because, as they put it, he had been greatly respected (*na sangap*).

Clan or lineage segments were traditionally given shape through opposition in feud and other sorts of violence in some situations, as Evans-Pritchard suggested for the Nuer (1940:142-149). But the levels-of-violence basis of fusion of segments, according to which those most closely related join forces to oppose a more distantly related segment, is as difficult to apply in the Batak case as it is for the Nuer or Bedouins (Peters 1967).[5] As can be seen from Figure 3.1, they are not in demographic balance to each other. It is likewise impossible to apply a model of structural equilibrium to the larger Toba Batak genealogy (Hutagalung 1961). Historically, Batak villages that were invaded and Islamized by marauding Padris from Minangkabau were prone to insularity and were unable to constitute a grand alliance to oppose the invaders (Dobbin 1983, chap. 5). The same problem characterized Batak opposition to the Dutch. Judging from informants' accounts, each village at various times had hostile relations with almost all other villages, except those with which its inhabitants had periodically renewed relations of wife-giving and wife-receiving. Contrary to the fusion-and-fission model of segmentary lineages, these accounts do not refer to cooperation among individual villages of the respective segments of subclan or sacrificial offering community (*bius*) areas. To

[5]For an account of difficulties with the application of the "balanced-opposition" or "fission-and-fusion" model elsewhere, see Emrys Peters (1960, 1967). This part of my discussion owes a great deal to Peters' essays and to their discussion by Michael Meeker.

the contrary, on occasion, minimal segments of two major Sagala subclans (or their wife-receivers) united to harass a common enemy who was lineage 'brother' of one or the other.

The place of women in the genealogies also contravenes notions of an agnatic or patrilineal "principle." This can be seen by reconsidering the main genealogical divisions in the Sagala community (e.g., the two wives of Sagala Raja gave birth to three subclans) and in the village of Huta Ginjang (the alliance with the Sigiros turns on the marriage of the daughter of a second marriage of a second wife). At present, a social and ritual distinction is made between descendants of the mother of the founder, who was his father's second wife, and those of his father's first wife. Only descendants of the second wife received a portion of the top of the tail section of sacrificial offerings. A model of invariant patrilineal descent and unilineal descent groups does not account for the customary division of portions. This ought to make us aware that such models are simply glosses of a complex reality; each helps us apprehend and make sense of some parts of that reality, although we also recognize that we are stretching the model to continue its use. (As noted earlier, I want to use the model to examine land holdings of different lineages and clans, in part because doing so addresses Leach's feudal analogy.)

There are several indications of what may be termed the strength of links established through women in the framework of Batak patrilineal-descent ideals. Many sayings enunciate another ideal of strong bonds between men whose mothers or wives are of the same clan (such men are each other's *pariban*, as are women of the same clan, as well as a woman and her father's sister's son—her ideal marriage partner). The only stronger bonds among men are said to be those of a man and his sisters' sons, which are likewise traced through a woman:

> A fork is still a branch, a worn mat is a mat;
> a mother's brother is a father, a sister's son is a son.
>
> (*Dangka do dupang, amak do rere; ama do tulang, anak ibebere.*)

Yet these same men also say that in tracing descent or establishing proper precedence, 'as for [ties traced through] one's mother's clan, [they] lack strength' (*molo marga ni ina, hurang kuat*), or, again, 'It is not followed, the clan of a mother' (*Ndang siihuthonon marga ni ina*). More will be said later on the importance of women's roles in Batak society. In concluding this chapter, I take up the precedence rights of descendants of the village founder.

Harajaon: The "Right to Rule" or Exercise of Ritual Perquisites?

'To open,' 'launch,' or 'found' a hamlet, *mamungka huta*, is said by J. C. Vergouwen (1964:110-111) to give a man and his male descendants "the rights to be masters there and freely to dispose over the admittance of others." Descendants of those who have been admitted have an unquestioned right to remain. If it were otherwise, the descendants of a founder in an overpopulated area would simply expel those of other lines. One would not find villages like Huta Ginjang, where half the men are of clans other than the founder's.

Vergouwen wrote that "the right to rule in the village, *harajaon*," is "the common right, *hatopan*, of every one of the founder's direct patrilineal descendants" (1964:112). What the people refer to as *harajaon tano*, which literally might translate as 'lordship of the earth' (*raja* = king, in Sanskrit; *tano* = earth), is indeed a *shared* attribute of the descendants of the founder of Huta Ginjang. How could this shared right have been thought by the Dutch to signify "the right to rule" or "chiefship"?

Although the word *raja* in Sanskrit signifies 'king' and the word *tano* refers to 'land' in Batak, the compound *harajaon tano* does not signify "sovereignty over land" or "rule over a territory," as its overt derivation led Dutch scholars to believe. In Huta Ginjang, those descended from the first man to pioneer the land retain the attribute of *harajaon tano*. This gives them the position of "master of ceremonies" and the concomitant right to divide the 'showing parts of the food' in ritual concerned with establishing permanent constructions—hamlets or tombs—on the land. This interpretation is borne out by an excerpt from an article entitled "Younger by birth-order, elder in *harajaon*" in a magazine of Batak culture. *Harajaon,* says the writer, does not refer to "the governing of some king who sits upon a throne":

> Rather, the *harajaon* of which they speak means something like 'cares for, [has] authority over what is done, the order of the ceremony, feast celebration, including who speaks, who receives the portions, who gives and receives shawls, and other things.' As we know, *harajaon* among us Bataks [is manifested when] one is put forward to be the main speaker, the one who gives the shawl, the one who receives the *jambar*-portion, and likewise, if one becomes the one who is listened to. (Anonymous 1977:31)

Thus *harajaon* refers to the exercise of ritual perquisites and *harajaon tano* to the exercise of those perquisites with respect to land. As a descendant of the founder said to assembled elders when challenged at a tomb-permit ceremony:

> As concerns [being of] this land (*partano on*), founding of a hamlet, building of a tomb, that is land-custom (*adat tano*), it is we. Because it was we who pioneered (*manombang*) the land of Huta Ginjang. . . . The hamlet cluster which is here in Huta Ginjang was founded by our ancestor, and it was he who made the prayer [to the earth spirits] (*manilupi*). Thus it is he who clamps the standard (*manolothon bane-bane*) [for founding a new hamlet]. Thus, those who have the right (*hak*) in that sacrificial offering community have the right in the land (*i partanoan i*). . . . And concerning the tombs that exist—there have been two or three—always, it is we who receive the stem of the tail section [because tombs are something which is] of the land (*taringot partanoan i*).

Although objections were raised by two men of lineage IV, they gave way, tacitly approving the proceedings with the statement: "Our words, so long as we have spoken them."

The founder or descendants of the founder of the first hamlet in a distinctly separate area like Huta Ginjang also have the right to exercise ritual perquisites with respect to the founding of adjacent hamlets by virtue of the need to ceremonially bless the breaking of ground for the enterprise. Their power to do this derives from the founder, because he was the first to break the ground, to pioneer an area that, in effect, had previously been the sole domain of spirits.

What we consider political sovereignty is distinguished from such ritual perquisites, even in matters of 'land custom' (*adat tano*). For instance, although the elected headman happened to be a descendant of the founder, a man of an older collateral line, not the headman, served as pre-eminent ritual speaker for members of the Ruma Pintu subclan of Sagalas on occasions when they all came together with their male in-laws, such as at the ceremony to give permission and blessing for a tomb to be built by members of another clan. Descendants of the founder were first in order of speaking and had 'the showing parts of the food' presented to them, but all their patri-cousins and other village elders were served a meal of rice and pork and were asked for blessings. After the meal, the top of the tail section and other 'showing parts' (*tudu-tudu*) were presented to the speaker for lineages descended from the founder, and he divided them. In this distribution of special portions, the hamlet headmen received theirs first by general consent, and only then did the village headman (considered a government official) receive his.[6] Further portions were distributed to descendants of the founder's brothers, his father's brothers, etc., and to their in-laws.

Political authority beyond the domestic jurisdiction of hamlet headmen (*tunggane ni huta*)—who could restrict residence in their hamlets, who participated prominently in territory-wide ritual, as well

[6]The office of village headman was first instituted by the Dutch, under whom two headmen served, one in the upper and the other in the lower Sagala hamlets of Huta Ginjang. Of four headmen who served under the Dutch and Japanese administrations (two of whom were still living in 1978), only one was a direct patrilineal descendant of the founder. Two were descendants of brothers of the founder, and one was a descendant of a brother of the founder's grandfather. It happened, though, that when this research was carried out, the man serving as headman (*Kepala kampung*), who had been in office for some eight years, was a direct patrilineal descendant of the founder.

The headman today acts as a transmitter of government directives, tax collector, and purveyor of funds for projects such as building a road to the village, a school-building, and a few drainage culverts. His ability to mediate or adjudicate serious disputes is very limited, and, indeed, that is not a function the government has delegated to the headman. Villagers know they can appeal to the police over the head of their chief elected official. One man, whose daughter-in-law reported she had been raped, left the headman no alternative but to lead a party with the accused man to the district police office, some 10 kilometers away. (Only in an instance in which two villagers were accused of breaking and entering a house in a nearby village did the headman succeed in mediation on their behalf.)

as in conflict and the resolution of conflict, and whose positions were essentially inherited by the oldest qualified male in their founder's descent line—does not appear to have been institutionalized. The authority required for colonial government at a local level had to be instituted by decree. Even with the centralization of political authority in the person of the modern village headman, the concept of *harajaon* is not used as "the right to rule." Thus, although the descendants of the founder maintained their ritual perquisites, and although the headman was a descendant, it was not claimed that they alone could dispense such blessings or give permission for the tomb to be built. All adult males of the Sagala Ruma Pintu subclan in Huta Ginjang were feasted, and all gave their blessing, because they are all 'of one land,' *sisada tano*. With one exception, their affines were also served the meal and gave blessings, but as 'elders' (*natua-tua*) and as members of the 'one-eating' community (*sapanganon*) or sacrificial-offering community (*bius*). (The exception, who received special portions, was the hamlet headman of the Sigiro hamlet, representative of the 'wife-receivers of the land,' *boru tano*.)

The "council" of elders from all the hamlets of the cluster comprises the village *bius* (territorial sacrificial offering community), a component of one of the four larger *bius* groupings of Sagala Valley. In the next chapter it will be shown that they share in the essence of the clans and lineages and that the latter are integral to the sacrificial communities.

Chapter 4

Bius: Religious Conflict and Accommodation

To the Batak, representatives of both church and state probably seemed to be the beneficiaries of a power whose source they imagined to be unitary, derived from special knowledge and special grace. The fact that missions and military conquest, here as elsewhere in the world, were not very far apart in their advances is perhaps less fortuitous than is sometimes thought. In fact, many of the nineteenth-century Europeans most directly involved in the conversion and colonization efforts directed at the Batak peoples were imbued with a notion of arresting the spread of Islam, which dated back to medieval Christianity. N. van der Tuuk urged prospective missionaries during the 1850s to work among the Batak in the north because they had not yet converted to Islam: "If we do not follow this plan it is my opinion that the whole society will become Islamized before we realize it" (cited in Pederson 1970:54).

By the nineteenth century, there had been a separation of the priorities of peaceful trade and spreading the gospel, both of which preoccupied the first European power, the Portuguese, in the Indian Ocean (Schrieke 1966:38). Yet, in 1912, when the Rheinish Mission was managing 494 public schools, 200 vocational training schools, a technical school, and a Dutch middle school, "the Dutch colonial Government. . . made a yearly grant to the schools of eighty thousand [guilders]" (Pederson 1970:70). For those subjected to colonization, the separation of secular and religious authority was perhaps unclear.

It is also significant that "[t]he conversion of whole villages and clan groups as social units served to preserve the kinship hierarchy, shaping the church organizations along familiar lines" (Pederson 1970:85). This, combined with the fact that, as Castles (1972:139-140) notes, "Batak magical concepts penetrated the popular interpretation of such rites as baptism, confirmation and ordination, and . . . [the Bataks] saw the missionaries as jealously keeping to themselves [the 'soul force' of the church] by specious excuses," has resulted in the formation of dozens of independent Batak churches. In the postwar era, it became incumbent on villagers to register as adherents of one of the world religions to avoid suspicion of atheism during the anti-Communist purges that, elsewhere in Indonesia, followed the presumed 1965 coup in Java. This resulted in massive registration of Samosirese, Karo, and Dairi Bataks as Christians ("*Kristen*") (Pederson 1970:187-192) for what, in our terms, were essentially political considerations.

Not surprisingly, the "continuing areas of conflict between [custom]-sanctioned traditions and Christian responsibility" listed by a Batak theologian remain: (1) eloping, "to avoid the expensive formalities of a church wedding . . . with an estimated 80 percent of the couples in [the city of] Medan choosing to elope"; (2) the unequal inheritance rights of women; (3) "the many *tugu* (ancestral monuments) that have been erected throughout Batakland . . . in the name of carrying out the commandment 'to honor thy father and mother'"; and (4) "the *gondang* or traditional Batak music accompanying any large social gathering or feast" (cited in Pederson 1970:85-86). The significance of both tombs and feasting is important for an analysis of the traditional sacrificial offering organizations called *bius*. This analysis, in turn, contributes to our understanding of what was referred to earlier as the "baseline" and subsequent changes.

Stone Tomb-Shrines, Ancient and Modern

One might say that Christianity has found a harbor in Batak society through the straits of the Fifth Commandment, which is most loudly and most often repeated in 'Ripe-old-age feasts' (*Gondang Saurmatua*):

> Honour your parents, so that you may live long in this land which God gave you, it is said in the Fifth Commandment

—to which, in disinterment feasts, the following is added:

> And these feast-givers are setting an example to be followed by all in raising the bones of their parents up to a high mountain, to a hard stone.

In the past, each major, subterritorial *bius* used a single, hand-hewn, covered stone urn or sarcophagus as a repository for the disinterred bones and skulls of deceased forebears of the inhabitants. According to Holt (1967:22), it was "the bones of high-ranking Batak dead" that were thus preserved. Informants told of several weeks when all four Sagala *bius* participated in an annual disinterment feast at which families that had so planned exhumed the remains of individual ancestors to be deposited in the common stone bone repositories, the 'place of bones' (*parholian*). The urns and sarcophaguses are no longer actively used, but massive concrete tombs that house the remains of ancestors of minimal lineages now dot the landscape. It is significant that the Dutch had ordered many stone sarcophaguses to be moved to locations outside and at a distance from the village squares, where they traditionally stood, for "considerations of hygiene" (Tichelman 1942:250). Thus the change in treatment of the dead may well have been conceived in response to regulations whose ostensible purpose was to promote sanitation.[1]

Other factors were perhaps more important, especially the technological possibilities of concrete. After being carved, the stones from which traditional sarcophaguses were hewn had to be transported over rough terrain by large numbers of draggers or bearers, and the cost of provisioning bearers would have been significant. The danger of breakage was also quite real (as the shattered frame of one by the side of the road from Tomok to Ronggur ni Huta makes evident). The use of concrete filled with stone rubble for recent constructions obviated

[1]In fact, hiking along the west side of the Samosir peninsula, I came upon two separate instances in which sarcophaguses had recently been moved back to their original hamlet sites, one in Lumban Suhi-suhi and the other (still supported by scaffolding) in Rianiate.

A carved stone sarcophagus, recently moved back to a hamlet.

Placing bones and skull (visible at the side of the ledge) inside a relatively small concrete tomb. Irrigated rice terraces are visible in the background.

that danger, since needed materials could be assembled piecemeal at a chosen site with a good deal less risk and difficulty. The effect has been to make the building of individual tombs economically feasible for many minor lineages in Samosir and throughout the Bataklands. In Huta Ginjang, where there are some twenty lineages, there were already eleven tombs in 1978, including two of wife-givers and one of a wife-receiving group.

In spite of certain changes, the belief in the power of ancestor spirits to affect the well-being of their descendants is still prevalent. (While countenancing the entombment process, churches consider it a problem.) Two or three disinterment feasts are held in Sagala at unsynchronized times after the main rice harvest each year. Typically, such a feast brings together the members of an entire lineage (many of whom come from afar) as sponsors, and representatives of all four main *bius* participate.

Territorial, Sacrificial Offering Organizations

At present, in the Samosir area, *bius* 'priests' give permission for and bestow blessings on disinterments and on a variety of other large-scale "Feasts of Merit" (as similar feasts have come to be called in Southeast Asian ethnology). The *bius* "sacrificial-offering communities" are constituted at successively more encompassing "levels" of what might be termed "ritual integration" of the society within each territory. The overarching '*Bius* of the Four Corners of the Rice Basket' is unique to the territory of Sagala. (That of Limbong Valley is termed 'the *Bius* of the Seven Ropes,' that of Pangururan, the '*Bius* of the Three Legs of the Buffalo.') The *bius* involved in a ceremony may vary. Indoor sacrificial offerings by members of a lineage, such as descendants of the founder of Huta Ginjang, require at least a goat and may be referred to as a "goat-eating community." A sublineage may use a small pig and be referred to as a "pig-eating community." But in order to hold a sacrificial feast at which either a cow, a buffalo, or a horse is slaughtered, a localized lineage must request the permission and collaboration of the component of the overall *bius* to which it belongs. Each of the four 'corners' of the Sagala *bius* (Sagala Huta Ruar, Sagala Huta Bagas, Sagala Huta Urat, and Suha [Siboro]) is considered a buffalo-eating union, 'a buffalo-eating community' (*sapanganon horbo*). Huta Ginjang belongs to Huta Ruar.

When the members of the Sigiro lineage with the status of 'wife-receivers of the land' in Huta Ginjang decided to hold a 'hamlet-shaking' feast, it required the slaughter of a bull. The 'feasting community' (*sapanganon*) was limited to the Huta Ruar 'corner' of the territory. Only Huta Ruar was represented at the 'fixing of the day' and only they participated in deciding the procedural issues that arose in the course of the main feast, to which representatives of all the *bius* of Sagala as well as many from neighboring areas were invited.

Mount Pusuk Buhit is believed by most Toba Batak to be the birthplace of their common ancestor. Likewise, most consider it the dwelling place of the most powerful of the *sombaon* (localized earth spirits). Ypes defined *sombaon* as "dwelling places of higher beings, which are likewise called *sombaon*," and noted that "the best known [is] the *sombaon* of Pusuk Buhit. It is invoked all the way to the highlands south of the Lake" (Ypes 1932:196). I also encountered an instance in which the *sombaon* of Pusuk Buhit (addressed as 'great Mountain,' *dolok na Bolon*) was invoked by Toba Batak at a feast near Sumbul in Dairi, some 50 kilometers west, over rugged upland plateau. For those who live on the mountain, it is an immediate presence. Huge boulders, cliffs, shoulders, forested chasms, and springs are considered the dwelling places of higher-order spirits. They refer to the one residing at the top of the highest peak as 'our Ancestor that is up there on the mountain' (*Ompunta na i dolok ai*) or simply 'that Ancestor of ours' (*Ompunta i*). Reference is sometimes made to 'our Ancestor, this great mountain' (*Ompunta, dolok na bolon on*).

Some villagers said that periodically all divisions of the *bius* of Sagala and the *bius* of Limbong cooperated in a feast to invoke the *sombaon* of Pusuk Buhit. However, it and other localized ancestral spirits are not invoked only at large feasts. Members of a localized lineage engaging in household sacrifices also make offerings to the *sombaon.* Spirits of the recently deceased are thought to require the prestigious recognition of public feasts of homage held by descendants in order to be transformed from ghosts (*begu*) to *semangot* (or *keramat*) and eventually to *sombaon.* Invocations made when sacrificial offerings are 'put up on the shelf' first address *Mulajadi na Bolon* ('The Great Beginning of Being') and then numerous other spirits, whose names designate specific topographical features such as the rock outcroppings, woods, and springs they are thought to inhabit. Particular ancestors, known to the memories of the supplicants, are addressed last, if at all (see, e.g., Sherman 1982:791).

Thus, *bius* groupings of any size may be considered "ancestral cults of the earth" and as such represent a widespread phenomenon in Southeast Asia. They might be compared, for instance, to the "local cults, tied to the soil" that Paul Mus posited (1933:378) in regard to megalithic stone images and epigraphic evidence dating back 1,200 years from Champa, the area of southern Vietnam, some 400 miles to the north-northeast of Lake Toba.

Colonial Views of the Functions of the Bius

H. Bartlett was struck by the concrete tombs as evidence of a "new flowering, or even survival, of native art" (1934:28), but since he saw few being erected between 1918 and 1927, he thought he was witnessing the withering of the new form, that the "forces bringing about cultural disintegration are too strong." One possible reason for the tomb-building hiatus that Bartlett noted may have been the Dutch ban on *bius* feasts. In order to understand how it came about, which will in turn help in assessing its effects, it is necessary to consider not only missionary pressures on the administration but also the government's own fears with respect to the *bius.* In addition to their religious functions, these *bius* played important traditional roles in economic and political intercourse among territories, some of which became superfluous with the advent of judiciary and other government agencies.

W. K. Ypes, like J. C. Vergouwen, was both a high official of the Dutch administration of the Bataklands and a scholar of the so-called indigenous legal community. He abstracted a number of aspects of the "ties" that traditionally linked the members of a large *bius* in the Samosir region (Ypes 1932:159f.). An outline of his views demonstrates the basis of administrative measures, such as a ban on feasting.

The first was "action of the *bius* as a whole in case one of its members has sustained grave injury at the hands of someone from outside it. In case of murder, arson, [or] poisoning of a member, it could demand extradition of the guilty party." In all likelihood, such purported "action of the *bius* as a whole" applied to *bius* of localized lineages or hamlet clusters. For large unions, adherence to the ideal would have been extremely difficult. It could have applied only in case of injury to those of very high status, with great and loyal followings.

The second aspect Ypes listed was the "form of the *bius* from a territorial whole and the division of the land therein between the affiliated clans." We have already seen some examples of how this comes about in Chapter 3.

Third was having "a collective secular head." This is hard to imagine. Each section of the four 'corners' of Sagala has an equal say in decision-making, and disagreements are resolved by formal debate and a drive for consensus. According to informants, formerly the *raja doli* could have issued directives (Indonesian, *patokan*) but functioned more as what one man termed "Information Minister" and "advisor" (*penasehat*). These accounts are borne out by Vergouwen's observation that "[t]he head of the [*bius*] officials enforces discipline in the corps, but for want of secular power they must be supported therein by the secular chiefs [i.e., hamlet headmen]" (1964:77). In Samosir, he notes, "the *bius* nearly always consisted of a number of fragments" of different clans. The "chief," he added,

> was recruited from the [clan] or [clan] branch to which the office belonged by virtue of primogeniture, earlier settlement or agreement of old. Each of the components . . . provided him with one chief as his assistant. (Vergouwen 1964:125)

Thus, it was not "having a collective secular head" of the *bius* but having a formal, hierarchical, territorially based organization, a kind of priesthood, with an array of assistants (ibid.:76) that acted as a bond among members.

Ypes (1932:161) considered the "united undertaking of large works such as construction of waterworks" to be the fourth aspect of the bonds among *bius* members. Two aspects of building an irrigation system stand out from a Batak point of view. First, it requires channeling of streams and rearrangement of the surface of the earth, thus impinging on the realms of earth and water spirits. Second, Lando's account (1979) of the history of an irrigation system south of the lake shows that the project was made possible by several localized lineages' agreement to serve as hosts for meetings *planning* the work. Such commensal meals are explicitly performed as rituals of strengthening and blessing.

Ypes' fifth factor again adduces politico-legal prerogatives, the "adjudication of intra-*bius* quarrels." This still occurs. I witnessed two instances in which one of the parties in a feast raised a complaint, first concerning an unpaid debt and, second, an unreceived inheritance. A gathering of the elders representing a union of *bius* of different clans ensures the most impartial resolution.

Ypes also considered the ties among *bius* members to stem in part from the "possession of one or more markets." This was based on the institution of a periodic "peace of the market," which had supernatural rather than military sanctions. As with waterworks, a periodic market was established by an agreement sealed with a ritual meal and sacrificial offerings.

The final link among members is said to be the celebration of communal offering feasts, "which consist in offering to the *sombaon*" (Ypes 1932:163). Ypes then describes some 22 offering ceremonies of the Limbong *bius*, all concerned with inducing bountiful yields of rice and general prosperity (ibid.:164-173). But categorizing the ensemble of *bius* rituals as simply one aspect of the ties uniting the members, on a par with the preceding ones, may distort the organization's nature.

Dutch attempts to characterize the religious and secular functions of *bius* were impelled by the practical problems of governing. The aim was both to define the indigenous "polity" and to neutralize whatever authority it possessed. It is therefore not surprising to find Ypes concluding that, "from all the above elements it appears that the *bius* is not only a sacrificial community, but also has a political character" (1932: 163). Vergouwen states that "the sole object" of the larger groupings was that "of celebrating the very large and communal sacrificial ceremonies," but he too considered them both secular and religious organizations, perhaps due to their territorial character, uniting fragments of diverse neighboring clans.

Yet, although Ypes documents it, he neglects to distinguish the most important *bius* function—that is, the conduct of what Firth (1929) called "productive magic." Judging from the repertory of small- and large-scale feasts and offerings of the *bius* of Limbong (Ypes 1932:164f.), their most common and obtrusive traditional effect was the ritual regulation of rice-growing, determining and publicizing the timing of the cycle, and placating or attracting help from the spirits concerned. As such, the *bius* were organizations with agricultural-ritual aims geared to the seasonal cycle. The rites affecting the unfolding of the yearly cycle of planting, care, and harvest were, for the most part, small sacrifices or offerings made to spirits of all the fields, by individual households, at the cue of the priests. The latter's role was to maintain prosperity by auguring the most propitious times for offerings and rectifying the causes of meteorological disasters.

As a territorial sacrificial-offering organization concerned with regulating the agricultural cycle and propitiating earth spirits, the *bius* can be compared with others in Melanesia, Africa, and Southeast Asia (see Malinowski 1935; Richards 1939:354, 359; Stevenson 1943). And although the ritual functions of the *bius* are now less centered on the timing of what have become multifarious agricultural pursuits, they remain focused on assuring continued access to the spirits that control the bounty of earth and sky.

From the point of view of the administration, however, its ritual aims gave the *bius* a degree of control over land and thus a political dimension. As Vergouwen put it,

> In the neighborhood of Pangururan, [the *bius* priests'] officiating at the agricul-

> tural ritual—it is they who give the signal to commence work in the rice-fields—entitles them to have a say in the control of the land within the . . . well-defined agricultural area of their own *marga* [clan]. (Vergouwen 1964:77)

Even this was a relative power: not sovereign control of territory, but a voice in its disposal among members of co-resident lineages. Certainly, the graded pyramid of offices resembles the hierarchies of lowland priesthoods. But the lack of definite criteria for selection of the highest official—"recruited . . . by virtue of primogeniture, earlier settlement or agreement of old" (Vergouwen 1964:125)—indicates that priests of the *bius* did not constitute a "theocratic class" comparable to the priesthoods of classical "irrigation societies" (Steward 1955:201-202). They were cultivators like everyone else, making their living from the soil and enjoying certain perquisites at large feasts.

The Dutch Ban on Bius Feasts and Its Effects

Undoubtedly, Ypes' analysis represents the quintessence of a long tradition of colonial analysis of Batak society. Such analysis provided a major impetus for the ban on large-scale feasts.

During the latter part of their administration, before their ouster by the Japanese, the Dutch maintained a ban on *bius* feasts. Exactly when the Dutch ban went into effect is unclear. It was apparently shortly after D. van der Meulen's tenure as Controleur of Samosir, which ended in 1920, for he writes (1977:77-78) of having opposed missionary urgings that he institute such a ban. Middendorp (1913:14) also noted: "I always give the permission which must be requested" for feasts with dancing to the *gondang* orchestra. But V. E. Korn, who became province head (Dutch, *Resident*) of Tapanuli in 1936, writes that in 1938 three priests from Pangururan came to his headquarters to ask that the "over twenty-year long ban" be lifted, because it was harmful.

> Inquiry in the archives showed that indeed there was such a prohibition. The sacrifice of buffalos had led to some fights while killing of buffalos with knives

> was called cruel. But the archives also contained requests from the local people that this prohibition be lifted. . . .
>
> Further research showed that the Rheinish Mission had urgently requested this prohibition. . . . I found that the old Nommenson [a missionary called 'Apostle to the Batak'] was bothered by the offering feasts because [converts] had to leave the community. . . . In 1939 not more than a third of the population of Samosir had been converted to Christianity. The other two-thirds were . . . still longing for the restoration of the offering feasts. (Korn 1953:32-33)

Korn decided that the ban on feasting constituted an immoral attack on a defenseless religion, and he lifted both it and the ban that had been instituted on the traditional *gondang* orchestra, considered a bulwark of paganism because, as Parkin notes, "the beating of the drums . . . is an essential . . . part of any . . . rite directed at communication with the spirits" (1978:189, n. 15). Putting an end to the ritual dancing at feasts (from the funerals of the well-to-do to the various feasts aimed at ensuring prosperity) had thus been justified from the point of view of the missionaries because it removed a burden of nonparticipation from converts and kept them from temptation.

Since the ban affected not only large sacrificial feasts but many much smaller ones as well, it also interfered with the indigenous economy of feasting. Whatever "surplus" was thereby liberated became available at just the time cash was coming into general use as a medium of exchange and nontraditional means of attaining respect and achieving status and wealth were becoming accessible to those who could afford the education necessary to qualify for salaried work as clerks, teachers, and church functionaries.

The ban on feasts may have appeared to be only one of a series of misfortunes to most Batak. One suspects that, for a time, as Firth (1929) noted of the New Zealand Maori, many Batak felt they had irreparably damaged their relationships to the powers responsible for their well-being, although, undoubtedly, small household sacrifices helped overcome this fear. In any event, the *bius* hierarchy and territorial organization did not disappear, and, despite the unrelenting moralizing of the preachers, it has been revived, at least in skeletal form, and enjoys a modus vivendi with the churches. While I did not encounter many of the small field sacrifices described by Ypes (perhaps because only 6 percent of the agricultural labor of Huta Ginjang is devoted to irrigated rice), the main rites at the start and end of the wet-rice cycle are still carried out. Responsibility for these rituals—'sprinkling of purificatory water on the seeds as they are taken to the fields' (*mangurasi boni tu balian*) and 'fetching the soul of the rice to the village' (*mangalap tondi ni eme tu huta*)—is rotated on a yearly basis among the heads of the four main *bius* of Sagala Valley.

In spite of the often nominal church membership of many villagers, feasting is again common. While many of the most prosperous households do not give feasts unless an elder dies, others do. Aside from funerals in 1976-1978 in Sagala, four localized lineages staged feasts ('Village Shaking,' 'Exhumation,' 'Ripe-old-age,' and 'Feast of One Agreement'). And the greatest feasts in the surrounding areas were held by a bank president, a judge, and a former Bupati (head of the subprovince) of North Tapanuli. In each instance, the *bius* heads, representatives of the local clan network, played central roles.

One may well wonder at Pederson's claim that, although by 1920 "there were still more than a hundred thousand Bataks who were not Christianized . . . many Bataks were ready to receive a new religion, either Christianity or Islam" (1970:68). It is misleading, and the fur-

The bius *heads make demands for recompense of their promised blessings.*

ther statement that "[e]vangelization proceeded from one Batak tribe to the next [and] the Toba and Silindung society was so thoroughly Christianized that to be a Batak was also to be a Christian" (ibid.: 1970:68-69) is even more misleading, since Pederson is using the indigenous topographical nomenclature "Toba" to designate the Balige Plain. Assertions such as these have been so often repeated by converts and missionaries that many people have accepted them as true without qualifications. Vergouwen's observation that "Christians are often disposed to revert to paganism for the sake of obtaining the office of [*bius* priest] and the honour and respect, *hasangapon*, associated with it" (1964:77) has been ignored—though it is still a common occurrence. Temporary expulsion (*tarban*) of so-called 'spirit worshipers' (who are literally called 'those who make offerings to ghosts'), that is, of anyone who participates in a feast at which someone becomes possessed, followed by confession of wrongs (*manopoti sala*) and readmittance, also occurs frequently (see Appendix C).

This is not to say that nothing has changed. A new annual cycle of Christian holidays has been taken up by church-going villagers (mostly women, who outnumber men in church attendance by about ten to one). The institution of a "day of rest" has co-opted Sunday morning for many, except in seasons of peak agricultural activity. Efforts are also made to satisfy as many relatives as possible in feasts by making offerings to the spirits the day or night before a feast is "officially" inaugurated by church officials. A common observation brings this out: "Offer to the 'powers' in the daytime; at night, a Christian feast, inaugurated with hymns"—or vice versa.[2]

One of the most striking examples of the general attitude to the cultural-meaningful disjunctions brought on or exacerbated by the new religion in contemporary Batak village life was a speech delivered by a possessed woman in requesting a particular dance melody from the orchestra the night before a feast was inaugurated by a church functionary. The analytically distinct aspects of "progress" and "change"

[2]For a sensitive and evocative treatment of Angkola Batak religious syncretism, see Susan Rodgers Siregar's *Adat, Islam, and Christianity in a Batak Homeland* (1981).

(e.g., political subordination, education, religious conversion, expansion of economic activity, and, implicitly, upward mobility) were joined together, as of a piece. The spirit—perhaps partly for my benefit—spoke as follows:

> As for our ancestor Raja Jakob, by his lifetime, the Dutch had already come, bringing the glad tidings, the news, in order to know about God (*Tuhan*). And Raja Jakob was already baptized, I know about that. And it is true that we in the past, before the coming of Religion, did not have religious ones inaugurate our feasts, we ourselves opened them. . . . As for me, I understand. If I have come [here] it indicates that I assent to the religious matters now. Why, those Dutch brought truly good tidings. They gave progress (*hamajuon*), they gave food, they gave all those delicious things [spoken in a tone of somewhat mocking disdain], they gave clothing. They ought to be thanked for coming from the other shore of that ocean, to bring the Batak people to its feet. Quite often the Controleur brought me to his office, I know about it. As for my descendants here, many do not understand well. . . . In my opinion, since I am the eldest son of the one known as Raja Jakob, and even in my lifetime I was the one who understood words, and feasts, my descendants here should ask each other's pardon [for disagreeing over whether a clergyman should inaugurate the feast]. . . . [As for me] I will explain to all the ancestors from before, so that they forgive their descendants, 'Why, they are seeking progress, as for this, and respect (*hasangapon*); it was the tidings which came, which gave it to those descendants of mine.' . . . Now [addressing the orchestra], you must play my request!

The speech makes clear the point of view that can be said to characterize Samosir Batak folk attitudes to Christianity and upward mobility. The glad tidings, the 'news' brought by the Dutch, tacitly adhered to, are seen by some as providing—or, rather, as improving—access to the power and respect associated with material betterment and official position.

Chapter 5

Ritual Expressions of Values and the Feasting System

This chapter has two purposes. The major one is to depict the process of contemporary feasts, both in terms of the ritual expressions of values they occasion and the economic transactions they entail. At the same time it provides an account of the values to which the people adhere. There are two main reasons, in turn, that necessitate this exposition of feasting system and values. Feasts are major undertakings and, as such, have economic bases and effects (Hill 1963:190). If we wish to gauge the significance of monetization, we must consider its effects on or interaction with the feasting system. In addition, we will later examine the differentials of production and resources of groups of households and therefore need to develop a greater awareness of the values that bind as well as those that provide them with the means of accepting inequality, and of the role of feasting in the maintenance of values. In Chapter 3 it was shown that there are built-in differences between those of the founder's clan and men of clans their women have married. Here we consider further what such marriages involve.

Leach set a major part of the agenda for this discussion by claiming that in a society in which there exists a preference for marriage of men with a mother's brother's daughter, the tendency is for wife-givers to hold their wife-receivers in a vassal-type relationship. Thus it is important to establish an understanding of the terms in which Batak view the interrelations of clans and lineages whose members marry each other.

The Ideologies of Descent and Marriage Relationships

The Batak summarize their ideal "code for conduct" with respect to all of their fellows by the oft-repeated saying,

> Revere wife-givers (*Somba marparajaon*),
> Request earnestly from wife-receivers (*elek margelleng*),
> Be wary of 'birth-companions' (*manat mardongantubu*).

Everyone falls into one of the three categories of kin—wife-givers, wife-receivers, and agnates. They are referred to as the 'Hearth of Three' (*Dalihan na Tolu*), a metaphoric reference to stones set in a triangle to support a pot of cooking food: 'If one is missing, the pot tips over.' The most frequent context in which the phrase is used is in reference to *adat*, 'custom,' as in the phrase 'Batak *adat*, the *adat* of the Hearth of Three' (*adat Batak, adat Dalihan na Tolu*), often employed to invoke the precedent of tradition to justify a ritual procedure.

All members of the Sagala *marga* (clan) are each other's 'birth companions,' but not all Sagalas have the same relationship with other Sagalas, nor do they all relate in the same way to those of different clans. One lineage may "give" women to the men of a lineage of another clan, while members of a 'brother' lineage "receive." So, as was shown in Chapter 3, even those who trace descent from one father or grandfather are distinguished by ancestress if their ancestor had more than one wife.

While the use of so-called classificatory terms of relationship is common, Bataks do not share any sentiment like that voiced by one of Firth's Tikopian informants, that "if you have no child, and there is your brother with children living, there are your descendants" (Firth 1963a:219). Adoption is rare. I heard of only one instance of the adoption of a village man who was of the generation of the household heads and one of the previous, mostly deceased, generation of their fathers.[1] In both instances, the lineage of the adopter would otherwise

[1]These are not indicated in my genealogical diagrams, since they were considered valid, almost unmentionable, adoptions. The term 'to make [an] offspring' (*paranakhon*) is the only one used to refer to adoption in which a hitherto childless couple gains a son. Yet two kinds of adoption, one

have died out. A man—blind from the age of three, married, and the father of two children—claimed, "If one has descendants 50 percent of the fear of death is eliminated; [one says to oneself:] 'There is someone to replace me.'"

This attitude also entails a patrilineally focused retrospect on one's ascendants, one's own line in relation to the lines of collaterals of one's ancestors. The 'soul force' (*sahala*) of a person who appears to have the best of fortune, who has many children, bounteous yields, fruitful livestock, and who is brave, generous, hospitable, and eloquent is thought to derive from a father or grandfather or other patrilineal ancestor, as well as from a positive influence emanating from the 'soul force' of one's wife-givers. We will come to the wife-giver/wife-receiver relationship after we first consider the relative status of those who are elder-younger 'brothers.'

The reason for the ideal precedence of elder-in-birth-order is that at birth he personifies the possibility of a successor for his parents and his grandparents. But the aphorism 'Younger in birth-order, elder in *harajaon*' (ritual perquisites) makes clear the relativity of rights of precedence in a hierarchy ideally based on birth order (Vergouwen 1964:39). As it indicates, rank due to an eldest son is often vitiated in practice.

There are reciprocal ritual duties of older- and younger-brother lineages. Because it is improper for the principals of a feast to do any overt supervision or work while it is in progress, a number of ritual functions—'master of ceremonies' (*parsinabul*), 'untier of the wrapped bag of cooked rice and meat' (*pangkangali*), 'giver of the closing benediction' (*panilupi*)—must be carried out by members of other lineages. For instance, men of Sagala lineage I always officiate at weddings of women of Sagala lineages II-VIII, and vice versa. At a funeral of a Sagala I, men from Sagala II and Sagala IX are supposed to set up a sacrificial pole in front of the house of the bereaved. For the

considered 'valid,' the other less so, may be referred to by the term *iparanak*, ('[he] was made an offspring by . . .'). In cases in which the mother's brother is not ritually replaced, 'the offspring can return to [its parents in fact], that is, he is like a borrowed item' (. . . *hira barang pinjaman*), as one of my informants put it.

death-dues payments at the funeral of a Sagala I, IX, X, or XI, a man from the lineages II-VII officiates.[2]

The proverb, endlessly repeated, says to be 'wary' of agnates. It is necessary for Batak meeting for the first time to question each other to determine their relationship. Although there are hundreds of clans, almost all stem from a dozen or so near the upper reaches of genealogical reckoning, and no matter how small or how recently "chartered" the *marga* (clan), it can always be found to 'enter' or 'be a branch of' a clan whose name and relationship is known to one's interlocutor. Generally, if two people are not agnates, they know of a relationship by marriage—be it ancestral or recent—and assume the attitudes and expressions of most general application by their closest agnates. If one's cousin twice removed has married a woman of clan A, one 'considers as wife-giver' (*marhula-hula tu* or *marparajaon tu*) any man of that clan, even if a more ancient marriage, at the upper level of the genealogy, was in the other direction.

If men of different clans cannot determine any relationship, they address each other by the general term *lae*, 'brother-in-law,' which is used reciprocally by wife-givers and wife-receivers. A man who believes he stands in a wife-receiving relationship to another and wishes to show deference, addresses him as 'mother's brother' (*tulang*). If the latter is older, he may respond with 'sister's son' (*bere*) or he may respond with 'brother-in-law.'

The injunctions, 'Revere wife-givers; request earnestly from wife-receivers' do not determine the course of every encounter between strangers who are both Toba Batak in the world beyond the home area. They do allow people to strike up relationships easily, although even in the home area the relationship of two men not closely related will depend on factors other than the demeanor enjoined by the code. And, generally, for people closely related by the marriage of respective

[2]At one planning session I recorded, the members of a large Sagala lineage talked themselves into a corner: they wish to control the ritual functions, but no one can officiate or perform such functions at his own feast; and they want to take them away from those who hold them at their feasts but are forced to admit to themselves that they would have to share them with yet others. In effect, such perquisites are rotated among quite a few lineages.

clanmates, the injunctions do characterize the tenor in which they conduct themselves—the flow of deference and services, in an atmosphere of mutual regard.

Ritual Enactment of Beliefs

There are many forms of symbolic action by which the Batak exhibit to themselves, and at the same time set in motion, forces that they believe their relationships with affines and agnates automatically engender. One set of these, the reciprocal ritual duties of older- and younger-brother lineages, has been touched on. Another set involves relationships established by marriage, as these are carried down through generations.

The blessings of wife-givers are bestowed in many ritual contexts. Whenever, either as the primary purpose of a gathering or at the end of a larger feast, a plate filled with hulled rice in which *Ficus* leaves and money are embedded is passed from the wife-receiver group to the wife-givers, the latter intone: "There has arrived here a firm platter [bearing] hulled rice, well-ordered leaves, and the clear-sounding doubloon. Pray tell, what is the purpose of this?" And in answer to the inevitable request for blessings, they bestow them both in words and, one by one, by cupping a handful of rice and, passing along the line of the seated wife-receivers, dropping a small pile of the uncooked grain on the heads of all—men, women, and children. This rice is called *boras si pir ni tondi*, 'the rice of the solid (hard, immovable) soul,' and the act of blessing in this fashion is called *marruma-tondihon* ('making a soul-house [of the head]').

The underlying belief that leads people to behave, in ritual, with a deference approaching reverence to closely related wife-givers is that one's wife-givers have what Leach termed an "uncontrolled mystical influence" on the well-being of their wife-receivers (1966b:22). In particular, one's wife's father or brother has this mystical influence over the well-being of one's children, as does one's mother's brother; the latter and one's father's mother's brother (or his/their descendants) have such influence over one's own well-being.

This belief in an "uncontrolled mystical influence" of a soul force having an effect on the lives of wife-receiving kinfolk has no equivalent in Western ideology or kinship beliefs. Yet it is central to Batak kinship beliefs, and its uniqueness must be grasped to get an inkling of its power in the thoughts and lives of the Batak. It is said to be involuntary and to require fulfillment of duties, such as occasional offerings (see Vergouwen 1964:83). A household that has been suffering misfortune will generally consult an augurer to determine the source. If, for instance, the augurer claims that the signs point to a dissatisfaction on the part of the 'soul force' of a deceased father's mother's brother and one wishes to assuage the 'hurt feelings' that have brought on the misfortune, one makes an offering, revering (*marsomba*) a living descendant of the father's mother's brother who has been divined. Or if a marriage has been barren, the couple will visit the woman's parents and present them with a meal of a specially prepared small pig.

The 'showing parts of the food' (tudu-tudu ni sipanganon), *presented to wife-givers. No matter how ample, the paucity of what is served is always excused.*

The salient steps of the ritual are the following: a speaker excuses the paucity of the food with words to this effect:

> You, our wife-givers, our fathers and mothers, however small [the offering] that we have brought, may it rule your souls (*margomgom ma on tondimuna*), may your soul force support [us] (*manumpak sahalamu*), so that we may get, yet again, that which is even larger to bring to you. May it be strength to your flesh, may it be luster to your faces (*Pamurnas ma i tu daging, saudara ma i tu bohi*).

After the meal, the husband or a speaker for the husband asks forgiveness for any unintended insults or injuries suffered by the 'heart/mind of the souls' (*roha ni tondi*) of the wife-givers:

> We are distressed because this daughter of yours has not borne any children; so in case we have done anything wrong, we have come to acknowledge it to you, dear sirs. May your *sahala* and your *tondi* give us succor, may God always shine his blessings on us.

When appropriate blessings have been pronounced and the couple prepares to leave, the woven *pandan* bag in which they brought the meal is given back filled with cooked rice and topped with a cooked fish, to be eaten on the return home: As they explain, "If one ties [a blessing shawl around a bag of food], one must untie" (*Molo manapol, ingkon mangkangali*). "The *balbahul* (woven pandan bag) should not be returned empty." This is one of several explicit expressions of the value placed on reciprocity, per se.[3] It is not, however, a directly balanced reciprocity: it is not tit for tat but, as Lehman (1963) indicated, an asymmetric reciprocity.

Dancing is in itself a ritual enactment of kinship beliefs. Lines of people approach, one by one—groups of guests greeting the hosts who dance in place. Wife-receivers meet their wife-givers in the dance with their knees slightly bent, so their heads are somewhat lower than those of their wife-givers. They reach out and stroke the jaw (*maniuk osang*) of their wife-givers with both hands, while the latter reciprocate with a semi-embrace, placing their hands on the top of the head of

[3]Another is found in Sherman (1987:872).

Dancing at a large 'soul force' feast in Sagala Valley: obeisance is shown to wife-givers (by stroking the jaw of the partner, maniuk*), and blessings are conveyed (by placing hands on the wife-receiver partner's head,* manabei).

At a smaller funeral ceremony, hosts and guests bless and do obeisance in the same manner, during one of many dances. Wives in line behind their husbands.

Co-villagers bless and do obeisance with even more fervor in a dance at a funeral.

each wife-receiver, or, with the same gesture, stretching out the shawl they are wearing, and, as they pass each dancer opposite them, wrapping the shawl over the other's shoulder, partly covering the head with it (*manabei*). When a blessing shawl is made a gift in dancing, laid emphatically on the shoulder of the recipient (*mangulosi*), the beneficial influence is thought to be even greater. (Agnates who are of different generation grades may also engage in these ritual acts without the use of shawls, the seniors giving blessings by placing hands on the heads of their juniors and the latter showing obeisance by stroking the jaws of their seniors. Generally, however, agnates maintain a kind of ritual parity by stroking each other's jaws.) There are many nuances of the caresses, the height of the hands being at the level of the ears or just above the ears or covering the top of the head, and for each intermediate position, there is a corresponding possibility of adjustment in the caress of a partner dancing past.

The distribution of the *jambar* (named portions) of a sacrifice at the end of a large feast is made to both affines and agnates. According to a variety of conventions, which differ from territory to territory, different ranks or grades of wife-givers receive specific parts of the sacrificial animal at a great feast. In Sagala, 'the wife-givers of origin' (*parbonaan*, father's father's mother's brother's descendants) receive part of the femurs, as do the *bona tulang* (descendants of the father's mother's brother of the feast-giver). The head goes to the mother's brother of the feast-giver, the *tulang*. The hindquarters go to the *pangolian*, those from whom the wife of a feast-giver has come. (Two additional grades of wife-givers, more removed in the genealogy, are *bona ni ari*, 'origin of days,' and *mata ni ari*, 'sun.') Again, such prestations serve a symbolic function, concrete expression of relationships by ritual sharing of consecrated food.

The Process of Feasts and the Rendering of Accounts

The word *feast* is a gloss that distorts as much as it describes. Batak feasts do not comprise a large multicourse meal to which hosts and guests sit down together. The guests at larger feasts may number from several hundred to more than a thousand people, many of whom attend for only one day out of three or four and receive only one meal of rice and meat. Gorging, as is found among the Tsembaga and other peoples, does occur but on a much reduced scale, without any intentional regurgitation to permit diners to eat more. (Most village women put about half of the meat served to them into small plastic bags to bring home to their households.) Vendors not related to the feast-givers often set up booths with coffee, tea, and snacks on the outskirts of the hamlet courtyard, and men who like to gamble frequent them.

Let us now consider more fully the giving and receiving, demanding and forestalling, that goes on at feasts. People engage in a great deal of nonsymmetrical exchange and a great deal of what we can call economic activity. But it should be borne in mind that the Batak carry out these procedures with their own, very specific economic purposes in mind. That is, in their ritual, they constantly articulate the livelihood-enhancing or livelihood-attaining goals that they pursue.

On the first day or night of a feast, wife-givers of the host lineage make contributions called *santi* (pronounced *sakti*), which consist of money or hulled, uncooked rice. In most cases, the gifts are brought

Marruma-tondihon *('making a soul house of the head'), blessing by dropping uncooked rice on the heads of (the blessers' husbands') wife-receivers.*

into the house where the principals sit lined up to the right of the door, and a little rice is dropped on the head of each by the wives of their wife-givers. The women give their bags of rice to a group of attendants, who record the amounts; then they and their husbands are served a meal. When they leave, another group enters. The hosts remain seated as each party of guests is shepherded through. Later, in the course of the dancing, cuts of meat are readied and an announcer calls out the names of recipients, presenting them the 'return' of the *santi* contributions (*ulak ni santi*) or the 'return for blessing shawls' (*ulak ni ulos*) bestowed on the feast-giver. These prestations are, then, literally, reciprocal gifts of food given in proportion to, but by no means commensurate in value with, the contributions made.

For a feast of disinterment and entombment of ancestral remains, as

Presenting gifts of rice in courtyard dancing at a feast. The bunch of leaves at the right is affixed to the sacrificial pole, to which a cow is tied.

for most large-scale feasts, preliminary meetings may be held more than a year in advance by principals and a few of their wife-receivers. To 'dig up the bones' (*mangongkal holi*) and 'raise them to a hard stone, a high mountain,' as the Batak put it, is usually prompted by visitations of spirits in dreams or during possession at curing feasts. When a decision has been finalized and an augurer has designated a propitious time, they send word to the *parbaringin,* the ritual heads or priests of the territorial sacrificial community, *bius*, making known their tentative plans and inviting them to attend and be regaled (*gallang raja*) on a given morning. At that meeting, they will 'set the day' (*maniti ari*) and arrange the schedule of the feast.

As in the presentation of a meal to propitiate 'the souls' of wife-givers and as in large-scale wedding ceremonies, the feast begins with a meal served to wife-givers, during which various wife-receivers of the host lineage feed meat by hand to the mouths of the guests (*manulangi*). After the meal, the assembled wife-givers (of a number of different clans) are asked to bestow certain shawls (*ulos topi-topi, hoba-hoba* and *laman-laman*) in which to wrap the skulls and other remains that have been dug up. One by one, the wife-givers send them to those seated opposite by way of an intermediary 'attendant.' They then demand recompense from the principals, their wife-receivers, for permission to exhume and entomb the bones of those who were 'blessed by our [ancestors'] souls' (*pinupus ni tondinami*). The return is generally deferred until the day after the feast. The first sounding of the *gondang* orchestra takes place just after dark of the first evening, and dancing is carried on late into the night.

Next morning, a sacrificial buffalo (or, in other feasts, a cow or a horse) is led around the courtyard and tied to a decorated pole in front of the house of the principal or (when there are several) the one who has undertaken the greatest expense and initiative in staging the feast. It is the duty of one group of wife-receivers to keep it standing and clean the ground during the dancing, prestations, and blessings or good wishes expressed by each succeeding group of kin for the duration of the feast.

In addition to the contributions brought and deposited before the initial meal by wife-givers, gifts are made throughout the dancing in

Leading a buffalo to the pole at the center of the courtyard at a feast of naming, Mamampe goar, *for naming grandparents as "Grandparents of (grandson's name)."*

Prestation of a large number of ulos *shawls at a disinterment feast. Paper tags pinned to them have names of donors written on them.*

the courtyard by all guests, whether wife-givers, agnates, or wife-receivers. Each party of dancers—beginning with agnates, then wife-receivers, and lastly wife-givers, often in separate groups based on village of origin—prepares to dance by pooling their individual cash contributions and listing them on paper. After those who wish to do so have made introductory speeches and dances, circling the courtyard to show themselves to the crowd, the lead dancer holds up the total between pressed palms and dances with it past the principals, followed by the entire party. He deposits the contribution in the hands of a principal, while others (if they are wife-givers) place shawls, to which they have tagged their names, on the shoulders of secondary principals. As the dance ends, following speeches of thanks by the hosts and, often, calls and counter-calls for additional dances to be shared, the gifts are turned over to a group of record-keepers seated at a table to the side, who make note of the donors and amounts and shawls given.

Occasionally, a group of wife-receivers of the principals announces that they are giving 'a chewer of grass' (*sigagat duhut*)—i.e., a ruminant or part of one. What Vergouwen termed "a symbolic presentation" is made. "A person giving cattle [or, some fraction of an animal] holds a small [twig] whip [with a note stuck in a slit at the top]. . . . [T]he actual transfer . . . follows later" (Vergouwen 1964:318). One of the principals may take the presentation, be it a whip or a number of large bills—sometimes affixed like leaves to a small stick-figure tree—and dance at a trot around the square, holding it upright between raised fingers, hands above his head.

On the final afternoon, the dancing ends as it began, with a set series of musical flourishes, the participants dancing in place. A procession carries the remains out of the house where they have been stored in large rice baskets. They are then sealed in a portal (or portals, if more than one ancestor of a lineage is involved) of a concrete tomb.

That night or the next morning, the sacrificial beast is slaughtered, and the *jambar* portions are cut up and distributed. There is some leeway as to the order of formalities at the close. Usually, sometime before the dawn of the next day, the principals meet with the members of the orchestra to reach an accommodation on their reward (*upa*). When mutual agreement is reached, the drummer and oboist give their blessings, which are necessary for the feast to be properly efficacious.

One or two days after an exhumation feast, the wife-givers of the principals gather to claim the debt (deferred on the first day) for having given permission to exhume ancestral remains. They are again fed a meal of rice and meat, referred to as 'revering wife-givers,' after which offering platters of husked rice, *Ficus* leaves, and cash are presented to them. When they inquire as to the purpose, their blessings are requested. Small increments are added in response to their (inevitably great) demands 'to add' (*ambahi*). The principals protest, as they do in serving food, that the smallness of the prestation is due to their poverty, promising that with their wife-givers' blessings there will be more at a later date.

A separate discussion takes place with the wife-receivers of the feast sponsors, who served during the feast as attendants and cooks. This involves a complete rendering of accounts. Expenditures made by individuals for cooking ingredients and other necessities are listed, as are gifts of shawls, rice, and money, and totals are publicly announced to those present. If, as is generally the case, expenses exceed income, shawls received from wife-givers of the principals are distributed among the wife-receivers, and they are asked to 'give support' (*manumpak*) by making a return for each shawl. It is often said that in this situation wife-receivers make contributions five times the value of the shawl they accept. "He who has many wife-receivers does not lose," one man said, but this rarely proves true. If there is great disparity between expenditures and the income of gifts and contributions, the wife-receivers often refuse the shawls that are passed across the room to them, protesting that they are unable to reciprocate.

Note that the shawls are never offered as payment for the many days and nights of effort just completed. The reason for offering them is always said to be to permit the sponsors to ask their wife-receivers to help bear the burden of the expenses. Nothing could show more clearly that such "Feasts of Merit" are not "Asian potlatches" (cf. Keyes 1977:47). These customary procedures imply that, rather than ascribing prestige solely to demonstrating the ability to outdo the largesse of others, as in potlatches, the Batak see nothing wrong with breaking even or turning a profit.

When a group of agnates of one or more minimal lineages has cooperated in sponsoring a feast, the final formality involves a private gathering to render their own accounts, each getting compensation in proportion to what he has contributed. In such instances, for example, all shawls received as individual gifts in the course of the feast (received *pribadi* or *persoon*, as they sometimes say) are brought together in a joint collection. The value of each is assessed and noted, and the total cash value is added to that of the remaining rice and cash. The *ulos* shawls are generally taken to market and sold to a dealer and the proceeds distributed as remuneration to each sponsor. The undertaking is then truly at an end.

The preliminary and terminating formalities are as integral to the process of feasting as the ceremonial aspects. Along with the ceremonial dancing, dedications, obeisance, and blessing that comprise the sanctified interval of the feast just described, similar formalities are found in feasts of 'Laying on of a name' (*Pampe goar*), celebrating 'Ripe-old-age' (*Gondang saurmatua*), feasts of 'Ancestral soul power' (*Gondang sahala*), 'Village-shaking feasts' (*Manghuntal huta*), feasts 'Making known the genealogy' (*Pesta paboahon tarombo*), and others I participated in. Ceremonies like the 'Exhumation of bones' (*Ongkalan holi*) involve long planning before their execution. But the same steps are followed for the funeral of an elder, which may be precipitated in spite of a lack of definite plans (Sherman 1982:300-304). Dancing, preceded by benedictory dedications, is of the same formal, measured pace and hand movements as at any other feast, and it is undertaken by groups standing in a similar relation to the principals—agnates, wife-givers, and wife-receivers.

Thus, the very process of Batak ritual consists of interactions with distinct sets of kin. In the relations of affines as well as of agnates, connections among the living depend on occasional invocation of both "maternal" and "paternal" ancestor spirits by offerings and invocations. As Singarimbun notes (1975:106, 139), Karo (as well as other) Batak kinship beliefs are bound up in religious beliefs. Indeed, were it not for their methods of augury (particularly astrological time-reckoning) and ideas of destiny or fate (Sherman 1982:345-366), the kinds of kinship beliefs Batak villagers hold would allow them little alternative than to consider misfortune to be the fault of (at best) unhelpful or (at worst) malevolent kinfolk. The days of the months, as represented on the bamboo cylinder that Parkin (1978) calls the Batak "calendrical oracle instrument" (*parhalaan*), range between being propitious and unpropitious—having positive and negative affects. When I asked if, given the length typical of feasts, at least part would inevitably occur on an unpropitious day, I was told that I had grasped a key point, and one man remarked, "Yes, if there is a celebration, there must be someone who is struck [i.e., some category of the hosts' kin—or the hosts themselves—that 'comes in contact with' an unpropitious day]. But it is possible to pass this to others [strangers], by using charms (*pagar*)."

The Ideal Feasting Series of a Household

In his *Economics of the Central Chin Tribes* (1943), H. N. C. Stevenson distinguished several "series" of feasts of that West Burma hill tribe: feasts of merit, hunting success, marriage, and funerals. For each type, he listed the ideal series of progressively larger feasts said to be undertaken by a household. Although I did not pursue this line of inquiry in the field, I gathered some evidence for the applicability of Stevenson's characterization of a Chin "feasting system" to the Batak. Informants often said that it was the custom to sacrifice buffalo to call upon *sombaon* (the highest order of localized spirits), cattle to call upon *semangot* (ancestral spirits of high status), and horses to call upon *Debata di ginjang* ("God on high"). Further, I noted down a statement made to me during one ceremonial procession (circling the courtyard with the buffalo to be tied to the decorated pole in the center, at the start of the first full day of a disinterment feast) to the effect that "that is a *santi* buffalo, or a *ripe* buffalo. One has to feast buffalo three times before one can have a *sungkot* or *sitiotio* buffalo [feast]."

In response to a letter in which I asked one of the village teachers to elucidate this statement, I received the following answer[4] (which I have interspersed with additional comments):

> Batak *adat* ('custom') has levels. . . . The steps (the succession) are as follows. . . .
>
> [Steps 1 and 2 have to do with getting married.]
>
> 3. When one marries, one usually 'establishes independence.' After establishing independence, one quickly makes efforts to seek livelihood. In addition to working, one 'takes care of a hen and a pig of others in return for part of the offspring' (*dipahani manuk dohot babi*). The chicken, if possible from a wife-receiver, and the pig from a wife-giver. The intent is that they reproduce because chicken can be the main side-dish served with rice to wife-receivers and pork, to wife-givers.

[4]Part of a letter from a Sagala man dated March 21, 1980.

4. If one has good luck, the pig reproduces well, its offspring get fat quickly, in a vigorous bunch: One must make an offering. If one does not make an offering, one will be beset by difficulties.

Note particularly that the need to make an offering occurs if the pig is prolific.

5. One's fortune must increase [as a result,] due to the vigor of that pig, a request of one's dreams. As a result one holds a feast called *manghalang gordang* [hanging the drums up in order].

Significantly, it is specifically a pig to be raised, given by wife-givers, that is held to be the ideal source of prosperity. Pork is not only prepared especially for wife-givers, but it is also a prerequisite of any large feast, when, in the course of four days, a dozen full-grown pigs may be slaughtered to feed newly arriving guests. So, a new household's ability to participate in the feasting system is attributed to the good fortune that stems from what begins as an effort to provide appropriate offerings to serve wife-givers. Correspondingly, the potential of the pig lent to a newly married wife-receiver stems from the beneficial effects of a mystical influence emanating from wife-givers. The initial step in the series rests on the latter's willingness to give up part of the offspring in return for the care and feeding of one of their sows.

The letter continues:

6. Next one has another feast called a feast of purification (*gondang uras-uras*), and at the same time one 'lays on a name,' for example, . . . Grandfather of Matio. At the time of this feast one purifies a horse [by sprinkling it with water from a sacred spring]. If one has no horse one borrows a horse from an older or younger brother; it should be a female horse.

7. After one's fortune continues to increase (one's rice is plentiful, and there are also cows, buffalo, horses) . . . one hosts a cow feast, called *lombu sitiotio* though some call it *lombu suhung* [or] village shaking.

8. After hosting a cow feast one hosts a buffalo feast.

9. [Next] one hosts a feast of a horse of god. We call it the horse that is elephant of the stable (a red-coated horse), that is why at the purificatory feast [see (6), above], one quickly purifies a female horse (in the wish that it will have a

male offspring of red coat), so there will be something to use at the time of a feast of a horse of god.

10. A *bius* [sacrificial offering community] buffalo (as for a *bius* buffalo, it is not a private endeavor). Those are the steps of that which is endeavored (*siulaon*) . . . from the time of marriage until old age.

It is notable that a married couple embarking on the series and needing to 'purify' a female horse, to set in motion the future sacrifice of one of its male offspring, simply borrows (*pinjamhon*) one from 'an older or younger brother.'[5] In fact, the head of any household will require aid from lineage mates.

By no means all households pursue the series described above—it is an ideal. One could undoubtedly elicit other, more and less elaborate accounts of the series from others (cf. the citation above, to which the letter was a response). Note, in this regard, that a number of the feasts named earlier are not specified in this series. What is important is not whether the series is one to which all informants would subscribe but that there is a notion of a progression of feasts of increasing size and prestige and the greatest (number ten) may only be cosponsored by those who have passed through the previous steps.

Since my correspondent was both a teacher and a lay minister and had already prepared a tomb for reburying his father, it is prudent to point out that he dissociated himself from being thought a participant in any such series by excluding exhumation and reburial from the progression. To the above he added, "As for a funeral feast, it is just like a prayer service = wedding feast (Reception)" (. . . *partangiangan* = *pesta kawin* [*Resepsi*]). But this statement is debatable. Neither at prayer services nor at weddings is dancing to the music of a *gondang* orchestra found; but it is central for a feast of exhumation, a large funeral, and all the other feasts he names.

[5]I have independent confirmation of this part of the sequence from field notes of a Toba Batak feast in Sumbul, Dairi: "After purifying [a red female], if a male is born, one can host an offering to god. If a female is born, one waits for its offspring in turn."

Rituals of Contract for Skilled Services

"Rituals of contract" for engaging and rewarding orchestra players (as for midwives, carpenters, and other 'skilled ones,' *pande*) culminate with the blessings of the specialist, signaling acceptance of the recompense. Here I want to consider them for feast orchestras. Their relevance to the broader themes of this study will be taken up in the chapter on labor mobilization.

When fairly definite plans have been made for a feast, one of the principals or immediate wife-receivers is delegated to speak with either a drummer or an oboist (each of whom will have a partner on whose participation he can count). They sit cross-legged on a mat, and the musician questions the visitor at length as to his purpose and plans, the nature of the feast, the proposed date, the time it will begin, and other particulars. After a pause, the musician asks for an advance partial payment of a total sum he names. Much bargaining follows.

A gondang *orchestra: drummer (center), oboeist (silhouetted to the right of center), and assistants, on a makeshift stage, for lack of a house balcony.*

At the appointed time, the orchestra is served a formal meal, after which the players are asked if they wish to be paid in full before they commence. They decline the offer with the assurance that payment can wait. During the dancing, they receive "tips" from each speaker who requests a dance. These *pinta-pinta*, as they are called, consist of coins or bills stuffed in a small bag lowered from the orchestra balcony for each speech of dedication. In Indonesian, *pintaan* is a "request," and *terpinta* means "predestined, fated" (Echols and Shadily 1961:280), which is significant in view of the frequent and explicit Batak requests that the musicians transmit the dedication prayers to the spirits through their music. In other words, the payment is almost literally a gift in return for "ritual efficacy."

When time for rendering full payment comes, after the feast has ended, the musicians again sit down to a formal meeting opposite the principals. An offering platter containing hulled rice and the balance of the amount promised is placed in front of the specialists. The latter invariably demand incremental payments and, in turn, are asked to be satisfied and make their blessings (*silup-silupan*) to signify full settlement and bring the proceedings to a close. Sometimes the principals argue with orchestra members for almost an hour. The tension that builds up with the intractability of both parties will finally be broken by a small added payment and the spoken blessings of those accepting it, to the effect, "Now that you have had this feast, may you be healthy and prosperous." Such blessings, like those bestowed during feasts, are embellished with a variety of rhymed couplets (*umpasa*).

The blessings of the musicians are highly valued. Without them, it is said, a feast would have only dire consequences. This gives these 'skilled ones' a bargaining power they would not otherwise have. Yet, in spite of their power to withhold blessings, they never do so, although they often settle for a smaller payment or reward, *upa*, than had been promised. Clearly, the musicians have little recourse; their efforts have been expended. The usual claim by those who have just held a feast that their resources are exhausted may often be true. However, from the point of view of the feast-givers, the feast is best viewed as setting in motion a series of further effects. To convince the musicians to accept less than they may have expected, they are sometimes promised that the just-completed feast is merely preliminary to a greater one (provided, though not so stated, that the desired prosperity ensues) and that they will have the opportunity to earn even more on the next occasion.

The Work of Feasts and Its Remunerations

Although no Batak willingly calls another 'master,' all allow themselves to be called *parhobas*, 'servant' or 'attendant,' when they serve at feasts of their wife-givers. Different grades of wife-receivers are considered appropriate for serving at feasts of differing size and importance. Before the main preparations at the site of a feast, the wife-receivers who have gathered at the behest of the principals, their wife-givers, arrange themselves 'according to level' or 'by share' or 'portion' (*mangihuthon tohap*, Indonesian, *taraf*).

Grown and adolescent children accompany and aid their parents in much of the work—feeding fires, carrying water, stirring cauldrons of rice, and serving meals to the participants. During a feast, the at-

An early morning shot of a group of young parhobas *(attendants) at a large feast.*

tendants receive and execute peremptory orders—"*Parhobas*, do this," "*Parhobas*, do that!"—from spreading mats for guests to refilling glasses with hot tea, washing dishes, or serving a late-arriving member of the orchestra. At appropriate times during the ceremony, they also join in the dancing. The principal host of a feast delegates the prime responsibility to one man and communicates mainly with him in trying to balance the needs of his guests against the limits of his stocks and to move the proceedings along with the exigencies of the passage of day into night.

As was noted, attendants do not receive remuneration for the work. Formal offers of shawls are always made to them in rendering accounts at the conclusion of a feast, and like musicians, they are expected to voice a salutory blessing to signal their satisfaction, whether they accept or refuse the shawls. If they accept, they are also expected to 'give support,' to make up 'the loss.' This seems puzzling. How can we explain the apparently untenable situation of wife-receivers, who not only serve as unpaid attendants at feasts but are also asked to make contributions to help erase a deficit rather than being remunerated at the end? Indigenous terms for feasts may hold the answer.

Among Samosir Batak of the Pusuk Buhit area, feasts are most often referred to as *ulaon*, 'works' or 'labours,' the root of which, *ula*, with an infinitive prefix, *mangula*, means 'to work,' particularly with reference to agricultural tasks involving soil-turning. *Mangula paremean* means "to be in the process of performing the necessary labor to prepare a field for planting rice"—i.e., 'to work a rice field.' But *marulaon* is 'to hold a feast,' 'stage a celebration.' How does it happen that the root *ula* is used in such apparently divorced meanings? Is it simply a matter of polysemy, of one word having entirely different meanings, as in English "fair skin," "county fair"? One might think so, were it not for the fact that a parallel conjunction of meaning occurs in Indonesian for the word *kerja*, which may mean, "1. work, labor, activity . . . , 2. occupation, job, 3. a celebration (wedding, etc.)" (Echols and Shadily 1961:184). Moreover, Toba-Batak has two traditional cognates of *kerja*—*karejo*, meaning "work" or "occupation," and the word *horja*. The latter, which is used interchangeably with *ulaon*, refers specifically to a large sacrificial feast. Among the Angkola Batak to the south, *horja* is, in fact, the main term for 'celebration' or 'feast.' These congruences may be shown more clearly in this fashion:

English:	to have a job, occupation	to work to labor	a celebration feast
Indonesian:	*bekerja*	*bekerja*	*kerja, pekerjaan, pesta*
Toba-Batak:	*karejo*[6]	*mangula*	*ulaon, horja, gondang*

What might account for these parallel usages? An answer may be sought in an analogy with M. Panoff's analysis of concepts of work among the Maenge of the New Hebrides (Vanuatu) (1977:11-12) and that of E. Schwimmer on those of the Orokaiva of northern Papua (1979:292, 301). Both refer to the yields of labor as being considered a return, part of a reciprocal relationship with "supernaturals."

Diligence in work is a valued and inculcated characteristic among Batak, but no one ever attributed the poverty of a neighbor to lack of diligence. Rather, such misfortune is attributed to 'fate,' to the dissatisfaction of spirits, or the effects of witchcraft. Bounteous yields are the result of one's general quality of bounteousness, *hagabeon* or *panggabean* (from *gabe*, blessings, good fortune), which stems in turn from harmonious relations with affines and compacts with ancestral spirits through reciprocity set in motion by offerings at feasts. Among humans and between humans and spirits, this involves the prestation of symbolic gifts, prominent among them special foods, including rice or rice-flour cakes, fruits, meat, or fish.

The work of attendants at feasts, centered mainly on the preparation and distribution of food, therefore, receives recompense in real, though often not immediately material, form. In the give-and-take of the whole gamut of social ritual that, in general terms, comprises Batak "feasting," the most common expression of reciprocity is one that fittingly concerns food: "*Molo manapol, ingkon mangkangali*," "If one ties [the woven pandanus bag of cooked rice and meat or fish

[6]*Karejo* appears in Warneck (1977 [originally 1906]) as *kharadjo*, used in the sense of 'work,' 'occupation.'

given to affines], one must untie [that which is returned for the first]." The same holds for spirits as for their human communicants. A proper relationship is set in motion and maintained, in the first instance, by the proper food being placed on the shelf and proper obsequies observed. It is perhaps for this reason that, in both Batak and Indonesian, the same roots signify what we gloss as "to work" and "to feast." These usages are paralleled by the Tikopian, in which the term for labor (*fekau*) is used as well for the series of yearly ritual offerings, which Firth translated as "the work of the gods" (Firth 1965: 110).

There is no confusion as to what is agricultural work and what is feasting. The Toba-Batak verbs, *mangula* for the first, *marulaon* for the second, certainly are distinct. But the use of one root for both is not a matter of polysemy. In a sense, the two activities have one stem in Batak because they both refer to life-giving endeavors. Although they involve different spheres of activity and different inputs of energy or strength (*gogo*), it appears that the labor of agriculture and the labor of feasting are both subsumed in the same root, *ula*, "an endeavor," because in both, humans are seen as fulfilling one side of a relationship, relating to the sources of supernatural bounty, through a series of reciprocal actions. Both require expenditure of effort and involve stated or taken-for-granted reciprocal relations. Both receive returns. Those of agriculture are tangible, while those of feasting, appearing to be intangible, are likewise considered tangible by most Batak. They are thought to manifest themselves over time in the size of harvests, the improved or continued health of a family, the increase of their livestock, and their own fertility. If positive results do not eventuate, then a ritual procedure, a misreading of the astrological situation, or the witchcraft of others provide ready scapegoats.

While theirs does not correspond to our economic model, the Batak have (or share) an economic model, a model of livelihood, based on a different but no less rational set of premises than that of formal economics. This assertion does not seek to give Batak motivations a Western legitimacy, but to establish an awareness of the difference.

PART III

AGRICULTURE AND TRADE

The ecological, historical, and cultural backdrops of the contemporary agricultural system have now been established. In the last chapter, a number of the economic and symbolic ritual uses of rice were shown in some detail—as gift, ritual payment, or blessing medium. In this part, we further develop our appreciation of this grain that served as a medium of exchange in Samosir before money—its cultivation and its current place in the economy. Since agricultural effort is not exclusively devoted to rice, some attention to other crops is also necessary.

Chapter 6 deals with the range of farming strategies pursued by villagers and the variations in household self-sufficiency of rice; Chapter 7, with the unusual cultivation of Imperata *grassland in ethnological perspective; and Chapter 8, with marketing products of the soil, credit, and investment. There we return to the complementary roles of rice and cash.*

Chapter 6

The Agricultural Cycle and the Cycle of Wants

I consider the people of Huta Ginjang to be a combination of subsistence and commercial farmers, though some might argue that it would be more accurate to call them "peasants" (Wolf 1960:2) or "gardeners" (Bohannan 1963:215). No doubt, the scale of their "farms" and endeavors can be rated only marginally productive of surplus by comparison to commercial Western farms. Eric Wolf rightly distinguishes peasants from "farmers or agricultural entrepreneurs as we know them," noting that,

> The American farm is primarily a business enterprise, combining factors of production purchased in a market to obtain profit. . . . The peasant, however, does not operate an enterprise in the economic sense; he runs a household, not a business concern.

But because most of the residents work the land full-time, often in acre-sized, monocultured plots, I will speak of them as "farming." They are "peasant" farmers—or, indeed, "tribal-peasant" farmers—making up what Firth calls "a socio-economic system of small-scale producers with a relatively simple, non-industrial technology" (1964a: 17).[1] But Hill (1986) details good reasons to avoid the term "peasant."

Having inherited a magnificently stone-terraced land, the villagers are able to irrigate crops on a small but significant portion of their holdings (see Chapter 12). Originally, the village water source was used to grow rice on flooded terraces. A changeover from wet rice to

[1] I wrote this passage before reading Polly Hill (1986, Chap. 1), "Why Country People Are Not Peasants." My equivocation is more than amply supported therein.

Part of the Galung area terraces with watercourses to allow plate-splashing of bulbs. People are visible planting below and to the right of the center.

bulb crops was said to have begun around 1937 and to have been completed in the early 1970s. (Indeed, in 1975-1976, one well-off returned emigrant grew a crop of wet rice in the precincts of the village.) The terraces are no longer flooded. Bulb crops grown on raised beds are watered by plate-splashing out of ditches, or, in the valley where water is more plentiful, by keeping ditches surrounding the raised beds full of water.

The downstream areas of fields, Parlumbanan, were the first to be converted from wet rice to bulb crops. The upstream fields, Galung, perhaps because their proximity to the source guaranteed a more dependable water supply, were not shifted to bulb irrigation until bulb prices had risen to five times that of an equal volume of rice, which was said to have occurred suddenly around 1967. Although bulb prices have undergone many fluctuations since then, these fields remain almost entirely bulb-growing areas, raised beds separated by water ditches, in place of formerly sunken rice terraces. The price of rice has been consistently under government control in Indonesia since colonial times (Timmer 1975), hence, we may surmise that there is thus no possibility of getting a windfall profit in rice cultivation, whereas, presumably, there is an incentive to grow crops for which such a possibility is ever present.

When I first visited Huta Ginjang, I assumed that all the villagers' fields were on the mountainside, but this turned out not to be the case. Quite a few villagers had irrigable terraces in the valley below, just as valley-dwellers cultivated dry fields a third of the way up the mountain, many abutting on those of Huta Ginjang. Of 112 subsistence households in 1976-1977, some 43 percent held wet-rice terraces in Sagala Valley; 77 percent of those also had irrigable terraces in the precincts of the village; another 31 percent had irrigable fields in the village only; while 28 percent had neither and farmed entirely on dry fields. For the most part, the ones who had irrigable fields in the village planted them in cash crops, mainly shallots and garlic, though they continued to grow a great deal of rice and other food crops, both in valley wet fields and mountain dry fields and some cash crops in dry fields. Households have an average of six parcels and work three or four at a time. Very few grow no rice (limiting themselves to cash crops), and very few grow only for consumption. The priorities of most are evident in the fact that they plant rice before bulbs at the onset of the rains. Many plant rice, bulbs, rice, then more bulbs.

The Agricultural Cycle

In 1977, the first harvest of valley-grown wet rice in the northern half of the Sagala Valley was reaped in early April, and the end of the Batak lunar year in Sagala was mid-April (the full moon at the end of April marked the middle of the first month of the new lunar year). At the end of May, with the onset of the dry season and the last of the wet- and dry-rice harvests, villagers finished planting corn in the harvested rice fields. They use a variety that matures in two and one-half to three months, corn that, in spite of being stunted by lack of water, has an amazing ability to bend with the wind and keep growing from a 45-

degree angle, requiring very little rain and only one weeding to produce at least one good ear per plant.

The dry season is sometimes referred to as the feasting season, *musim pesta*. Following the vegetational profusion of the wet season and the year's largest harvests of shallots, garlic, and rice, it is best suited to staging feasts. Most of the effort required for opening fields for the coming year's dry rice, while strenuous, can be spaced out during the dry season, from June through September, according to the demands of ritual. Watering bulb crops during this time is difficult, requiring hours of bending from the waist, but it is interspersed with days and weeks of the more slow-paced, though equally demanding, concentration of weeding.

With the coming of the rains, the pace of preparing the remaining fields for rice and bulb crops quickens. In a good year, like 1976, when the rains come in late August or early September, planting of dry rice begins then, in the earliest-readied fields at the lowest altitudes and progresses to higher ones, until, by late October, the highest dry fields (about 1,750 meters above sea level) have been planted. Most families plant more than one plot of dry rice (the average number for all households being 1.7 plots), and the hamlets are deserted on most days at this time of year. The dry field rice needs weeding at least once every four to six weeks; it may need thinning if seeders are inexperienced, or it may need replanting (from thinnings) where germination is poor or young sprouts are eaten by mole crickets (*singke*). Many villagers plant bulbs immediately after rice, although they are aware that the torrential afternoon rains of the first half of the rainy season may waterlog the earth and prove as harmful to the bulbs as a prolonged dry spell. Wet rice is transplanted in December and January.

From mid-January onwards, most households are primarily engaged in readying fields to plant the main shallot and garlic crop of the year in the second, more moderate half of the rainy season (see Figure 6.1). Tubers and the minor cash crops (peanuts, chili-pepper bushes, coffee trees) must also be planted during the rainy season. As rice begins to ripen, it requires protective measures such as guarding from birds or setting poison for rats. The quickest-growing dry rice matures in four months in the low-lying fields. At warmer, lower altitudes, it begins setting grain by late December, and harvest is possible there by early February, several months before that of any valley wet rice. From then until May a series of fields ripen at times that depend on altitude, date of planting, and seed variety used. The bulk of dry-rice fields are harvested during March and April. In the higher-altitude, colder fields of the village, it takes seven months to mature, and harvest tends to coincide with that of the irrigated valley fields.

The rice-harvest period, beginning in the second half of the rainy

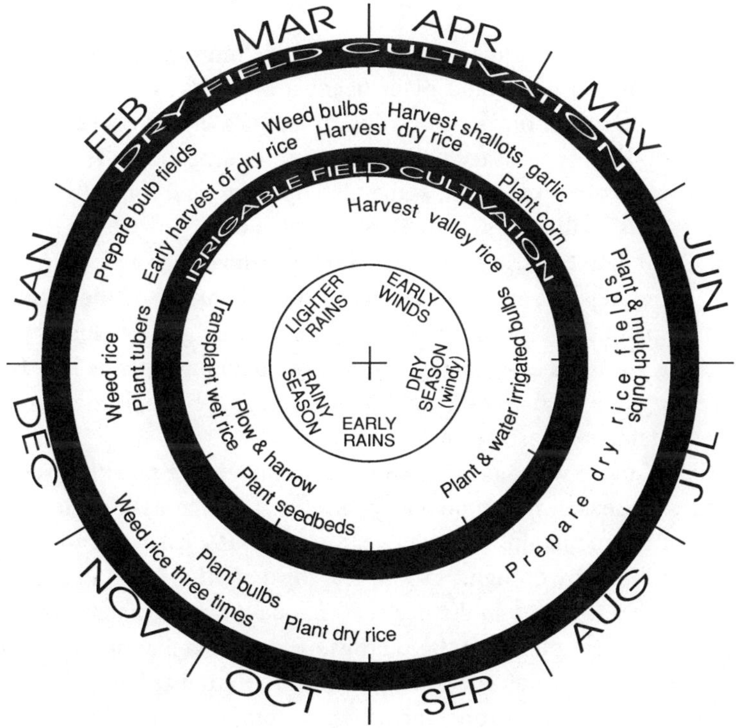

Figure 6.1. The range of village agricultural activities in a yearly cycle.

TABLE 6.1
Seasonal Bulb Plantings in Huta Ginjang (1976-1977)
(1 *rante* = 0.04 hectare)

Season	Number of households	*Rante* (average)
Haleon (first half of the rainy season)	81	3.1
Sipahatolu (second half of the rainy season)	96	4.3
Logo ni ari (dry season)	93	2.5

season, is hectic. A farmer may cut rice in the morning, help thresh an earlier cutting at noon, and plant peanuts or bulbs after the midday meal. At nightfall, further threshing of another pile cut several days earlier might be necessary to keep it from overheating. Household members are often scattered, some also opening land for bulbs, some picking bulbs, still others, coffee, in separate fields.

The bulb harvest, from plantings done in January through March, is nearly complete by early June. Some three-quarters of the farmers begin to plant dry-season bulbs during June in irrigable fields or dry, mulching with rice-straw and grass, and the planting extends into July in the irrigable fields. As would be expected, the smallest areas are planted in the dry season (see Table 6.1).

Most of those without irrigable fields in the village plant bulbs during the dry season in the powdery, dark soil on the eastern, leeward slopes of the mountain. In a bad year, such as 1977, large amounts of bulbs are killed by drought. About one-third of all the irrigable valley terraces are left fallow in the dry season, one-third are planted in rice, and one-third are planted in bulb crops. But double that proportion of village-held *sawah* was left fallow then, and a third was lent for valley-dwellers to grow bulb crops, for which no return is asked. This is because most mountain-dwellers, caring for dry-season bulb crops in the village and preparing dry-rice fields for the following rainy season, were unable to match the planting schedule of valley residents. Late planting, when only a third of the wet-rice fields are in rice, is dangerous. There is a community of the "preyed-upon" in the cultivation of rice. If one's crop is too far behind those surrounding it, rats and birds from already harvested fields converge on, and devastate, it. This holds especially for those who plant flooded-field rice in the dry-season, *mareme tamba* (to [grow] rice in addition), when two-thirds of the terraces are not so used. Only five households from Huta Ginjang sharecropped the fields of others. This highlights a second factor that discourages Huta Ginjang villagers from planting their valley fields in the dry season. A shortage of water, as is apt to occur even in the valley in the dry season, can seriously impede the growth of wet rice. Water depth must be regulated while the rice matures. Again, that requires Huta Ginjang farmers to visit their fields several times a week or trust valley kin to oversee them. This tends to discourage those whose time is devoted to other pursuits from attempting a second valley rice crop.

Of the 46 households with valley wet-rice fields, 25 had inherited them and 21 had taken fields as security for loans. Sixteen of the 46 gave out all their fields for sharecropping during the rainy season, and 9 others worked some of their *sawah* and gave some out to be sharecropped. Most of those sharecropped were given to valley villagers.

Cultivation of the Major Food Crops

The tubers—mainly sweet potatoes and cassava—are generally planted and harvested piecemeal rather than in large lots. They are harvested, one basket at a time, at the rate of two or three baskets a week, because tubers are subject to relatively quick rotting (one to two weeks) once they have been dug up. Any member of a household may harvest tubers, although generally the work is done by women and girls.

Households, including those that have wet-rice fields, plant from one to two stands of dry rice in mountain fields. (Seven households had only wet rice, while only three, all headed by women, planted no rice.) Those without irrigable fields plant an average of 1.7 stands, with seed averaging 24 liters per plot. Those who grow both irrigable and dry rice plant an average of 1.6 plots of dry rice, with an average of 28 liters of seed—around ten percent greater area than those who do not have access to wet-rice fields. Note this paradox of the greater area of dry rice planted by those who already grow wet rice. An explanation will be offered in a later chapter.

About half those who work their own irrigable fields hire Sagala residents to do the transplanting because they consider their valley neighbors more adept at the task. The wage ranges from Rp. 250-300 per day, whereas other field-labor wages range from Rp. 400-500 per day or, alternatively, 2 liters of husked or 4 liters of unhusked rice, worth about Rp. 400 ($1.00, at then-current exchange rates). Men generally dibble (*martaduk*, *mangordang*) the holes for dry-field rice using two poles some two meters long. Women, girls, and boys follow, seeding into the holes. The field is then smoothed over with the flat side of a large wooden rake.

In both wet and dry fields, ripening rice must be protected from birds by shouting and cracking whips of woven grass, as well as by special constructions such as scarecrows. Poles with noisemakers, at-

Children guarding ripening rice in some of the lowest village dry fields.

tached by lines of rattan to a center post that can be set moving from any of the poles or lines, cover many of the fields. Much of the guarding (*mamuro*) is done by children before and after their schoolday (8:00 A.M. to 1:00 P.M.). Because birds are active at the first sign of dawn, a number of adults sleep in field shelters to avoid the tiring walk in the half dark, which others choose to endure. Guarding continues for two weeks after the harvest of a particular field has begun, since the first part harvested may take in only the portion of the field that receives earlier light in the morning, due to topography, than does the rest.

Since most children go to school, even adults who have children must spend time guarding rice. Many therefore locate a part of their seed-bulb crop of the second half of the rainy season or the early dry season adjacent to their rice so they can work the ground while guarding, pausing every so often to shout at thieving birds. Similarly, to conserve effort, in cutting a swath of about 10 meters' width around a dry-rice field to keep away field rats, they separate brush from mulch grasses, burning the former or bundling it for cooking fuel.

As rice in the higher locations on the mountain reaches maturity, the danger of loss to birds decreases, but that due to field rats increases. The ripening of rice also brings with it an increase of hunting activity, aimed at eliminating the threat of wild boar. For the rats, which attack even unheaded rice stalks, poison is a common but ineffective countermeasure (because there is no concerted effort). In recent years, farmers with fields in higher cultivated areas have come to depend on encircling their fields with a half-meter-high wall of polyethylene plastic, using a roll of some 5 kilos for the average field. The plastic is cut to a width of about 0.6 meter, tacked to small posts, and buried along the bottom with dirt and rocks to keep it taut. This is by no means an effective remedy, but since most fields are now fenced with plastic, those without lose a greater part of their crops. In a bad year like 1977-1978, when I saw field rats in broad daylight with bodies as big as a man's forearm, some farmers guard their rice at night with dogs and spend time each day gathering gnawed stalks to prevent the

A young man and his cousin on a hunt for wild boar. Background: a newly planted rice field, below the rise they are climbing. In the foreground: Imperata cylindrica *and the fern* Pteridium aquinlinum.

rats from building their nests in the very fields they are decimating. (Such extreme invasions are said to occur about once in ten years.)[2]

Rice is harvested with a sickle gripped with the whole hand. Sheaves are gathered, brought to a central point, and stacked in a ring with the heads of grain facing the empty center. The rings (*luhutan*) are 3-4 meters in diameter and may reach 1.5 meters in height; more than one is generally required for a crop being harvested in stages. The last sheaves are filled into the center ('the head'), which is stacked higher than the edge so that it becomes conoidal.

After a few days, the stack heats up so that the grains fall off the stalks easily when threshed. The heat prompts many villagers to bring out pressurized kerosene lanterns and do their threshing at night. Men and some young women thresh the rice by "stamping," gripping a staked, horizontal pole with both hands and crushing sheaves between their feet on mats of woven pandan, somehow passing them along,

[2]Darling (1956:784) remarks that "rodent irruptions" are "characteristic of pastoral areas in several parts of the world." One might add that being sedentary, farming grains and tubers as well as tending livestock, as do the Batak, on periodically burned-over vegetation is not incompatible with such 'irruptions.'

down the line of two or three of their fellows, who repeat the process. They are resupplied by women and girls, who remove the straw and shake out the remaining grains. The crop is winnowed before being measured out in 2-liter cans into gunny sacks by men or women, loaded on pack-horses, and brought to the hamlets for further drying and storage in large wooden bins.

An unmarried young woman, in typical work garb, harvests rice.

Father and sons building a ring of rice, before stamping.

Kin and neighbors help stamp and winnow a household's grassland-grown rice.

Like rice, corn is also generally planted by women who follow behind men. For corn, men make shallow hills into which the women dibble holes with their heels, drop the seed, and cover it with a pass of the foot as they go on. Corn is sown in groups of three or four plants about 1 meter apart, and is generally weeded only once. It is dried on the cob, and the kernels are removed by hand or by pounding with a pole in a basket. Unlike rice, corn cannot be saved in large volume for more than six months because it is vulnerable to 'worms.'

Variability of Yields of Rice in Successive Years

Most dry fields are used for three years, and some up to five years, before being left fallow. Between each crop of rice, the fields are often used for secondary crops such as bulbs, tubers, and corn. One area of dry fields (Na Hul Hul), set just above the hamlet cluster, was largely undisturbed by the rats during both years of this research. It is therefore possible to compare the overall yields of rice fields in this area for the two years and derive a figure for average variability of yield under "normal" conditions.[3] Many of these fields had already

[3]Hanks (1972:57) remarks on a paucity of data on the variability to which different methods of growing rice are subject.

TABLE 6.2
Comparison of Rates of Yields for Rice in Southeast Asia

Region and cultivation method	Rates of yields (kg/hectare)
Averages for Southeast Asia[a]	
Six cases of shifting cultivation	1,446
Seven cases of transplanting (wet rice)	2,185
Averages for Tapanuli Batak areas[b]	
Unfertilized wet rice, Angkola	2,870
Unfertilized wet rice, Silindung	2,790
Unfertilized dry field, Toba plateau	1,480
Unfertilized dry field, Dolok Sanggul	1,560
Averages for Huta Ginjang (1976-1977)[c]	
Average dry-field yields (129 fields)	1,494
With respect to fertilizer use	
Fertilized fields (22 fields)	1,680
Unfertilized fields (75 fields)	1,596
By cover vegetation	
Imperata grass (87 fields)	1,696
Mixed bush and grass (42 fields)	1,238
By length of use and cover vegetation when opened	
Newly opened grassland (27 fields)	2,095
Two (or more)-year-old grassland (59 fields)	1,371
Newly opened bush-grass areas (12 fields)	1,967
Two (or more)-year-old bush grass (29 fields)	943
By soil type	
Andosols (61 fields)	1,560
Regosols-lithosols (68 fields)	1,435
Huta Ginjang wet rice	
In Sagala Valley (26 sawah)	2,068

[a]After Hanks (1972:56, Table 4.2).
[b]After Mohr (1944:459, Table 96).
[c]Includes 15 near-failed crops.

been in use for three years in 1976-1977, when the average yield was 34.1 *kaleng* (1 *kaleng* = 20 liters) of rice per *kaleng* of seed planted. In 1977-1978, this declined to 25.1 *kaleng*, a decrease of 26.4 percent. This corresponds to the approximately 25 percent decreases reported by farmers for successive yields on dry fields. Table 6.2 shows the comparative yields of dry rice grown in Huta Ginjang in 1976-1977, with respect to whether fertilizer was used, according to prior cover vegetation without regard to length of use, according to the length of use and cover vegetation of the land when first opened by the users, and according to soil type.[4] The effects on yields of differences in these variables is much smaller than appears by comparison to the effect of differences in previous state of fallow or farmed. Note particularly that while the amount and kind of labor differ, and while there is less insurance from drought, newly opened fallow *Imperata* grassland is almost as productive of rice as are many flooded fields.

Cultivation of the Major Cash Crops

The zinced, corrugated-iron sheeting that covers the roofs of most village houses was bought with the proceeds of shallots and garlic. "Bulbs made that zinc," as a number of informants said. Bulb crops rank second only to rice in the amount of time and effort devoted to growing them. Since many of the fields are used in semipermanent fashion, the time devoted to opening land for planting bulb crops is, on the whole, not as great as for rice. Generally only two weedings,

[4]On soil types, see Sherman (1981; 1982:34-37). As can be seen from Table 6.2, less than one field in four is fertilized with chemical fertilizer; manure is applied only to bulb crops. Manufactured urea (N, 46 percent) became available at subsidized prices from the government in the late sixties. Diammonium phosphate (N, 18 percent, P_2O_5, 46 percent) became available for the first time in 1976 as part of a mandatory package of 100 kg urea and 50 kg of DAP. No source of potassium was provided. Fields in the sample were spread at the rate of 28 kg urea and 17 kg diammonium phosphate (DAP) per hectare, far below the recommended rates of the Indonesian National Fertilizer concern, PUSRI, of 200 kg urea, 50 kg tri-super phosphate, and 50 kg muriate of potash per hectare for rice. Data on fertilizer, like those in the table, were gathered by the methods and with margins of error described in Appendix B. See also Greenwood (1976:58-59, 215-216, n. 31).

rather than the three or four required for dry rice, are necessary. Except when the bulbs are mulched and hand weeded, weeding is done with the same pronged tool used for rice, 'to allow the roots to move easily.'

Those who have livestock or care for the stock of others spread dried and powdered manure on fields just before or shortly after they plant the bulbs. (Farmers who do not keep animals sometimes obtain manure by requesting it from those who do.) Over 60 tons of dried, broken-up manure, dug from stalls under the houses and swept from the courtyards and paths of the village, were spread on fields in 1977. The coffee trees, which were grown on Dutch orders before World War II, were cut down during the Japanese occupation, and few people replanted saplings until the 1970s. Of 40 households with coffee orchards in 1976, only eight had mature stands, with an average of 170 trees. (The trees bear well for about fifteen years.) By 1978, 33 among them planted an average of 300 new saplings, and 32 other households began orchards, each also planting around 300 saplings. This flurry of activity was induced by a doubling in price from Rp. 600 to Rp. 1,200 for 2 liters of skinned beans during the period October-December 1976, an increase caused by a world coffee shortage. Villagers were aware that they had a tendency to plant more coffee trees during periods of high prices than they had inclination to care for during periods of low prices.

The rainy season of 1976-1977 was the first time a substantial number of households sowed peanuts in Huta Ginjang. Twelve households planted an average of 24 liters of shelled seed. Most people claimed that the main drawback to growing peanuts was a high rate of pilferage by schoolchildren. It turned out, however, that the real losses were to depredation by rats. Both in the ground and in storage, peanuts are easy prey for the rodents. Grains are stored in large wooden bins, which are not capacious enough to hold peanuts. Moreover, few households have cats. The other export crops—the bulbs, coffee, and chili peppers—are not eaten by rats. Though no one foresaw the rat problem, the majority were apparently content to let others take the initial risks of judging the best planting time and whatever other haz-

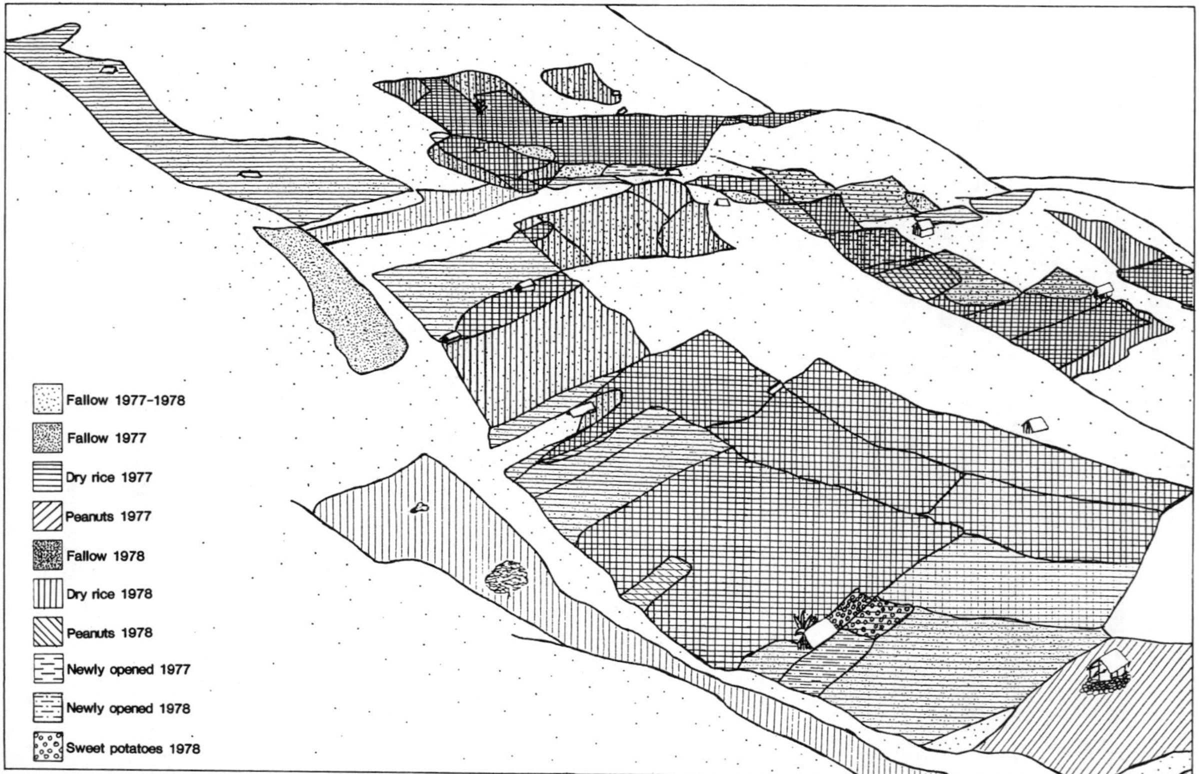

Figure 6.2. Schematic of cultivation in one area over two years.

ards might be involved in trying a new crop. The risk-takers were all more than moderately successful farmers, but only one was reputed to be among the half-dozen best off.

The impression that villagers were looking for another cash crop in attempting to grow peanuts was borne out the following year, when a large number of households planted both irrigable and dry fields with chili pepper. In part, this was due to news that the two households already growing chili had received high prices for them in the market. The productive cycle of the spindly chili bushes can be prolonged for a year or more. Three people can pick 100 kilos a day at least once a month from 1,000 bearing plants, which at that time would have earned about $170. By contrast, 200 of the best coffee trees in the village yielded some 60 liters of skinned beans per week, or $300 per month, for the heaviest months of the fruiting stage during the brief price inflation. Most households purchased seedlings for pepper planting at nominal cost rather than growing them from seed. This may have been due to the fact that—as was true to some degree with coffee plantings—when the decision to plant chili was taken, it was often for lack of hoped-for seed bulbs.

Rice and the Rest of the Diet

The main constituent of any Batak meal is high-carbohydrate, filling *indahan*, which means "cooked rice" but can also refer to other starchy foods such as boiled corn, cassava, or sweet potatoes. In a general sense, *indahan* means 'food' or 'sustenance' (as when it is used in reference to meals eaten by students living in city rooming houses).

As in much of Southeast Asia, the preferred staple is cooked rice. It is common knowledge that only the well off in Huta Ginjang eat rice as *indahan* three times a day. Most households that have corn in stock mix it with their rice at least for breakfast. Very few eat corn unmixed—or so it is claimed. One man said he refused to eat corn that had been served plain in North Samosir. For it to 'have taste,' he said, required two parts rice to one part corn, and he would rather go hungry than eat unmixed corn. Nevertheless, since corn matures in half the time as the quickest-growing dry rice, it does provide a stopgap against hunger, and only 14 households grew no corn.

Only ten households raised no tubers. Most others have them boiled for breakfast. The peels and "leftovers" are the main food fed to dogs and pigs, and the feeding of both is essentially reckoned into human needs. Most of those who raise pigs can quote a fraction of the household's tuber consumption that is set aside for these omnivores.

Almost all of the locally grown rice varieties are "brown." They are, in fact, closer to red than to other colors, the grains having deep red flecks when pounded to remove the husks. They take on shades of dull pink after cooking and give off a delicious nutty aroma. Even the most well-to-do villagers prefer them to white rices, though they rarely pass up an opportunity to observe self-deprecatingly that rich, corpulent city dwellers eat only white rice. (As in China and elsewhere in Asia and the Pacific, corpulence is an infrequent and admired characteristic, taken as a sign of well-being and supernatural favor.) Usually, a condiment (*ingkau/lompan*) such as ground chili pepper, fried dried salt fish, curried *ikan jahir* lake fish (*Tilapia mosambica*), or cooked vegetable (e.g., prepounded cassava leaves, termed *ingkau rata*) accompanies the starchy base of the meal. Salt is usually supplied in dried salt fish, mixed in chili, or added to cooking food.

Midday meals are cooked in the fields or brought there by women. Typically, the mother and daughter(s) cook and serve the meal on individual lacquered "tin" plates. Men sit with legs folded, women with knees together and legs under them. The woman of the household or one of her daughters remains outside the circle of diners, postponing her meal to refill tea glasses or serve additional hot rice as needed, and forcing more than enough on any guests. Formerly, entire households ate from a common *sapa*, a stand made of a log with a shallow depression in one end. The person who described the eating stand intimated that there was more generalized reciprocity in that way, since everyone did not have a plate on which to hoard food. I assume, though, that children were more easily crowded out. Speaking to Sahlins' consequence number 4—"even household commensality may be rigidly supervised" (1972:225)—I would say that in neither mode was consumption "rigidly supervised." There are a host of factors which govern such interaction in any given household, and the change to plates probably had to do with their availability, imitating the Dutch, and economizing on the amount of food dropped.[5]

Fishermen's wives sell fish at small early morning markets or roadside gatherings of women dealing in spices and a few other needs. Fish prices vary with the season; if demand rises or supply falls, prices rise. Since harvesters and field hands should, by convention, be fed fresh lake fish rather than the more common salted, dried, ocean fish, prices rise at harvest time, as well as in the dry months, when most fields are being opened, and at planting time for valley *sawah.* About one-third of the villagers said they hardly ever ate fresh lake fish; two-thirds ate it several times a week, depending on availability of the fish and the price being asked.

Some 90 percent of household heads reported eating vegetable dishes at least five times a week. Only rarely, on formal or festive occasions, are curried meats or golden carp eaten. Occasionally, a wild boar from the small, impenetrable groves in the hollows at the upper reaches of the mountain is killed by a group of hunters. The spearer gets a hind leg, and division of the meat is carried out in a rotation, with small pieces passed by the butcherers to each hunter in turn, as well as to all those villagers who make their way to the scene in time. (Sahlins does not deny that such generalized reciprocity occurs in meat distribution among hinterland Southeast Asian peoples [1972:225].)

Although cattle are more valued than pigs for ritual sacrifice and gift, villagers prefer to eat pork. Many also prefer raising pigs because, they say, "pig meat increases [itself] more" (*umganda jagal babi*). This is so because pigs—waste consumers that roam every nook

[5]It is significant that I was told about the *sapa* during a meal I agreed to share with a family in their field. Moore (1986:291) notes that, among the Chagga, where accusations of sorcery and poisoning are made, as they are among the Batak—I was often warned not to accept food from people in a settlement 'over there' whom I intended to visit—"one comes to understand that eating from a common pot constitutes a precaution against poisoning. It is not simply a matter of a lack of separate containers." This may also have been a factor in earlier times among the Batak. (With regard to the plausibility of such accusations, it should be kept in mind that dysentery is not uncommon in such communities, due in part to the lack of appropriate treatment of human feces.)

and cranny behind, between, and court-side of the hamlets and their interstices—put on weight faster and perhaps also because the use of pork in ritual is much less restricted. Cattle are generally slaughtered only in large rituals, while pigs of any size (even a few kilos) may serve in appropriate situations as the basis of a commensal meal. Purchase of butchered meat in market is a modern innovation. It serves mostly to fill the needs of town restaurants, although villagers occasionally buy meat to serve some minor ritual obligation. A more expensive chicken or piglet, purchased live, is so much preferred for such rituals, however, that usually only one cow was slaughtered for the weekly Pangururan market, serving much of the west side of Samosir, and one pig a week for the Sagala market. A disproportionate amount of market-butchered meat is consumed by well-to-do townspeople, storekeepers, and those who hold government appointments.

The Cycle of Wants

During the first part of the rainy season, which lasts from September or October until January or February, stores of corn and rice run low, and about half the villagers buy or borrow additional supplies until the harvest (37.5 percent of the households bought rice, 6.3 percent borrowed, and another 4 percent had a deficit that they made up with other starches).

While being put in sacks at harvest, rice is measured quite precisely using 2-liter cans called "*tumba*" or "liter," which are leveled off with a cylindrical piece of wood. The yield of each field and of each season's harvest is remembered clearly in figures "rounded off" to the nearest *kaleng* (20 liters), and calculations of the coming year's needs play a large part in determining the amounts of corn planted. Householders calculate rice needs on the basis of one *tangkar* (a third of a liter) of hulled rice per person, adult or child, two meals per day. Parents of several babies may not actually cook that much, but by figuring their needs on that basis, they provide some leeway so as to be able to sell some rice. The following table is based on this method of reckoning needs. For each household, the number of adults and children was multiplied by two-thirds of a liter per day, by 365 days, and the total was subtracted from one-half of the total of unhusked rice (*eme*) produced—that is, from the amount of husked grain (*boras*). When compared to the reports of 81 respondents whom I asked if they had had to buy rice or had been able to sell any, the figures arrived at in this way corresponded to their answers in almost all cases. In some instances, discrepancies were due to the rule-of-thumb's failing to provide for feeding of cooperative or wage labor and for contributions made at feasts. Table 6.3 includes rice grown by households themselves and rice received from sharecropping arrangements. Nearly one-quarter of village households had a substantial surplus, and an additional 20.5 percent produced or received as much as or slightly more than their needs. On the other hand, half the households did not grow enough rice to supply their wants and had to buy rice for at least part of the year.

Given this situation, which (judging by the lack of remarks to the

TABLE 6.3
Distribution of Surplus and Deficit in Rice Production (1976-77)

Surplus or deficit	Number of households	Percentage
Substantial surplus	27	24.1%
Minimal surplus	14	12.5
Sufficient rice	9	8.0
Small deficit	22	19.6
Large deficit	31	27.7
SUBTOTAL	103	
Lacking data	6	5.4%
Grew no rice	3	2.7
TOTAL	112	100%

contrary) may be taken as normal for recent times, it is evident that for many households cash crops are an alternative means of supplying rice that might otherwise be grown. And the other staple crops, corn and tubers, emerge as major sources of subsistence for three-quarters of the villagers (since the calculations are based on a reckoning of two meals of rice per day per person, the third having to be made up largely of other staples). On the other hand, for the households that produce a substantial surplus of rice, it is both a cash and a staple crop; they have disposable surplus.

The data for corn contrast with those for rice. Seventy percent said that they grew enough corn for their needs, 20 percent said they bought some (usually small amounts), and about 10 percent sold corn. The difference in the number of those who grow 'enough' or more than enough corn as opposed to rice—80 percent in the first instance, as opposed to less than 50 percent for rice—is a function of several factors. Since most households run out of corn several months before their main rice harvest, and since the price of corn is roughly on a par with that of rice (volume for volume of the milled or pounded product), and its price follows that of rice (Dixon 1982:253), villagers generally buy rice rather than corn when they require additional supplies. (Purchased rice is termed *matubaba*—literally, 'to the mouth.') Yet some do buy corn. In general, they are not simply those with deficits of rice, but rather those who want to conserve rice supplies for sale or other uses and so mix corn with rice for one meal a day.

In normal times, no households attempt to subsist on either corn or tubers alone, and none buy tubers. During a severe drought, such as occurred in 1947, however, women took woven shawls to Dairi on the high plateau to sell or exchange for baskets of tubers that they then head-loaded back to the village.

Rice as a Focus in Subsistence Strategies

The dispersal of fields in the area of Huta Ginjang, from the valley (about 1,000 meters above sea level) to above the village (1,750 meters) and the noticeable fragmentation of holdings presumably spreads risk so that failure in one area is not catastrophic to a household. Similarly, a range of subsistence strategies is pursued—with rice as a first preference and corn or tubers second and third. Strategies thus include three major crops of differing growth habit and taste. There is no particular mix of corn or tubers or, indeed, of cash crops grown by any grouping of households relative to the method by which rice is produced or acquired. Nor does surplus or deficit production of rice correlate with a particular mix of other crops (Sherman 1982, tables 1.5 and 1.6).

When a household has too much pressing work to do, subsistence concerns are always given primacy. Commodities are worked on or harvested only in order of their current price and future importance as seed. Although several of the older farmers made coffee their priority, it was generally low on the scale. It was said that when coffee prices rise, everyone goes out and weeds it.

Based on extensive sampling (over 17,000 records) of field labor of villagers and their children recorded in 1977, 55 percent was devoted to food crops and 45 percent to cash crops (see Table 6.4). Though the survey was by no means complete, the data are a representative sample (see Appendix A). The greatest distortion is probably in the percentage found for tubers, since most planting and harvesting, done in tiny increments in comparison with the area being grown in tubers, simply was not observed. (Totals do not include processing time for either food or cash crops.)

Whether to produce for use or for exchange is sometimes decided on the basis of rather fluid criteria. In some instances, farmers pre-

TABLE 6.4
Relative Amounts of Work Devoted to Food and Cash Crops (1977)

Predominantly food				Predominantly cash			
Dry-field rice	Wet-field rice	Corn	Tubers	Bulbs	Coffee	Pepper	Peanuts
42.7%	5.4%	6.1%	0.7%	39.3%	1.7%	0.6%	3.5%

pare a field even though they are uncertain of what they will plant. A man opens a field to plant bulbs if he can harvest or afford enough seed; as one said, "If not, maybe I'll plant corn." Such choices are not solely dependent on resources of land and seed capital or even of currently available labor. The future work load entailed by a planting is also taken into account. The Batak plant manageable plots of rice or bulbs in succession because they have a rough idea of how much they can care for at any given time.

Weather patterns, size of household, and other tasks projected are, of course, equally important considerations in such decisions. All strategies bear a heavy element of risk. Bulbs mature best when, after several months of sporadic rains, a dry spell of about a month occurs. Those who have rice maturing at the same time as a crop of bulbs feel torn. As one man put it, "If I ask for rain, the bulbs will be damaged. If I ask for a dry spell, the rice will be damaged." This can serve as an epigraph for the agricultural change that has occurred since the 1930s. There are irreconcilable tensions, and villagers attempt to strike a balance as best they can. Most spread their risks, while a few decide to specialize.

Yet the bases of the system are still largely intact. In the following chapter, we examine one of the most striking in comparative perspective: the grassland component of Samosir agriculture. As has been pointed out, not everyone has access to irrigable fields, but those without are not entirely bereft of resources. Before we examine mobilization of labor and distribution of land in more detail from a sociocultural standpoint, we need to develop an understanding of the methods and requirements of grassland farming.

Chapter 7

The Ecology and Ethnology of Batak Grassland Farming

The agricultures practiced in Southeast Asia are usually grouped under two main headings: swidden (shifting, "slash-and-burn") cultivation of dry fields and *sawah* (wet rice on irrigated terraces). B. J. Hagreis was the first to depart from the accepted wisdom and argue that with sufficiently long fallowing, shifting cultivation was economically and ecologically viable. His work (Hagreis 1930-1931) has been ignored, but that of other scholars (Conklin 1954, 1957, 1963; Pelzer 1948) has made some progress in dispelling the universal condemnation that European administrators first heaped on slash-and-burn cultivation. Nevertheless, as M. R. Dove shows (1983, 1985a), official policy still condemns it. Hagreis and Vonk (1927-1928:688-689) also described Toba Batak grassland farming, but their work too failed to alter accepted viewpoints or East Indies agricultural policy of claiming eminent domain over grasslands, or, as the Indonesian government still calls them, "empty land."

I was, thus, surprised to find Huta Ginjang villagers adept at growing rice on land opened from nearly pure stands of the much-decried "swordgrass," *Imperata cylindrica* (L.) Beauv. According to conventional wisdom, once established, it was impossible to eradicate—the grass had "turned . . . much of Southeast Asia into a green desert" (Geertz 1963:25).[1] In this chapter, I show that the Samosir Batak sys-

[1]Most of this chapter appeared as part of a more extensive review and treatment of the subject, entitled "*What* 'Green Desert'? The Ecology of Batak Grassland Farming," in *Indonesia* 29 (1980):112-148. R. Pendleton (1939-1940) epitomizes the negative school of thought that flour-

tem of grassland cultivation is by no means unique in Asian, Oceanian, or tropical contexts, and I explore some of the primary interpretive economic, cultural-ecological, and political-economic questions raised by considering the case in ethnological perspective.

After about a year in the village, I ascertained that some fields were indeed being opened from what I had assumed to be an unfarmable condition. I also saw buffalo and cattle eating the "inedible" fodder. In 1977, 22 percent of subsistence households in the village opened new grassland fields, many of which had been fallow for so long that no one remembered who had last worked them; 21 percent of the households widened grassland fields that they had first opened in 1976; and 38 percent opened mixed grass-bush fallow fields they had inherited. (Those who did more than one of the above are counted in only one category; 19 percent of the subsistence households did none of the above.) The average newly opened field was 0.7 acre—0.28 hectare—and several might be opened by the same household in a given year on different parts of the mountain.

While much of this chapter is comparative, it should be clear from the outset that the Samosir Batak methods of cultivating grassland are, if not unique, certainly unusual, and, insofar as they are, the ecology of grassland farming casts light on the value that rice still has. It should be kept in mind that long fallows, largely covered with *Imperata*, are almost always opened ('pioneered') for the planting of rice. Thus, the question of production for use versus production for exchange (and whether monetization has occasioned fundamental sociocultural changes) becomes a little more complicated. Not only has a change occurred—from production for exchange being exclusively of rice to a much broader range of options—but we also come to recognize that rice-growing (even with irrigation) has traditionally involved great difficulty. The reputation of *Imperata* and other such grasses, while inaccurate, is not entirely undeserved in one respect—eradication is not "economical" of time and effort in Western terms. According to

ished in colonial times, blaming the grass for everything from climatological features to the fall of the Angkorian and Mayan empires.

van Beukering (1947), it requires twice as much time to open comparable areas of grassland and jungle swidden, and the figures he gives for grassland are compatible with my findings. On the other hand, the maintenance of *Imperata* grassland is largely the result of livestock raising, and since bovine livestock cannot forage in jungle, there is complementarity between farming grassland and raising livestock. It also has other benefits, to which I will refer.

Opening the Savannah Grassland

It is usually said that too frequent cultivation of the same plot without a sufficiently long fallow period endangers the continuation of the swidden (or "shifting") agricultural cycle. As Hanks puts it:

> When the land is overtaxed because the period of fallow has been too short to regenerate needed fertility, nature responds with soil erosion and nearly ineradicable weeds. This latter signal of impending trouble is *cogon* grass (*Imperata cylindrica*) . . . resistant to hoe, mattock and fire. . . . Here lies the terminal point for shifting cultivation, for though settlements may continue, economies must change to other techniques of cultivation or some other way of making a living, such as herding cattle. (Hanks 1972:31)

But although the grass is resistant to the mattock, it is not immune—certainly not to Batak methods. In fact, Hanks' description suits the Batak case. Swordgrass tends to dominate long fallows that are not overgrazed but are burned periodically. They farm it by other than typical swidden methods (particularly in that they turn the sod and break it up), and they keep cattle as well. Although fire is often employed and land is used in a pattern of alternating long fallows with shorter periods of cropping, the parallel between grassland and forest "shifting" cultivation ends there.

The method of working grassland is difficult; success requires foresight, hard work, and patience. Those opening fallow grassland start, for the most part, in June after the rice harvest, with a view to planting rice when the rains arrive between October and December. *Imperata* is often cut and taken off for mulch or thatch (though most houses now

A cooperative work group opening burned-over, long-fallow Imperata *grassland.*

Having struck the ground in near-unison, the men pose, pulling a section over.

have corrugated iron roofs). If the vegetation is dry enough, the field may be burned. The ground is broken up and turned, usually by four or five men who drive their mattocks into the sod, section by section, in unison and then heave and pull a section of sod over (*mamahal*). On the average, they can turn a 1-meter-long, 1/3-meter-wide, 20-centimeter-deep pallet of sod at a time. They move in rows back and forth across the field. It requires some 35 man-days to open an acre (0.4 hectare), and the result actually resembles a field that has been turned by a moldboard plow. The field is then left to bake in the hot sun so that the rhizomes of the *Imperata* lose their resilience. The size of the pallets of sod reduces the number of new shoots sent up, since these come mainly from the edges exposed to light. After a month or six weeks, the field is reworked, and the pallets of sod are chopped up into small chunks. This and further steps of the process are carried out by individuals, including women or couples working together.

The smaller chunks of sod are again left to dry for as long as a month. Once the hold of the rhizomes on the soil has been loosened by sun-baking, a third working breaks the sod down completely, knocking rhizomes and roots of bushes loose. Plant residues are then raked out of the soil and are either burned or left in rows perpendicular to the slope to prevent erosion.[2] Ditches for rainwater runoff are also dug above many fields lying on steep slopes.

The differences between grassland and swidden cultivation are clear. The cutting and disposing of the cover vegetation remains a preliminary step to opening the land (a step often bypassed), rather than being the primary tasks, as in typical swidden cultivation. Burning of raked-out plant residues is also of isolated piles or rows, rather

[2]While hoeing sods is *mamahal*, preliminary hoeing of a field not covered by sod is *mangombak*. Shallow hoeing of low weeds is *manggisgis*. The process of smashing dried pallets of sod to free the rhizomes of grasses and the roots of bushes is *manggargari*; a similar process for land that has not been covered with sod is *mamaspasi*. In each case, root residues and other plant wastes are raked (*manggarpu*, also called *mangumbanghon*, 'to sift') and burned (*mamuruni*) in small piles, wherever convenient, being reduced to ashes by what is more of a slow smoldering process than an actual fire. The last hoeing and fluffing of the soil (*mamali*) is followed by a final raking (*manggargaer*) with a very wide, shallow-toothed wooden rake. (Middendorp [1913:19] described a similar process with somewhat different tools.)

than of a layer spread over the whole field, as in swidden and *citimene* (Richards 1939). But as in those methods, fire is used to get rid of vegetational wastes, to facilitate sight and movement, and to add ash to the soil.[3] Timing is the most crucial factor in working grassland. In a typical swidden cultivation system, drying out cut vegetation is important for a proper burn to provide soil-fertilizing ashes (Sherman 1980:124f.). Under grassland conditions, it is not the burning that is important in the process of field preparation, given the much smaller bulk of plant material, but the fact that the parched conditions are conducive to killing the rhizomes in upturned pallets of sod.[4]

It is testimony to the appeal and logical consistency of the "breakdown" model of "degeneration to grassland"—the supposedly irrevocable dissipation of what was thought to be soil fertility in a cycle of forest regeneration—that C. Geertz and other scholars did not consider the degree to which the model was conducive to the intensification of colonial agro-economic policies. Yet it is clear that the Dutch anti-swidden stance helped in the virtual enslavement of Java, which Geertz (1963) documents. For instance, he tells us that in 1870 the Agrarian Land Law codified "the convenient notion . . . that all uncultivated 'waste land' is inalienable state property . . . making it possible for private plantation concerns to lease such land on a regularized long-term contractual basis from Batavia and to use such legal titles for the purposes of obtaining credit" (1963:84). Yet this and other laws, such as the 1879 law against burning of grassland, fail to alert Geertz to the possibility of built-in political bias in the reports of *Imperata*'s perniciousness.

It is ironic that the Dutch, who branded shifting cultivation "robber agriculture," practiced it on a wide scale themselves in the East Coast

[3]Burning over a field, setting undergrowth on fire, is *manutung* (from *tutung*, a cognate of Hanunóo *tutud*, 'burned swidden' [Conklin 1957:31]). *Mamuruni* (from *purun*, a pile of weeds) means 'set fire to wastes.'

[4]I have proposed an explanation of major differences between forest and grassland ecosystems that would account for the widespread cultivation of grassland (Sherman 1980:124-132). In addition to the sources cited there, see also Kellman (1969), Zinke, Sabhasri, and Kunstadter (1978), and Dove (1981).

region of North Sumatra. For the first thirty years of the existence of the tobacco plantations there, yearly planting was done on land cleared of primary forest for the purpose. After that, in the 1890s, "an interim fallow period of approximately eight years between use was discovered to be sufficient to allow the land to . . . be able to support another tobacco crop. . . . By the time this discovery was made Deli was 'one great grass plain'" (O'Malley 1977:147).

Fire and Fodder in Grassland Ecology

Burning is necessary to the continuance of a grassland ecosystem. To repeat, there is complementarity between raising livestock and farming grassland. The prevalence of grassland in Samosir has made it possible to raise large numbers of livestock for export to the surrounding regions of Dairi, Simalungun, Toba, and the East Coast, and this export has continued in spite of reductions in pasture area and a ban on burning during and after the colonial period.[5] Although *Imperata* is often denigrated as coarse and unpalatable for cattle, that characterization applies only to the mature stage of growth. Furthermore, even authors who denigrate it have come to admit the necessity of burning tropical pastures. Thus, while Sanchez claims it is "practically worthless for grazing," he points out that the practice of burning (as the Batak do, to renew their pastures)

> is easily condemned by people unfamiliar with the system, citing ecological damage. . . . An examination of the available data, however, indicates that periodic burning is essential for maintaining the stand and productivity of many natural grasslands and that the frequency and timing of burning operations are important . . . to destroy the dry, unpalatable grass stands and to promote the regrowth of younger, more palatable grass shoots. (Sanchez 1977:538)

[5]See W. Middendorp (1913:26-29) on the export of horses and buffalo, where he records an export of 600 horses and gives the price of these and other livestock found in the Pangururan market. (These prices are reported in Chapter 2.) W. Haibach (1927:22) gives livestock population of Samosir as 9,218 buffalo, 4,870 horses, 5,244 cattle, 14,282 pigs, 7,142 goats, and 3,530 sheep and reports an export of buffalo worth *f* (guilders) 80,840, horses worth *f* 11,820, cattle worth *f* 15,600 (about 800 buffalo, 300-400 horses, and 300-400 cattle), and smaller amounts for other animals (1927:23).

What is involved in condemnation of such practice, of course, is another instance of deceptive appearances, of the difficulty of reading the significance of the landscape from its overt appearance. Indeed, it is shocking to see blackened, seemingly bare and easily erodable swathes in the landscape during and after a burn. But the *Imperata* rhizomes, unharmed by the fire, continue binding the soil and resprout with increased vigor after a few days. What on first sight appears to be a vast black wound in the landscape turns light green within a few weeks. As Sanchez notes,

> Burning is a rapid process: a curtain of fire travels quickly along the grass. It is likely, therefore, that its effects on soil properties are less marked than those of forest burning. . . . Native grasses . . . are well adapted to this process. (Sanchez 1977:538)

The villagers also know that cattle prefer young shoots of *Imperata*. Although villagers are unaware that the protein content of such shoots is higher than of mature grass (Soewardi *et al.* 1974), they distinguish between the two. Mature *Imperata* is called *ri* or *lalang* (Indonesian, *alang-alang*), while grass in the process of resprouting is referred to as *tulmok*, which Warneck (1977:273) translates as "short and thick." "Yes," said one man with whom I was discussing the matter, "we always tell the children, 'take the cows to that *tulmok* over there.'"

Pan-Batak Evidence of Grassland Farming

At present, the Toba Batak farm grassland not only at the fringes of their region (as on Pusuk Buhit) but apparently in areas as diverse as the vicinities of Tarutung (in the earlier-colonized Silindung Valley), the seat of the regional capital, and of Dolok Sanggul as well. Protests against the expropriation of such ancestral lands for government forestry programs were often reported in *Sinar Indonesia Baru* (the largest Sumatran daily) during this study. For example, a news report from a village near Tarutung said: "The reason given [for the protest] is that from the earliest times to the present these plains had been used by their ancestors for dry fields. They constitute the only subsistence resource . . . to supplement the yields of working their barren *sawah*."[6] The following citations from Burton and Ward (1827) confirm the people's truthfulness. Traveling in the same area in 1824, they observed:

> For two hours the path lay over a grassy plain or valley, having at intervals patches of cultivation. (1827:486)

> The woodlands had already given place to grassy plains; and the mountain on which we stood had been cleared on every side for cultivation, merely retaining its original forest in a tuft at the top. (1827:488)

> The whole plain was perfectly free from wood, and presented, as far as the eye could descern, a vast unbroken field of verdure. On a farther examination with the telescope, it was discovered to be thickly studded with small detached huts of straw. . . . To each of these was attached a field or patch of mountain rice. (1827:493)

These passages were cited by H. H. Bartlett (1961:127), who remarked,

> If the last observation was correct (doubtless the interpretation was that of their well-informed Batak companions) the inhabitants of the Toba plateau . . . were probably practising shifting agriculture on *lalang* (*Imperata*) grassland, a laborious form of agriculture. . . .

Moreover, it was not only the Toba Batak who farmed grassland in precolonial times. In 1847, F. Junghuhn, a German botanist, wrote of a journey through the Angkola region of Southern Tapanuli, where he

[6]From *Sinar Indonesia Baru*, November 7, 1977. See also September 20, 1977; October 21, 1977; November 18, 1977; December 1, 1977; February 22 and 27, 1978. The translated titles of the relevant articles are: "53 inhabitants ask the attention of the Forest Service because of the measuring and fencing of the flat area 'Parbalean Parrongitan'"; "It is still being investigated how many hectares of pines got burned near Parapat"; "The residents of Parlombuan in Sipahutar object to 200 hectares of pastureland being taken by the regional government"; "800 women 'walk together' to the police station of Dolok Sanggul"; "The head of N. Tapanuli orders the *Camat* of Siborong-borong to stop the digging up of the area of Simartolu which is becoming disputed"; "Five hectares of young pines which were just planted (reforestation) in Dolok Silom, Muara, is burned."

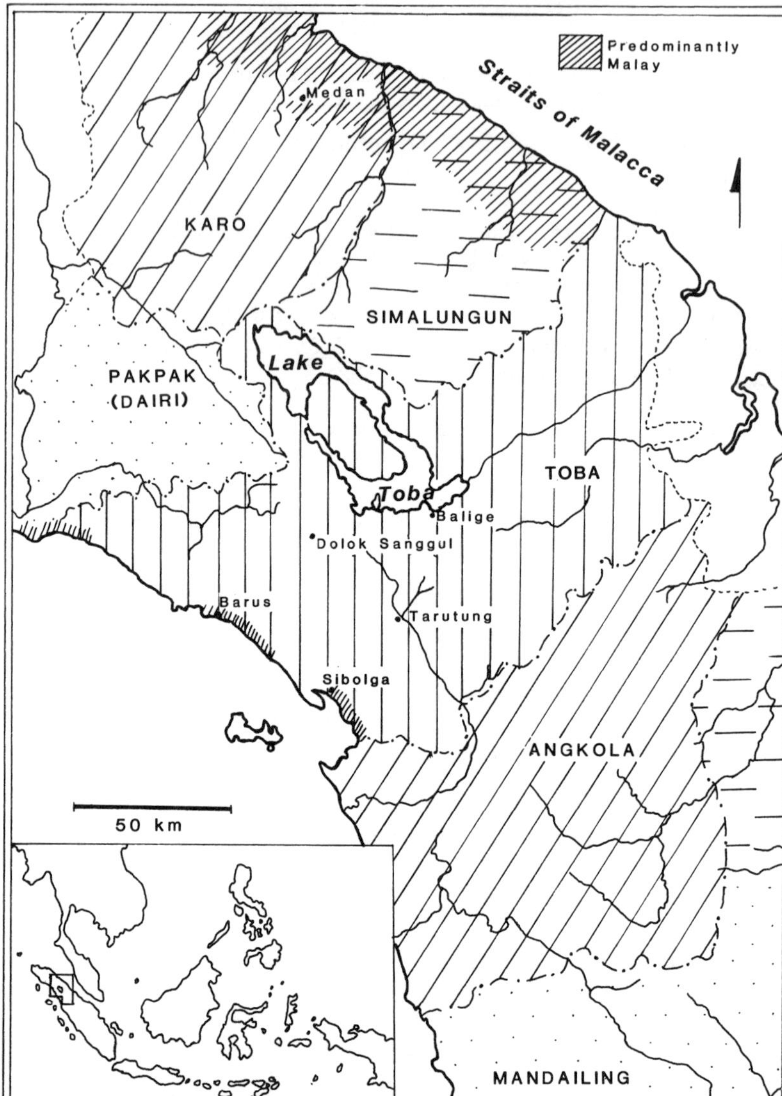

Map 5. Traditional Batak "subtribe" areas and languages.

found half the agriculture to be on wet-rice fields and the other half on grassland (Junghuhn 1847, II: 190-191). The Bataks of the Angkola region, he reported, preferred working *Imperata* grass fields to cutting forest. Later in the same passage, he noted that even on newly cleared forest or secondary forest ground, they turned in the ashes by rooting up the soil with a wooden pickaxe (G., *hakke*)—a practice not commonly found in swidden cultivation.

This report went unremarked until Bartlett noted the paradox:

> Junghuhn said that the ashes of burned-over 'wilderness' provided enough fertilization for renewed cultivation, but he did not tell clearly how a crop could be obtained after only a short fallow during which woody plants had not yet supplanted grass. He did speak of cultivating the land with wooden hoes, but that was in connection with newly cleared land. . . . This might have included uprooting the clumps of *galaga* grass, for in Karoland, farther north, the Batak actually turned the refractory *lalang* sod with digging sticks to make gardens in choice and accessible spots . . . and the more southern Batak may have done the same. (1955:332)

The existence of similar methods may be inferred among the Simalungun Batak, east of the lake. Tideman (1922) wrote that the Simalungun's elimination of the forest had "reduced some cultivators to the necessity of using [*Imperata* grassland] plains" (cited in Bartlett 1955:514). According to Dr. P. Voorhoeve (personal communication, 1978), in fact, there were two types of farmers in the Simalungun Batak area: *urang rih* (Toba Batak *ri*, *Imperata*) and *urang harangan* (*harangan*, the pan-Batak word for forest), and the terms were applied to the districts they inhabited as well.

Before the introduction of the heavy iron mattocks that Hagreis (1930) observed, Toba and Simalungun undoubtedly used digging poles similar to those Bartlett saw being used by the Karo Batak. Thus, four of the major Batak subtribes (see Map 5)—the Toba, Karo, Angkola, and Simalungun Bataks—practiced similar methods of farming *Imperata* grassland in areas where the need arose.

Grassland Farming in Other Areas of the Tropics

Reports of grassland farming from other areas, like the Batak cases, have failed to alter the generally accepted models of tropical ecosystems and their human adaptations. Gerlach (1938) described burning and shallow hoeing in the south and east of Borneo, which, he noted, may be in imitation of a more intensive hoeing method practiced there by Javanese migrants. Contemporary eradication of *Imperata* in the same region by plowing has been detailed by Dove (1981). An account of Javanese migrants in Lampung, South Sumatra, also describes methods of eradicating the grass (Suryatna and McIntosh 1976).

Agricultural systems based exclusively on grassland cultivation are rare. The Batak have other methods, including flooded terracing. The Kofyar of Nigeria (Netting 1968) have both semipermanent cultivation on manured fields and shifting cultivation of bush and grass fallows. However, the Batainabura of the central highlands of New Guinea, who live in an area that is almost entirely grassland (including *Imperata*), cut and burn the grass, and then turn the soil and work it into mounds, "a process that may be repeated consecutively for several years before the plot is abandoned to a short fallow period (five to ten years?) under grass" (Clarke 1966:354). Other New Guinea peoples such as the Kapauku (Pospisil 1963a:7-8), the Chimbu (Brookfield and Brown 1963:43-44, 62), and the Tolai (Salisbury 1970:61, 91, 95, 109) successfully cultivate terrain covered with *Imperata* or other Andropogonae, as do the Tiv (P. and L. Bohannan 1968:14, 42-44) and the Bemba (Richards 1939:302f.) in Africa. The Kachin also merit attention in this regard.

Leach explicitly notes the existence of what he calls "grassland *taungya*" (*taungya*, Burmese for swidden cultivation). In fact, the overall picture that he gives of Kachin agriculture is quite similar to that of the Batak given here. As already noted, many analogies can be drawn between Kachin and Batak practices and beliefs. Leach led the way in providing an extensive list of their "corresponding structural characteristics" (1966a:91-94), and he deemed Batak society "a kind of structural duplicate of that of the Kachin."[7] From the present vantage, the characteristic forms of Kachin agriculture make it something of a mystery that the usual stereotype of "hill tribes" as swidden agriculturalists could have persisted. Leach's description in "Some Aspects of Dry Rice Cultivation in North Burma and British Borneo" (1949) was expanded in *Political Systems of Highland Burma* (orig., 1954), but with one significant omission. In the essay, Leach wrote:

> A Kachin village in North Burma. . . . cultivated rice in four different ways. These different methods were complementary to one another, rather than alternative. . . . The Kachin preferences for different types of cultivation were obvious. Irrigated wet rice with animal traction was recognised as much the most advantageous; anyone possessing such land was rated a rich man. *Hkaibang grassland cultivation came next. Ordinary jungle taungya [swidden] was rated rather lower than hkaibang in popularity.* (Leach 1949:27, emphasis added)

What has gone unnoticed in subsequent discussions of the Kachin is that grassland was *preferred* to "ordinary jungle" swidden for dry-field farming—much as it was by the Angkola Bataks Junghuhn described in 1847. Leach omitted to note this in his subsequent book on the Kachin and instead pointed out that the forms of agriculture were associated with decidedly different "ecological zones." Grassland, the cultivation of which he had come to impugn, was largely associated with the drier zones (Leach 1965:22-27).

In *Political Systems*, Leach goes to some lengths in examining the degrees of correlation between given ecological niches—or what Hanks (1972) calls "holdings" that humans maintain therein—and forms of political organization (Leach 1965:228-238). He is forced to conclude that there is no correlation between the culture and political organization of Kachin communities and the ecology. He further comments:

[7]See Leach (1966a), especially pp. 81-95, for a comparison of the Kachin and the (mostly Karo) Batak. Unfortunately, Leach's source for many inferences was E. M. Loeb (1935), whose chapter on the Batak, Parkin (1978:41, n. 1) justifiably suggests to have been "uncritical" of its sources. See also Kipp (1983); Nugent (1982).

> A village which relies exclusively on [grassland farming] can seldom be self-sufficient in foodstuffs. There is consequently a much more marked tendency in the [dry zone than in the wetter jungle zone] for the hill villages and valley villages to be interlocked in some sort of more or less permanent economic and political interdependence. (Leach 1965:26)

This is certainly relevant to the Toba Batak case of Huta Ginjang. The problem is that such economic and political interdependence does not sit well with Leach's thesis of inevitable oscillation between "social structures of a fundamentally different type," *gumsa* and *gumlao* (autocratic and democratic), among the Kachin (1965:87).

Although ecology and political organization are not definitely correlated, there is some degree of correspondence. However, it is not what one would expect. *Gumsa* ("aristocratic") political organization predominates in the wetter Zone A of jungle shifting cultivation, whereas *gumlao* type ("democratic," "equalitarian") organization seems to persist throughout most of the drier, demographically denser northeastern areas of Zone C—regions not of jungle but of predominantly wet-rice and grassland farming (see Map 2 in Leach 1965:23). In this context, the anomaly of Leach's previous remark on grassland's leading to "interdependence" is accentuated. Why should the swidden-farming western Kachin have maintained autocratic control over other Kachins and the valley Shans in swidden-system conditions (of low population density), while in what are usually considered the more ecologically deprived areas of grassland, hill villages established interdependent relations with, but were not subordinated to, their more economically advantaged valley cousins, who, as we tend to view it, would be more capable of exercising domination? Is it attributable to hill-dwellers having the advantage of the high ground? One would rather expect political organization of the "autocratic" type to be more prevalent among Kachin who live in the more demographically concentrated, wet-rice "intermediate zone," given the shorter distances that would be involved in controlling large numbers of subjects.

A partial explanation is implied in Leach's statement that "a *gumlao* ['democratic'] community, unless it happens to be centered around a fixed territorial centre, such as a patch of irrigated rice terraces, usually lacks the means to hold its component lineages together in a status of equality" (Leach 1965:204). Apparently what is intended is that being tied to a fixed territorial center with provision for at least a modicum of livelihood makes it possible to establish social equilibrium. This is a suitable description of what the Toba Batak of the Samosir region have achieved through their ecological "holding," the culturally based social organization of their livelihood and a process of outmigration.

To return to the analogies Leach first drew between Batak and Kachin societies, his gloss of the ideal type of Kachin "democratic" organization—in which "the political entity is a single village and there is no class difference between aristocrats and commoners" (1965:57)—indeed recalls the anarchic political scene with which the Dutch had to contend when they sought to govern the Toba Batak through "native rulers."[8] Nearly all Samosir chiefs or headmen "laid claim to the few chieftaincies which the Dutch government had instituted" (Vergouwen 1964:126). The contrast between the Toba area and South Tapanuli is also significant: "One does not find the social classes in the Toba Country such as exist in South Tapanuli" (Vergouwen 1964:110; see also 327). In other words, in areas such as South Tapanuli (Angkola and Mandailing), *gumsa*-type (autocratic) organization was much more prevalent.

As might be expected, given what is probably a kernel of truth in Leach's oscillation model, in the *gumlao*-type (democratic) areas, there were also exceptional disturbances of the democratic equilibrium. As Vergouwen observed, referring to the Toba, "almost every region has known periods in which powerful and still renowned *radja* have exercised a wide-ranging authority" (1964:133). This is, of course, reminiscent of Leach's *gumsa* pole. But in Vergouwen's next sentence, we find a clear intimation of what Leach described for Kachin as *gumlao* ("equalitarian"):

[8]In addition to the references below, see Castles (1972), especially chap. 7, "Harajaon Politics in North Tapanuli." Much of this work on the Bataks' absorption in parochial conflict rather than in an awakening nationalism could be read in this light.

> Theoretically the development of a strong personal authority over large groups belonging together could have come about had it not been for the vigorous, ambitious, and obstinate character of the people. (Vergouwen 1964:133)

Although the climatic zones and farming systems used are not as well demarcated in the Batak highlands as in the Kachin Hills, it is remarkable that both grow irrigated wet rice in even the driest zones, while in the wetter zones, where most forest swidden is carried out, the pattern is "monsoon *taungya* in the hills; wet rice in the valleys" (Leach 1965:231). This set of parallels applies, for instance, to the relatively dry Samosir area and the Dairi Batak area west of the lake crater, which receives far more rainfall. The Simalungun Batak area, with swidden and grassland farming, had small kingdoms (Liddle 1970:20-1) of up to 10,000 people. But the "political organization" of the Angkola Batak, who farmed both wet rice and grassland, also resembled Leach's aristocratic *gumsa* pole, while the Toba areas, especially the Samosir region, with holdings of wet rice, grassland, and bush fallow, appear to have been democratic.

Difficulties of a Cultural Materialist Analysis

The fact that the congruences of Batak and Kachin agricultural systems occur in societies that Leach described as "structural duplicates," it might be argued, exemplifies Harris' determinist claim that

> similar technologies applied to similar environments produce similar arrangements of labor in production and distribution, and that these in turn call forth similar kinds of social groupings, which justify and coordinate their activities by means of similar systems of values and beliefs. (Harris 1968:4)

But besides the differences of agricultural method and preference among the various Batak subtribes, the materialist viewpoint may be called into question with the example of other hill tribes in Southeast Asia, such as the Chin, that are as much structural duplicates of the Kachin as are the Batak, although they do not farm on grassland (Lehman 1963:88f.). On the other hand, the Kofyar of Nigeria farm grassland and bush fallow as well as semipermanent "homestead fields," but they live in patrilineally inherited homesteads rather than in villages or hamlets, as do the Southeast Asian hill tribes. From still another perspective, the Batak, the Ifugao, and other Southeast Asian peoples devised extensive irrigation systems without resorting to large-scale bureaucratic autocracies. Yet Ifugao society is in no sense a structural duplicate of Batak society. The Ifugao have a bilateral mode of reckoning kinship relationships, while the Batak have what can be glossed as patrilineal, segmentary lineages. Like the Batak, the Chin have segmentary lineages and voice a preference for matrilateral cross-cousin marriage—but they do not build floodable terraces, despite their monsoon climate. These examples should discourage any attempt to apply a simplistic materialist determinism in analyzing the similarities between Batak and Kachin agricultures.

The implications of grassland farming have gone largely unremarked in descriptive and theoretical works on both the ecology and political economics of Southeast Asia. It has been the ideal-typical poles, either wet-rice or shifting forest cultivation—and never grassland farming—that have been taken as keystones for both social anthropological analyses and for the teaching of regional ecology. Two such dissimilar reinterpretations of Leach's *Political Systems* as those of A. T. Kirsch (1973) and J. Friedman (1975) use the demographic limitations of a swidden system as determinant of the limits of social cohesion attainable in such societies. But given the Batak and Kachin examples, as well as others I have cited, many previous assumptions concerning the carrying capacities of monsoon Asian grassland regions are put in doubt. Contrary to long-accepted wisdom, the advent of grassland may be said to herald a beneficial adaptation. Although it requires different kinds of work and perhaps twice as much time (but not, I believe, twice as much energy) to prepare "equal" areas of grassland and forest for planting, the yields of grassland are generally better, fallows can be shorter, and thus its cultivation allows higher demographic concentrations to develop.

The labor expended in physical alteration of the environment in the building of both dry- and wet-field terraces and in what amounts to a system of deforestation near settlements is also evidence of a desire for permanent settlements and of the ability to maintain them in a permanent sociocultural developmental cycle. Whatever may be the agronomic basis for the practice of grassland farming (see n. 4), there remain the questions of what social, cultural, and historical factors lead people to create and maintain the kind of ecological holding described and of the role of rice in their adaptation, social economy, and system of values. One thing is clear: to go to such lengths to cultivate rice, they must value it highly.

To begin answering these questions—not simply to explain what the Batak are doing, but also its meaning to them, and what it is in their views that keeps them doing it—we must take into account both their system of beliefs and values and the social organization of their livelihood. The bonds among, and divisions between, villagers, their sharing and limiting access to resources are related to their cultivation. All are communicated in word and deed, some in traditional ways, others innovatively—always, over time, with some input of foreign words and even foreign religious and other doctrines entering a pre-existing system of meanings, as has already been described. Before we turn in Part IV to examine how the social organization and values of the Samosir Batak are reflected in their allocation of resources or factors of production, the following chapter is devoted to equally important background aspects of the agricultural economy—namely, marketing, credit, and investment.

Chapter 8

Marketing, Credit, and Investment

As we have seen, most villagers devote substantial effort to production of crops for sale. Only a small number produced no commodities, deriving their cash income mainly from wage labor. The rest are, to a greater or lesser degree, part-time marketers of their own produce. For this and other reasons, the social parameters of marketing are significant for this study. As will also be shown, the use of credit and interest are closely related to the existence and "pull" of the market. A grasp of these subjects will also allow us to address the absence of commercial agricultural cooperatives in the village.

Part-Time Marketers and Full-Time Traders on the Toba Circuit

Traders, who divide their time between taking, selling, and paying for consignments of bulbs, as well as storekeepers and weekly circuit-making merchandisers, who spend most of their time engaged in retail selling, differ from the bulk of the resident population in the degree to which they depend for their livelihoods on buying and selling.

The Pangururan marketplace is of partly roofed galleries surrounded by four outside walls made of adjoining buildings, comprised of shops and eateries facing the outside streets and others facing the inner square. In the largest, as in the smallest, the positions of full-time traders—of shawls, fruits and vegetables, utensils, etc.—are constant from week to week. Different kinds of goods tend to be concentrated by area as well: all fishmongers gather in one corner and in the same lineup from week to week; next to them are those selling pigs, then those with chickens, all in front of a row of bays whose boarded-up fronts open to reveal bolts of cloth and treadle sewing machines.

Some traders farm during the off days, while many attend other markets, either to buy supplies (as in Haranggaol on the northeast shore of the lake, Pematang Siantar, or Medan) or to spread a bale or

Women bargaining for small stock in front of a row of tailors' bays.

Market woman displaying containers, pots, and other cookware.

two of their goods on the concrete floor of the unpartitioned, roofed gallery of a local, territorial market.

Traders of Chinese descent have not penetrated the ancient marketing infrastructure in the Toba highlands, although in the cities they are often involved in the upper and middle levels of bulking exports and debulking imports (Jasin and Smith 1978:165f.). As in Acheh to the north and Minangkabau to the south, there is an apparent resistance of Batak society to small-scale trade by Chinese merchants.[1] Whereas in the cities of North Sumatra, as elsewhere in Indonesia, the most well-stocked "general stores" are owned and run by people of Chinese descent, every Batak town has "home-owned" stores carrying a wide variety of goods (from notebooks to lanterns, cassette decks to soap, furniture, motorcycle batteries, umbrellas, and hats), specialty shops (hardwares, photography studios), restaurants, and artisans' shops (jewelers, tailors, and shoemakers). For every shop or store, moreover, the Pangururan market has numerous permanent storage stalls (shuttered when closed) that are rented by smaller-scale traders of cloth, tools, packaged goods, kitchen utensils, necessities like matches, coffee, and sugar, snack and drink sellers, and others. The lanes of the market, deserted on off days, fill on the day of the main weekly market with scores of additional traders offering prepared foods, subsistence items, medicines, combs and face powder, dried fish, baskets, mortar-and-pestle sets, rice-winnowing trays, colored ices, and the like.

Clearly, the proliferation of manufactured goods has given rise to entrepreneurship on a scale that dwarfs precolonial trading enterprises, since traditional markets had no facilities for storage of goods other than nearby hamlets. Market 'pull' draws shoppers to fill previously non-existent needs (Siegel 1986:166-168). People who have money generally do not spend it on wages but on such things as tape decks, furniture, clothes, as well as feasting, and education. In many ways, as in Java, money is "converted into the idiom of status" (Siegel 1986:168).

[1]Siegel's analysis (1986) of Javanese attitudes toward the people of Chinese descent in the city of Solo (Surakarta) is extremely useful in understanding their absence in the hinterlands. See also, among others, A. Dewey (1962:103-104, 191-193).

Women outnumber men both as buyers and sellers in the market.

A spice and squash seller, with some of the ingredients for curries.

To all appearances, villagers never go to the market with the intention of buying anything on credit (although partial, preliminary downpayment in ordering tailor-made clothes—the cheapest kind—is common). If they do not have cash, they take some commodity to sell before making their purchases. Of course, buying on credit, referred to as *marbon* (from Dutch *bon*, voucher, check) or *mananggung* (Indonesian, be responsible for payment), occurs, but market traders resist requests for credit precisely because many have gone bankrupt after too many credit sales. Delinquency in paying small debts is the bane of village enterprises. Two small-scale "open-only-when-home stores" failed in the village during the period of this research, both having dealt in cooking oil, sugar, cigarettes, and snacks.

Few households offer items like bananas for sale in the village, perhaps fearing (as expressed on a few occasions when my wife or I noticed such things being put out of sight) that "the neighbors" (*angka dongan*) and, probably more so, close relations, would ask for them. By implication, it would be unseemly to request payment. This may seem to be in accord with Sahlins' predictions, though one wonders what a shortage of fruit has to do with rice export in any direct fashion. Let us, however, examine how Sahlins' predictions apply precisely to the marketing of rice from the village.

Village women and men sometimes took as much as two sacks of rice strapped to a packhorse to sell in the market, even though co-villagers went there to buy rice. Most women took a *kaleng* (twenty liters) on their heads to sell, and both parties could have saved the effort of transporting a load each way if an arrangement had been made in the village. (Of course the trip may have social and other attractions, but those don't necessitate portage.) The absence of any Huta Ginjang market does not mean that rice and other items are not sold in the village, but with the exception of shallots and garlic, it appeared that villagers bought and sold more goods outside the village than within it. This is probably because the price that can be demanded in the market for rice or bananas is some 5 to 10 percent higher. Although the likelihood of receiving an unreasonable demand is small, the possibility entices many women to make the attempt, particularly when they are intent on purchasing goods.

Again, we find support for Sahlins' prediction that export of rice means surplus is not liquidated in favor of need. This is something we have already accepted as given in the nature of this society. Does it have the other consequences postulated? Certainly, "intensity of sharing is low," if sharing means sharing with all comers, but why would village shops be such tenuous enterprises if not for the fact that sharing is too intense to permit them to survive? Furthermore, one of the main reasons people do not market rice in the village is that it would be unseemly to do so—to haggle with co-villagers over price. This is in complete accord with the "sociology of primitive exchange," which Sahlins sets out, but from which he claims rice export excludes Southeast Asian hinterland peoples. Sharing with all comers would constitute extremely "generalized exchange," but Sahlins' own examples (1972:231-275) show that it prevails only among close kin—even in hunter-gatherer societies like the !Kung. Indeed, what is involved here other than an example of generalized reciprocity pertaining to close kin—of the need to get outside the immediate home area to market a good such as rice? So, too, as Sahlins points out, citing Marshall, "!Kung do not trade among themselves. They . . . avoid it because it is too likely to stir up bad feelings" (1972:232). Even more to the point, Sahlins cites Bohannan (1955:60) on the Tiv, to the effect that "the presence of a previous relationship makes a 'good market' impossible: people do not like to sell to kinsmen since it is bad form to demand as high a price from kinsmen as one might from a stranger" (quoted in Sahlins 1972:246). This means that, even in the societies which Sahlins argues form the basis of a "sociology of primitive exchange," people sometimes sell or exchange with strangers rather than giving to close kin. More will be said on this in later chapters.

The Marketing of Bulb Crops

As noted, most of the main cash crop of shallots and garlic is given on consignment to one or more "full-time" traders who make the trip from the village to Haranggaol twice a week. A few of the largest village growers take the bulk of their crops to market themselves after harvest, and women may occasionally take a few gallons of bulbs for ready spending money (as do those who grow coffee).

Three Huta Ginjang men were bulb traders (*toke bawang*), two Sagalas and a Naibaho, and they were later joined by a Sigiro. (About

15 percent of the bulb traders in Sagala Valley were women.) Village traders did not make a practice of lending seed bulbs: they are not patrons involved in financing the planting of produce whose market they control. Traders make the rounds of the hamlets twice a week between the Monday and Thursday markets in Haranggaol, paying for bulbs taken to the previous market and quoting prices according to the quality and amount of bulbs offered for sale and their relationship with the sellers. They mix the poorer grades with better ones and count on being able to receive 5 to 10 percent more than they have promised to pay out. On the boat to and from market, one sees many traders bent over notebooks, figuring prices and debts. During slack times between harvests, some traders take sacks of rice to market because they have to keep abreast of price trends even though they have no bulbs to sell.

Wholesale buyers, to whom village traders have consigned their previous day's bulbs, pay them at the next market. Prices quoted in the village are based on the most recent market prices, on nonbinding promises of the wholesale buyers, and on apparent trends. This means that the traders sometimes get caught in the unprofitable situation of having contracted for bulbs at a price higher than they can get. When abrupt, unanticipated drops in the price occur (whether due to imports from Java, as was claimed, or to overabundance from Samosir, as was likely the case), traders refuse to sell and return to the Sagala port of Tulas with gunny sacks full. On such evenings, the news precedes them, and no one expects to be paid more than a portion of the money promised. Being caught out by the "live price" of wholesale buyers (Dewey 1962:107), village traders become chary of incurring further debts. They either take consignments without promising any specific price or offer only very low prices. Since both shallots and garlic keep well for a season, traders run the risk of having farmers withhold them at such times. Since traders must pay the amounts promised before the drop, they hold out for higher prices at the market, though they also incur added freight charges and market taxes with each trip. But if, after two or three further markets, the price seems to have settled at a new, low level, they can make much the same argument to the villagers that wholesale buyers make to them—if farmers will not accept less, traders will be forced out of the business.

The traders competed fiercely, but mutedly, bandying prices under their breaths; there appeared to be no collusion among them. If two simultaneously entered the same courtyard from different ends, they would rush from house to house to conclude deals before the other had a chance or would both accost the same seller and attempt to outbid each other (*marlomba*, 'to race'). While, for some villagers, a relationship with one or another of the traders determined the consignee for their bulbs, the relations of many to two or more traders were roughly on a par. Thus, other considerations, particularly prices, determined their choices. A number of farmers also made a practice of consigning fractions of their yields to several traders, even if they received the same price, to maintain good relations with as many as possible.

There are definite limits on the degree of exploitation of the villagers by the traders (e.g., through the use of "doctored" scales), for growers can sell their produce in Pangururan or Harrangaol—and several of the largest growers do—bypassing the village middlemen, just as some traders on occasion go to city markets by bus with their loads of bulbs. But few villagers actually do bypass the traders. Forty-five of 71 household heads said they had never tried marketing their own bulbs outside the village. Of the 26 who had, 10 said the effort had been worthwhile, 4 said they had suffered losses in comparison to the price they could have gotten by selling to the village traders, and 12 claimed to have "broken even." Note that it is in the interest of both the wholesale buyers and the traders to maintain the farmers' incentive to produce. But while the risk of driving too hard a bargain is very real for the village trader, vis-à-vis each individual producer, the wholesale buyer has the advantage that on any given market day there are hundreds of traders from scores of territories who are in need of money and anxious to sell.

P. and L. Bohannan observe that among the Tiv, before the middle 1940s, few "became professional traders. . . . Economic activities, like any others, were organized by the father of the family, by the compound head, or in some cases . . . men of political influence in the course of their familial and political duties" (1968:7). In Huta Ginjang, the largest-volume bulb trader was a former headman. Another ex-headman had been a cloth smuggler during World War II. On Burton and Ward's 1824 pioneer trek from Sibolga to the Tarutung area, they encountered a hamlet headman who was returning from a trading trip (1827:489). In other words, economic activities were perhaps part of "familial and political duties." On the other hand, trading was probably one traditional way of acquiring the wealth needed to attract followers—as a means, for instance, of establishing one's own hamlet.

The former headman trader had substantial irrigable holdings in the village (and two others had small irrigable fields). Generally, his wife and a son or daughter led three horseloads down the mountain for every two taken down by younger men and their wives. In part, this was because he had more close agnates than the others and was therefore involved in providing more ritual gifts and contributions than the others. Thus, more villagers were likely to be beholden to him, in spite of his alternating irascible and jovial humors. In addition, having more irrigable land and older children, he was assured of more consistent yields from his houshold's endeavors and may have been able to take greater risks in underbidding his competitors.

Indeed, it is significant that men who are traders depend in large part on their wives, who not only help load and lead packhorses to and from the lake steamer on market mornings but also return to tend their children and crops, as usual, for the rest of the day. As J. Kahn put it,

> If it is remembered that costs of commodity production and of distribution are determined by the cost of the labour power of individual producers and merchants . . . then clearly access to subsistence land will have an important effect on the individual's ability to enter certain branches of production or distribution. For [it] guarantees that a proportion of the cost of reproducing the peasant's labour power will be borne outside the commodity sector of the economy altogether. (Kahn 1980:126)

For traders, it is not only access to subsistence land but also the willingness of wives and children to maintain a high level of production on it that provides invisible support in trading enterprises (as it does for pioneers, itinerant peddlers, etc.).

Indigenous Notions of Traders' Acumen

Such trade, carried on at very low or negative margins of profit, has several other parallels in Indonesia (Dewey 1962; Siegel 1969; Kahn 1980). As Dewey showed for Java, people can make an incredibly small margin of profit and still be willing to work long hours. Among the Batak, as among the Javanese and the Achenese, making profit is attributed not so much to effort on the part of the trader as to astuteness (Dewey 1962; Siegel 1969). The following example illustrates the Batak attitude.

At the "arrival meal" for a newborn child of a village bulb trader, the midwife expressed her blessings:

> Verily, Father of N., and you, Mother of N., you have carried out the arrival [meal] of this grandchild. May the heart of God our ancestor be merciful. May you, sir, get livelihood; may difficulties keep away, from now on. May clarity come, wherever you, sir, visit. May you have good fortune. . . . May he be merciful. . . . May the money of Jakartans always come to all of us. May their hearts be soft in giving it to us. May our souls all be staunch henceforth!

It is clear from the invocation that there is a belief that success in trading stems from something more than the diligent effort of the trader. It is a belief that some have the power to best others in commercial transactions. As she finished, the trader's older brother chimed in, "Say, 'Just you be allowed to swindle. Be not swindled by others.'" There is, indeed, no contradiction between "Just you be allowed to swindle" (*mangoto-otoi*—literally, 'make others stupid') and the invocation "May the money of Jakartans always come to all of us. May their hearts be soft in giving it to us."

Unlike the Achenese, then, the Batak do not attribute the astuteness to which success in trading is due to the faculty of *akal* (reason), which is God's gift to men who obey His precepts (Siegel 1969), but to an acumen thought to derive from a compact with supernaturals. Some claimed that the ability of successful traders derives from magic (*ilmu*) exercised (*ipasang*) by them or by their ability to 'cast spells' (*mambahen sangkiat*). Further explanation consisted of names of specific spirits involved. It was said that one man did not even have to trade to acquire goods: "He would go to the market without money or goods and return with 5,000 rupees' worth of purchases. That was the robustness of his magic. If he exercised it, [people] would agree [to the patently unprofitable]." Another informant said that the man had been heavily in debt when he died; nevertheless, the fear of a believer in this kind of trading prowess is evident. As Dewey said of Javanese who fear being swindled in trade with strangers:

> Less experienced and less sophisticated carriers . . . are suspicious of settled prices and are unused to judging weights by the kilogram. They feel that they will be cheated in some way by the [wholesale buyers using scales] and prefer to sell to a regular [middleman trader] who will bargain with them in terms they understand. (1962:130; see also Siegel 1969:239-242)

The kinds of fears described by Dewey, the beliefs noted with regard to the abilities of traders, and the expenses involved in making market trips partially account for the fact that 63 percent (45/71) of the Huta Ginjang villagers sampled had never tried to market their own bulbs.

Credit, Interest, and the Roles of Rice

One way of characterizing "traditional Batak economy" is in terms of rice serving in several roles—as a medium of exchange, a standard of value, a unit of account, and a means of payment. The uses of rice for what are generally considered "functions" of money persist to the present, despite the fact that money often takes precedence as a medium of exchange, unit of account, and means of payment. Specie was also a standard of value, as in pawning land, for decades and perhaps for centuries before becoming a medium of exchange, but money is no longer a true standard of value. As was noted in Chapter 2, pawns of land are now phrased in volumes of rice, whereas, according to Vergouwen's informants of the late 1920s, land was traditionally pawned for specie.

The fact that both rice in the husk and money as we know it have the quality of durability renders their common use in loans and other transactions understandable. Rice had all the functions of money, and it retains them. This is not to say that, for the Batak, rice *was* money, because obviously, in addition to being valued for its liquidity and for what we can abstract as its various economic roles, it is valued as food. That is what gives it liquidity. Money, on the other hand, has all the functions Jevons identified—medium of exchange, etc. (cf. Codere 1968)—but it has them simultaneously and intrinsically, as L. M. Fraser argues, and is valued for its liquidity alone—i.e., "*exclusively* as a means of purchasing other forms of wealth" (Fraser 1937:137, 294).

Although rice is kept in the husk for storage purposes, husked rice is often loaned, and agreements involving cash loans, such as the pawning of a field, are phrased in terms of the husked product (which, in this area, is one-half the volume of the rice in the husk [cf. Drake 1982]). It is a frequent medium of payment for wage labor in village agriculture and for making contributions to kin at feasts, as well as being a component of "living expenses" for those at school or pioneering.

As a rule, farmers who are saving prefer to keep their assets in forms other than cash. Since rice is durable and always in demand for subsistence requirements, it has proven a definite standard of value, a hedge against inflation. In spite of government efforts to keep the price at a reasonable level by importing and lowering the price below cost on millions of tons annually, during the time of this research, the price of rice rose continually with inflation since Independence (1949), and the prices of other indigenously valued assets have done likewise (see Timmer 1975; Mears 1981).

Cash is often spent on rice for subsistence purposes, as well as for feasting, and no one buys goods for rice in the market. Like other crops, it is sold for cash before purchases are made. But in the village, when, for example, an animal is bought for slaughter by a group of households to provide meat for a Gregorian calendar holiday, it is said, "It is possible [that a household's share of the total cost] be made over to husked rice; when the harvest comes, [it will] be paid."

To an extent, shawls, gold jewelry—for the well off—and livestock are also used as local media of exchange. All have traditionally served as tangible assets, inherited wealth, *harto*, kept until needed. But they were never general media of exchange, nor are they today. For large loans, the pledge of some valuable as security is usually required—in most cases, a terraced field. Other items such as houses, gold earrings, and the like are also used for the purpose.

Both rice and money were traditionally borrowed with interest (*marlali, manganahi*) and without interest (*marsali*), and both still are. Before the Depression, loans of cash "often stipulated that payment of interest [was] to be made in rice and not in money" (Vergouwen 1964:334). This is no longer the case. Generally, interest on money loans is paid in cash, at the rate of 10 percent uncompounded interest per month, 120 percent of the principal per year. For loans of rice that bear interest, the rate is 50 percent per year, a common rate among Southeast Asian hill tribes (see, e.g., Mills 1937:74). In fact, such loans come due after harvest, generally within five months of having been made, and thus also yield approximately 10 percent per month. In Sagala Valley, the price of rice rose from Rp. 1,700 per *kaleng* in May, just after the main harvest, to Rp. 2,200 at the end of 1977, before any of the wet-season harvest was in, when the rice stocks had run out or were quite low. A person who loaned 20 *kaleng* of rice in December could have sold it for Rp. 44,000. Assuming that the price fell back to its previous low, the 30 *kaleng* expected after harvest would have been worth Rp. 51,000. Thus it would have yielded the lender a net profit of only some 16 percent of the loan's initial cash value (see also Firth 1964a:30).

Some farmers who have a surplus from the year before, prior to the main harvest, sell several sacks even if they know they will not have enough to last until their fields are ready. They expect that once most others' harvests have gotten under way, the price will decline, and they will be able to purchase what they need at a net profit.

Two households in the village engaged in "financing" (*mardagang*). They made loans equivalent to about $250 to support nonvillagers pioneering irrigated rice in the swampy East Coast lowlands. In return, the creditors were guaranteed either two-thirds or four-fifths of the harvest. Hence, such loans yielded approximately 800 percent of principal within a six-month period, barring catastrophe such as (fairly frequent) flooding. They were said to be made without security. The lenders had kin living in the areas concerned who sent word when the rice was ready for reaping. Since these swampy lowlands sold for between $50 and $100 per hectare (the limit that could be worked by a household) and since the pioneers who had to borrow a stake were too poor to have much in the way of assets, it is clear that even if—contrary to informants—the fields were pledged as security, the lenders were taking greater than usual risks in return for greater potential gain.

This "financing" of pioneering at a distance "fits" the context of the predominantly Muslim Malay and Javanese population of the East Coast of Sumatra. In what Firth calls "the Muslim *mazarebat*, the profit-sharing enterprise,"

> the proper method of using capital is the partnership system in which capital cooperates with labour, and gets a profit on the joint result. This profit should be allocated in an agreed . . . proportion . . . of the joint product, and not as a fixed percentage of the principal sum invested. (Firth 1966:152)

According to these strictures, the practice of "financing" pioneer ventures would be acceptable to Muslims, in spite of what appears to be a usurious rate of return. On the other hand, the loan of rice or money for a set amount of interest and a far lower percentage of principal, as found in Samosir, would be considered usurious, for, as Firth adds, "what [Islamic thought] objects to is a situation in which only one party bears sacrifice or the risk, and the other remains immune" (Firth 1966:152).

In the village, it often appeared that debtors were spared the strict terms of their pledges. Foreclosure on a one-room house named as security for a loan of 60 *kalengs* of husked rice was just being set in motion (with a threat of going to court) in 1978, eighteen years after the loan came due (according to a written agreement specifying repayment in seven months). This is not what one would expect to occur if "intensity of sharing" were, indeed, "low," as Sahlins claimed.

Loans of Seed

Seed for bulb crops and peanuts is also loaned for a share of the harvest, though not the same proportions for all crops. The loan of bulb seed is referred to by the same term as that for sharecropping someone else's wet-rice field, *mamola pinang* (to split the areca nut). But no one makes a practice of giving out seed bulbs for profit. Between the fluctuations of weather and market, the risk is too great. In one instance, a man borrowed 20 kilos of shallots worth Rp. 400 per kilo. He paid back 30 kilos a few months later, but the price then stood at Rp. 250 per kilo. The lender thus got back one and a half times the weight of his loan but formally 'suffered a loss' (*rugi*).

Small amounts of seed bulbs are more often given than loaned at interest. A sister asks (*mangelek*) her brother, for example; a father's sister, her brother's son; a daughter, her mother; a neighbor of one lineage asks a neighbor of another. None of the 20 percent of the villagers who admitted having been asked had refused to give a little (generally in the neighborhood of 10-20 kilos, 1 or 2 *kaleng* of seed bulbs), although one refused another in my presence. As with many things, if one has something and is asked for some of it, as one man expressed it, 'one must give a little' (at least to certain people). Again, this contradicts Sahlins' analysis of the consequences of rice export.

Itinerant Cloth-Peddling and Other Ventures

Between June 1977 and June 1978, four men who had farmed in the village the previous year took up itinerant cloth-peddling (*marjaja kain*), and one became a utensil peddler. Two of the cloth peddlers went to Minangkabau and two to the environs of Medan.

They drove trishaws along residential streets, hawking cloth "door-to-door" and making sales on credit. The two who went to Minangkabau peddled for kin who owned market stalls, and both took cash to defray the initial expenses of additional inventory: one pawned a wet-rice field for about $400; another who went to Medan raised $500 by selling surplus rice and getting loans from his village kin, and he took about half his cloth on credit from a Chinese merchant (*saudagar*). The peddlers revisited the same neighborhoods every few weeks, collecting a few coins from each debtor and leaving new cloths with some. Over a six-month period, with the accrued interest, they supposedly realized a profit of 100 percent. The trade near Medan is mainly with Javanese plantation workers, and, apparently, the population remains stable for long periods, because no security tokens were given in return for the cloths. But in view of the fact that Batak villagers, from the time they are children, know a market system in which little is bought on credit—and certainly not cloth, a relatively expensive item in household budgets and a sign of status—it is somewhat incongruous to find numbers of them engaged in this type of peddling. I was also surprised to learn the news of a girl of sixteen who left for Bandung, Java, in 1977 to "help out her sister," a cloth seller. She wrote back a few months later that she was engaged in money-lending/pawn-taking—making loans of small amounts of cash to the indigenous Sundanese in return for items taken in pawn at an interest rate of 10 percent of the principal per day!

While itinerant cloth-selling and money-lending, like middleman bulb-trading and retail marketing of imported and domestic goods, involve risk-taking and management of assets and while most serve necessary functions of distribution and transport, they do not produce anything. Such endeavors often involve what amounts to the pooling of village funds and stores of rice for sums required to set up as peddlers, but most are limited in personnel and in potential to grow beyond the circle of trusted family, rather than being expandable group enterprises.

There are, however, some large-scale productive enterprises founded by emigrant villagers. One son of a former Huta Ginjang headman ran a fleet of twenty trucks in a lumbering business set up with his father when the latter accompanied him to the Karo area with six buffalo for hauling logs in the early 1950s. Villagers who set up such labor-intensive businesses are able to draw on trustworthy workers from the pool of village youth who seek work abroad. This occurs widely in the construction firms and lumber operations that have been established by Samosirese in Karoland and Medan.

Investment in Agricultural Needs

In contrast to the large amounts of cash spent on feasting, education, trading, and pioneering, the investment in village agriculture (for tools, seeds, fertilizers, and the like) is minimal. The amortized investment or capital outlay for a mattock is an imprecise, small amount. Many farmers spent the cost of a mattock for the short-lived plastic sheet used to "fence" the perimeter of rice fields to impede invasion by rats. However, the expense of "seed" (bulbs that could be sold) makes the major cash crop capital-intensive by comparison to rice. A rice seed may yield from 25 to 80 new grains, whereas a shallot bulb often yields no more than five. Since very little chemical fertilizer is used for rice, and less for bulbs, seed is the main expense. To plant the same area of rice as of shallots during periods of median prices required seed worth half as much, and the yield would have been four to ten times as great in volume. But given government efforts to control rice prices, there is never a windfall to be anticipated.

Most bulbs are saved from a previous harvest. In a sample of 75 villagers, 49 had not bought seed bulbs in 1977. Fifteen did so in the village, and 11 in markets. Nineteen of them purchased an average of 33 kilos (some 3 *kaleng*), at a median cost of $16.00.

Carrying baskets made from split bamboo were mostly purchased at market. Local producers are residents of villages where there is no dry-season irrigation. In other similarly situated villages, women engage in weaving shawls or plaiting pandanus mats in the dry season. The mats, which are large but light and can be rolled up and stored easily, are also important in crop-handling and are often the main furniture. Some are used for stamping rice and drying rice, corn, and other crops, others for sleeping. When they become too worn, they are spread under finer mats for seating during outdoor feasts and to cover the floor for indoor dancing. While most Huta Ginjang households buy the mats, a third of the 75 women asked grew pandanus or gathered it at the lakeside and plaited their own. Indeed, the wife of the man who appeared to be the richest in the village did so.

Villagers bought only some $300 worth of manufactured fertilizer. As can be seen from Table 6.2, the increment in average yields for dry-rice fields in which it was spread was a mere 5 percent. No villager used potassium, which was not supplied in the government program of subsidized fertilizer loans, nor was the loan program synchronized with the local agricultural cycle. Fertilizers, which should be spread before planting, were not made available until the dry-rice crop was half grown and wet-rice had already been transplanted. The farmers, however, do not complain, since they prefer to see how their rice is doing before investing in fertilizer. They remain wary of purchased fertilizers and are reluctant to subscribe to the loan program. On the other hand, based on chemical analysis, it would have cost the villagers over $2,500 in 1977 dollars to purchase fertilizers containing amounts of nitrogen, phosphorus, and potassium equivalent to the contents of the more than 60 tons of dried manure spread on village fields (mainly for bulbs) in 1977.

The Dearth of Long-Term Village Cooperatives

Samosir and other Toba areas have loosely organized irrigation associations, with formal requirements of one day's labor per year for each terrace irrigated. These are under the auspices of the sacrificial organizations, *bius*. The lack of other agricultural cooperatives was striking by contrast with those found in the Andes, where there are communal lands of which "the crop is sold with the proceeds going to *barrio* funds for community projects" (Mayer 1974:39), or closer at hand, the copra marketing cooperatives of the Tolai of New Guinea's East Coast (Salisbury 1970:216f.). For lack of cooperatives, certain major capital investments in Samosir purchased by well-meaning emigrants, such as imported steel windmills for irrigation, were not maintained or used.

The term *kongsi* is Indonesian for "commercial organization." Yet *kongsi* was most often used to refer to the joint undertaking of a localized lineage in giving a feast. Such occasions are certainly "investments" in "intangible" social and spiritual well-being (Hill 1963:190), and they are serially recurring, but they are not continuously operating cooperatives. Vergouwen noted that trading societies, established around 1920,

> in which the common men, *na torop* [the many], could participate by taking a few shares, have all rapidly broken down because of the elaborateness of the plans and insufficient organisation of the mutual control. (1964:344)

He gives examples of a lineage "mutual relief fund," a clan branch's education fund, an "agricultural society," and a "funeral society." People who had emigrated to the cities described "*koperasi*" associations like wedding societies that kept all the plates, cookware, and serving ware for large feasts in storage (in the village they have to be rounded up anew each time). In others, members were committed to bestowing an expensive shawl on a new couple at the marriage of a member's daughter, and each was able to use the promise for persuasion in bridewealth negotiations. Such formalized cooperative agreements do not arise in the village, given the nexus of reciprocal duties among kin, which is a feature of life there—however much grumbling and public debate takes place over the carrying out of obligations. Rotating credit associations are also found among city Batak, but not in the village. Members contribute a stake and draw lots to determine to whom the right to use the fund will pass, interest-free, for a month. Again, though, these are not continuously operating but recurring cooperatives.

Vergouwen (1964:346) dubbed "the *huria* [parishes], built up by the Rhenish Mission," "native corporate bodies. . . . organised internally". Although I did not encounter any, such as he described, that "own money and loan it out" (loc.cit.), I was told that previously, a rice bank, called *kas huria*, "parish coffer," had been set up by the

Protestant church in Huta Ginjang. Each participating household had contributed 2 *kaleng* of unhusked rice, and anyone short of rice could borrow at the normal 50 percent interest per year. "But," as a minister said, "the members came, took rice from it, and refused to pay. They reckoned it to be their initial stake" (*Ietongi pangkalna hian*). By contrast, according to Salisbury, the Tolai

> see investing in worthy projects as a duty, and treat collections for clan copra [coconut meat] driers in the same way as collections for the church's mission activities, Council tax, or for sending the village school choir to a competition. The contribution is lost and not to be demanded back. (Salisbury 1970:273)

Such an observation could be made with regard to a collection taken up for school tables and chairs in Huta Ginjang, but my point here is not that there is a complete lack of cooperative pooling of resources (it also makes building churches possible, for instance) but that there is a dearth of pooling directed specifically to commercial or economic purposes. Perhaps because the Dutch required corvée labor in lieu of taxes, villagers treat government calls for "mutual self-help" (*gotong-royong*) as onerous impositions. A steep one-lane road from the valley, begun with government funds, remained unfinished for five years and was worked on at the rate of one day per household per year during 1976-1978.

Some potential benefits of agricultural cooperatives, were there to be any, might stem such projects as: (a) setting poison and traps in a campaign against rats, (b) making available soil tests and optimal amounts of ground limestone and fertilizers, and (c) acquiring storage space for bulb crops on the east side of the lake so as to hold out for higher prices or bypass the middlemen when necessary.

Cooperatives were also absent in the area of manufactures. This resembles the situation described by Kahn (1980) for much Minangkabau productive enterprise: there is little or no large-scale production of such things as metal tools, clothes, mats, etc. A brick maker in Samosir, for example, had four employees. Moreover, unlike their Minangkabau counterparts, Samosir women do not, to my knowledge, contract to do piecework in weaving shawls and sewing clothes.

Rather, so-called "petty commodity production" prevails among artisans in general—tinsmiths, blacksmiths, basket-makers, carpenters—paralleling the small-scale, narrow profit-margin enterprises of most of those who constitute the distributive network in market trade. Livestock raising might also be viewed as consisting of multiple small-scale enterprises. As will be shown, it often involves cooperative arrangements. But the kind of large-scale cooperation necessary to undertake a program of pasture improvement appeared to be unthinkable.

There might be some justification for arguing that the dearth of cooperatives lends credence to Sahlins' analysis of the consequences of hinterland rice export. As I noted in the Introduction, however, the degree of economic cooperation among villagers lies in the eye of the beholder. For all the New Guinea Tolai willingness to pool resources, rich and powerful leaders, on the pattern of traditional "big men," appear at least as likely, if not more so, to come to power among them than among Samosir Batak (cf. Salisbury 1970). Moreover, though I could not suppress my own tendencies to think up and assume such projects to be feasible, and this in turn gave rise to my wondering why windmills for irrigating fields were not a widespread goal and did not seem to succeed when attempted, it is not a foregone conclusion that they—or cooperative marketing or fertilizer provision—would be feasible or ultimately beneficial. Leaving aside such caveats, however, the theoretical question at hand may be addressed more fully. The question is whether the apparent "atomization and fragmentation" evinced by the dearth of long-term village cooperatives is, in major part, the result of or a "complement" to "restricted sharing" of the subsistence/export staple—namely, rice.

It should be clear that the restricted sharing of rice for subsistence purposes has an obvious complement in its widespread sharing as a ritual gift. Once we admit that there is, in fact, *some* sharing of rice as part of the continuous ritual give-and-take, we may then ask what social and cultural predispositions might make commercial agricultural cooperatives impractical among Batak in the Samosir area. One factor—perhaps the major one, which would apply equally to other hinterland peoples on whom Sahlins drew for his examples (Iban, Dayak, Lamet)—is the fragmented physical landscape. Alongside the Bataks' patrilineal ideology and their affinal alliances, there is a clear tendency of agnatic descent groups to fission, though as noted in the Introduction, there is a taboo on marriage of clanmates, so the clans are not "insignificant." It is a facet of Batak village and regional social organization that no one person is given too much trust and support in attempting to organize his fellows. Although this places limits on the mobilization of capital in potentially profitable joint ventures, it likewise puts limits on swindlers and despots. The smooth and rationalistic, double-entry bookkeeping needed for the running of such an organization presumably is not abetted by the constraints of ties of wife-givers and -receivers, and of older-younger brother lineages, involving ascribed deference and hierarchy. Nor is it abetted by sometimes conflicting ties of locale, and recollections of disputes and feuds. It is to such particularistic social bonds and ruptures and cultural, ritually inculcated, ways of expressing them, and to the resulting impediments to communication (as well as, secondarily, to the rugged and isolating landscape)—not to rice export—that we must ultimately look for explanations of limits on cooperative enterprises. Other "organizing principles," such as the asymmetric reciprocal bonds of wife-givers and wife-receivers, provide different parameters for economic endeavor, and these the Samosir Batak have put to wide and fruitful use.

PART IV

ACCESS TO RESOURCES: LABOR AND LAND IN INTERPRETING THE ECONOMY

The preceding accounts of Samosir Batak history, social institutions, values, and human ecology, in whose contexts agriculture has developed and is pursued, provide the groundwork for a meaningful description of the allocation of resources. In the following four chapters we will examine the interaction of social factors and cultural values in affecting labor mobilization and the distribution of livestock and land.

Focusing on land and labor follows Western economic traditions. So many economists of different schools have done so that one tends to do so as well, in order to see how the data can be construed in (and how they fall into) preconceived categories (Gudeman 1986). Perhaps, though, it can also be argued that the procedure is justified, in the case of the Samosir Batak and of many other non-Western peoples, in that both land and labor are fully though differently cognized by them in their rural social life and culture. In Samosir, as we will see, land is sometimes made a ritual gift, and labor is one of the main means of establishing and maintaining relationships.

Chapter 9 treats the development of households and the effects of inheritance and other institutions on age and gender differentials in the work force. Chapter 10 focuses on modes of labor mobilization; 11 treats modes of ownership, sharing, and transfer of livestock; and 12 deals with the ideology concerning, and distribution of, land. Each focuses on differences of access among villagers by clan, by age, and by available household labor.

It is necessary to examine differential access to factors of production in detail to adequately assess one of the major arguments of E. Leach's Political Systems of Highland Burma*—namely, that the Kachin and, by implication, other highland Southeast Asian peoples who express a preference for matrilateral cross-cousin marriage, tend to be class stratified. This is one reason that I devote so much attention to the degree to which access to factors of production correlates with the number and age of children present in a household. A further aim, which will be developed in Part V, is to go beyond a preliminary refutation of the "class-stratified" assessment to forestall the related view that such societies have become stratified due to the rise of a cash economy and to examine the significance of the circulation of "prestige goods" (among which livestock and land are prominent), in relation to marriage alliance.*

Chapter 9

Age and Gender Differentials in the Work Force

The first part of this chapter focuses on the composition and formation of residence and subsistence household groups. Almost by definition, these are the primary economic units. The second part considers gender differentials in inheritance—that is, in the process of replacement of households. And the third part focuses on factors that lead to disparities of age and numbers of men and women workers. It will be shown that the larger number of women, especially younger ones, is related to culturally determined inheritance and marriage customs and to the process of household formation.

Residence and Subsistence Groups

Households that share residence do not usually share the main inputs of production. They work separately on different plots of land. One cannot learn the makeup of "subsistence households" by a residential survey, but only by coming to know the villagers and their separately worked mountain fields. There is no indigenous category that includes all groups that make up the range of subsistence/livelihood-seeking units. The villagers use the term *ripe* (pronounced "ree-pay") interchangeably with the Indonesian/Malay term *rumah tangga* to refer to what we call a couple or nuclear (or conjugal) family.

At present, the institution of *manumpang*, sharing "room" without "board," reinforces a disposition to provide shelter for those needing it—one-third of the subsistence households shared dwellings. Unless the "guests" are newly married, they do not have any expectations of receiving daily rice from their "hosts," but cook separately. While this may seem to involve less-than-ideal generosity, for those in need of shelter, it reduces the risk of a potential lack of hospitality, as might occur if it were considered an obligation to feed as well as house them.

Although a transition from multihousehold to single-family dwelling has occurred over the past 70-80 years, it cannot be assumed that coresident households previously shared the products of their fields to any greater extent than at present. As many as six related households formerly shared one large house. The interior was divided into separate living spaces, demarcated by walls of unrolled mats at night, as is often still the case. Rice stores were kept in separate bins, shawls and other valuables in separate caches. Traditional subsistence households, like contemporary ones, probably had attached dependents—elders too incapacitated to work or children of an overburdened daughter. But most of those sharing residence in multihousehold dwellings were not primarily engaged in joint subsistence endeavors. The smaller, single-family houses that now predominate are mainly attributable to changes in building technology. In the past, wood was roughly hewn into timbers or split into boards by means of wedges before being carried or dragged out of the distant, high plateau forest by buffalo. The introduction of two-man saws by the Dutch undoubtedly facilitated the task a great deal. Later, a diesel-powered sawmill at the Sagala port of Tulas made wood even more readily available—for cash. Thus the proliferation of single-household dwellings is attributable to the easier accessibility of wood (and the end of feuding) rather than to a breakdown in some facet of social organization.

Of a total population of 596 men, women, and children living in Huta Ginjang during 1976-1977, 98 men and 113 women were married or had been married and survived their spouses. Note the gender disparities of those under 25 years old in Table 9.1.

Subsistence/livelihood-seeking groups are invariably married couples, nuclear families, or remaining members of former nuclear fam-

TABLE 9.1
Marital Status of Residents (1976-77)

Age Groups	Males			Females		
	single	married	widowed	single	married	widowed
13-18	7			25		
19-24	2	5		16	21	
25-30	4	15		4	21	1
31-36		13			11	
37-42		18			18	1
43-48		9			14	2
49-54		13			12	1
55-60		10	1		3	7
61+		11	2		3	6

ilies—i.e., they are households at various stages of development. Thus, "the" composition of residential groups, the basis for analysis of household development and, later, of production, is of necessity a synchronic abstraction.

Of 112 subsistence/livelihood-seeking groups living in 99 houses or huts at the beginning of 1977, the basic conjugal family functioned as a subsistence/livelihood-seeking household in 68, about two-thirds. The ways in which subsistence households are joined in common residence is shown in Table 9.2. Variants of the conjugal family include: the wife and children of a cloth trader who was away from the village most of the time, two couples who had not yet had children, couples who lived with their unmarried children and a grandchild 'on loan' from a married child, a couple who shared their house with the husband's widowed sister, and so forth.

In all, there were nine widows with unmarried children maintaining separate residences in the village, two of whom shared their houses with a married child's family and one with a stepson. In addition to their children, two also had 'borrowed' grandchildren. One lived for the most part alone in a house built by her emigrant son, which was

TABLE 9.2

Residence Group Composition, Showing Separate and Joint Residence of All Subsistence Households (1976-77)

Relatives living together	Residence groups	Subsistence units
(a) A couple and their unmarried children	68	68
(b) Wife and children (husband a migrant trader)	1	1
(c) Couple without children	2	2
(d) Couple, unmarried children, and grandchildren	2	2
(e) Couple with grandchildren	1	1
(f) Couple with husband's widowed sister	1	2
(g) Living-in (*manumpang/manginsolat*)		
i. nuclear families sharing house	5	10
ii. childless couple sharing house	1	2
iii. widows with unmarried children sharing house with son and daughter-in-law; daughter and son-in-law; step-son (1 each)	3	6
(h) Widows (other than 'g-iii') with unmarried children (including 2 with grandchildren 'on loan')	6	6
(j) Self-supporting widow with son's family	3	6
(k) Dependent widow with son's family[a]	4	4
(m) Solitary widow	1	1
(n) Widower and unmarried children	1	1
(o) Widower, unmarried children, and widowed mother[b]	1	1
(p) Dependent widower, unmarried children with son's family	1	1
(q) Dependent widower with daughter's family[c]	1	1
Residence group subtotal	102	
Subsistence unit subtotal		115
(Both excluding 3 [k, o, q]):		
TOTAL RESIDENCE GROUPS	99	
TOTAL SUBSISTENCE UNITS		112

[a] One instance already under 'g-i.'
[b] One instance under 'k.'
[c] One instance under 'g-i.'

sometimes used as a sleeping place by adolescent girls and young unmarried women. These are but a sampling of the alterations of time and circumstance.

Setting Up a Household

Although a far larger sample would be necessary to generalize, it is striking that all but one of the four young men and one young woman of the village who married in 1977 did so between June and August, the period that follows the rice harvest and precedes rice planting. Some newly married expressly counted on their paired abilities to ready the fields, calculating the shortest practical time in which to reap their first harvest and become independent of parental provisioning.

At its inception, what constitutes a household is indeterminate and circumstantial. The process of establishing one formally begins with a ceremony called *manjae.* Sixty of a sample of 103 couples lived in the house of the husband's parents both before and after the *manjae* period, and 22 of them remained 'in the presence of' parents until the latters' deaths. When questioned about the length of time before their *manjae* ceremonies, a number of respondents answered, "I did not *manjae*, I 'spoon-fed' my parents" (. . . *husonduhi natuatua*), or, "I was continually in the presence of my parents" (. . . *torus ijolo ni natuatua*). Generally, though, a few weeks to a few years after a man gets married, a simple ceremony is conducted: he presents his parents with a meal, informs them that he "wishes to establish independence" (*naeng manjae*), and requests blessings and a *panjaean*, a gift that symbolically effects the separation, usually one measure of unhusked rice and one of salt. The ceremony makes explicit the transfer of the good intentions of the father's soul (*tondi*) through his spoken blessings. If the father is able, he will name one or more fields as 'the path of life' (*dalan ngolu*) of his son, particularly in the case of the eldest. Some young men pawned fields received in this manner, which shows that the transfer had indeed given them possession of the fields. In a few instances, the *panjaean* gifts included a house.

The most common use of the concept *manjae* is with reference to those men and their wives who are 'still in the process of *manjae*,' (*na manjae dope*), who are called *panjae* (cf. Vergouwen 1964:217f). They are almost, but not quite, full members of the community. They dance, for example, at the end of the line that includes their elders or in village ceremonies as a separate group. The first question asked in assessing the anticipated size and cost of a gathering is, "Will it be including the *panjae*?" (*Dohot panjae*?). No further distinctions were drawn between the various *panjae* in terms of purely formal characteristics, such as having a house or children or both or neither. For this study, they are considered household heads. The difference in their general economic position will become clear in the following chapters.

Two reasons may be suggested for the prolonged indefiniteness in social status of a new couple. First, a marriage only becomes binding if they produce offspring. A male heir who shows an aptitude for survival is preferred, though with the birth of either a boy or a girl, a marriage is considered securely established (but that is not a sufficient condition for transcending the status of *panjae*). Second, there is what might be termed a delaying contradiction between the wishes of the father and the son for the latter to attain adult standing and an implicit conflict between senior and junior of what is, in a sense, identical lineage position. It is an unstated conflict between a son becoming adult and a father, usually in middle age, who is still an active participant in the community. It is impossible for two men of the identical line to participate as equals in social ritual. Perhaps this is why recently married sons often do not attend rituals.

This delaying contradiction is overcome slowly by a social ideal that supersedes it: that all one's children marry and that at least one have a child. Those who become grandparents attain the coveted status of *saurmatua*. Thus, as younger sons marry in turn, their older brothers become more and more fully fledged adults, giving priority to their elders in ritual yet also participating.

Male Heirs and Their Mothers and Sisters

Now let us turn from household formation to dissolution of households. Just as the inception of a "household" is difficult to pinpoint, its demise, the end of its cycle, is also indeterminate. Widows and widowers are both referred to as *na mabalu*. Like the *panjae*, who have not yet proven themselves a complete and procreative household, they appear to lack full status in village affairs. Widowers are unable to participate by speaking in ceremonies—"As for a widower, he cannot even bring a contribution of rice to a feast; his daughter must carry it for him"—even if they maintain a household and continue fulfilling their obligations.[1] While there are exceptions, the norm highlights the social pressures that prompted three-quarters of the widowers to remarry.

In 116 marriages of which one or both spouses remained alive (not counting previous marriages of widowers who had remarried), 87 women (75 percent) had moved to Huta Ginjang upon marriage. Both spouses were alive in 71 instances. (All the widowers had resided in their home village—virilocally—and 12 widows originally moved to the village upon marriage.) Nineteen marriages had been between Huta Ginjang villagers, with both spouses alive in 15 cases (four widows had also been born there). In only ten instances was the wife village-born and the husband from another village (uxorilocal residence).

In former times, widows had been routinely taken in leviratic marriage whether the younger brother of the deceased husband was already married or not. (An older brother cannot marry a younger brother's widow; indeed, they are forbidden to address each other—a speech prohibition which applies even to those who have lineage mates who intermarried.) A widow who was a second or third wife could

[1]Similar attitudes are in evidence among the Karo Batak. Singarimbun writes, "A widower . . . may not maintain his own household; there is a customary rule against this and, furthermore, looking after a household is woman's work" (1975:36). He states that, "While in certain circumstances a young man may be alone with his mother, in no circumstances may a man be alone with his adult daughter" (ibid.:48).

also be taken in leviratic marriage by an adult stepson. The levirate is now rare, perhaps as a result of church teaching. Villagers say that women do not remarry because their duty is to raise the children of their deceased husband. For example, I was told that if anyone tried to marry a certain man's stepmother, who had several small children, the suitor would 'be sliced!' (*Sineatna ma!*). The speaker added, somewhat ambiguously, "*Hak milikna ma*," ([It is] 'his right of ownership'). None of the 18 widows in the village had remarried, though a few cases outside it were mentioned when I pressed informants. It might be thought that the widows are left in social limbo, but they do not appear to be, and, to understand why, it is necessary to envision a separate "stage" of the developmental cycle of domestic groups.

Vergouwen tends to depict the Batak inheritance process as a succession of principals and heirs in the male line. It is true that a widow cannot inherit permanently, that her husband's property cannot pass through her to her siblings or parents. Vergouwen implies, however, that the widow is dispossessed on her husband's death, and this is not so. Widows, strictly speaking, do not inherit, but they retain a large measure of control over their husband's 'estate' (*tading-tadingan*, literally, 'the leavings'). Surely this is a form of inheritance.

As long as they are still rearing children, widows maintain the households of their husbands in place. Even when several sons are married and have independent households, widows with children whom they support, either at home or abroad, remain in control of the house of their deceased husbands and of as many fields as they can cultivate. Those who have no sons are far more powerless than those who have at least one, for although a man's sons have "exclusive rights in his estate," these are mitigated by a duty to their sisters and of course to their mothers. Vergouwen singles out unmarried sisters for the purpose of whose dowry, he claims, control of the property is ideally left in the hands of their widowed mothers.

> [T]here is conflict between the narrow and strict law of the patrilineal system, according to which girls and property accrue to the [heirs] who can decide at their discretion what part of the girl's father's estate should go to them, or can

> adopt the more tolerant practice, supported by the demands of the *adat parboruon* = custom towards the *boru* [wife-receivers], which provides that an adequate part of the deceased's estate should go to his daughters. (Vergouwen 1964:287-288)

Generally, elders followed "the more tolerant practice" in Sagala (another instance of the inadequacy of strict patrilineal segmentary models of Batak social organization), though in some cases heirs took usufruct of the choicest fields.

The process during which the widow, as a kind of representative of the *ripe* she had comprised with her husband, retires from the social life of the village continues until she is no longer able to provide her own sustenance or all her children have married. The parameters of the process appear to be largely circumstantial, the transition unannounced.

A developmental point of view of the domestic group, in which the widow appears to be a surrogate for her husband for as long as their offspring remain dependent on her, offers a more adequate explanation than the rigidity of codified and automatic patriliny—the official ideology, as it were—as it gets depicted by some of Vergouwen's statements. I observed an inheritance custom involving daughters that makes it likely that there was traditionally such a "phase" of surrogacy—that even in cases of leviratic marriage, widows were still, to an extent, surrogates. For, while the Dutch may have legislated a greater regard for "fair play" toward women, they cannot have affected village funeral custom in the manner found in the following account.

Briefly, one of the four dependent widows living with the family of her only son worked but grew no crops on her own. All finances, planting, harvesting, and sale of produce were in the purview of the son and his wife. The man, a teacher, had also had his own house built. Like other widows, his mother looked after grandchildren, tended animals, and helped to plant bulb crops or rice. In a sense, her son and daughter-in-law were as dependent on her as she on them, although she was too weak to grow her own crops and differed from those widows who kept separate stores and lived with sons. It would seem, then, that the process of replacement had been accomplished. Two of the man's sisters also lived in the village, the older, like her brother, having married a co-villager, and the younger's husband having moved there. When the mother died, a large funeral was held, and on the last night, after the younger sister and her husband had had a small pig served by other wife-receivers to 'all' the Sagala (the clan of the deceased woman's son), both sisters received special "death-dues." The elder got a valuable shawl, but the younger demanded and got public transfer of 'a path of life' (*dalan ngolu*), a field. (It was said that on the death of a father, the oldest daughter received a similar field.)[2] As the demand was put by the speaker for the wife-receivers, representing all households of which the wives were of clan Sagala,

> We are honored, we are blessed, God has granted our wishes. Our mother, this *saurmatua* [person all of whose children have married and one had a child] . . . can be so blessed that we can have such a great feast for her. You asked that your daughter dance here at the feast. Well, our request to our parents-in-law is that you present her *hoba-hoba* shawl and her *hande-hande* shawl, her earrings, her eating [fields] (*pangan-pangananna*), livestock, satchels. Present them here. Only then will your daughter(s) condescend to dance.

The way in which social pressure was brought to bear on the brother, "the legitimate male heir" in patrilineal ideology, is remarkable. All the wife-receivers of the Sagala clan sat as a group, men and women together, on one side of the coffin, and their wife-givers, the Sagalas, sat on the other side. The request, voiced by several main speakers among the wife-receivers, was on behalf of the widow's daughter and son-in-law and, explicitly, for the honor or prestige (*iang*) of all wife-receivers. This is the *adat parboruon* ("custom towards wife-receivers") that conflicts with "the narrow and strict law" of patriliny.

After a long debate with the speakers for the principals, who wished

[2]The special 'portion' given to the youngest is referred to as the *adat ni boru partohon* (custom of/to the daughter "most directly concerned," the one who is *tohon*). Since there are only two parents, only two daughters can be *boru partohon* at their death. Middle daughters do not receive this special *adat*. If there are no married daughters, a stand-in takes the place of the appropriate (i.e., oldest or youngest) daughter. (On the concept of *partohon*, "the one most directly concerned," from the point of view of ritual standing, see Sherman 1982, appendix 4.3.)

to 'open the cupboard' in private, the demands were restated:

> What does she ask?
>
> The paths of life of your grandchildren; there are some that we observed.

At this point, the woman's brother rose to settle the issue. After excusing his long reticence on the grounds that he had hoped to make the presentation in private so as not to be shamed by the smallness of the transfer, he said,

> As concerns a path of life, as you put it earlier, the [dry] field Saerpaet has already been given, a hectare, there. And it was from there, originally, that I derived my livelihood [lit., life]. You are well aware that there were no great undertakings of my father for me to follow, up to this very day. And that [field] was the source of my livelihood. . . . I repeat, I received no heirlooms from my father, nor my mother.

Strikingly, he directly invoked his *father*, although on this occasion, he and his sisters were bereaved by the loss of their mother:

> As for what was opened by my father, may his heart be merciful, and his spirit (*sahalana*) hear, it was Saerpaet, the path of life for us. And it is dry. As for the wet [irrigable], [you know my father's valley field was destroyed by a flood].

While the brother claims to have "already given" the field (i.e., as dowry), the transfer is not "official" (Indonesian, *resmi*, *sah*), according to informants, until after the demise of both parents, when it must be officialized (*diresmihon*) in a public declaration. (Note that the brother is not pressed, nor does he offer, to give irrigated valley fields he himself has taken in pawn.)

This episode of a funeral is called the *adat pandungoi*, 'custom which causes to stand,' though the reference is not to the daughter's or wife-receiver's standing up and dancing, but it is 'the wealth/estate which stands' (*arta na dungo*), or, as we might put it, "is manifested." It has important implications for understanding the position of women. Those who remain in their natal village and have anything to inherit do so if they are oldest and youngest daughters. Beyond that, it is important with reference to the definition of the domestic group and to the parameters of its developmental cycle. The deceased had not been a widow with unmarried daughters holding a large portion of "the estate" to ensure them a dowry. Not only were her daughters married, but their brother had already long controlled the estate. The fact that the transfer of a field to the younger sister and her in-married husband did not occur until after the death of the dependent widow shows that a stem household does not entirely dissolve on the death of the male head nor after all children are married, but only when he has truly been replaced by his son, whose mother was a surrogate.

Note that, in contrast, on the death of a woman who is survived by her husband, there is no special inheritance to her children. Indeed, why should there be from the Batak point of view? The domestic group that he heads persists. Perhaps this is the kernel of the "patrilineal principle." On the other hand, since a man's death leaves his wife a surrogate, an indefinite interstitial period passes during which the demise of the stem household and the establishment of its offspring's overlap.

Gender Differentials in Education

About half the adults, mainly those over 37 years old, had no formal education. By 1978, not only were almost all children of primary school age attending the village school, over 80 percent of those 18 years or younger (196 out of 240) were being schooled. Nearly equal numbers of boys and girls attend primary school, but the number of girls decreases at each succeeding level. Sixty percent of those from the village enrolled in the Limbong Valley junior-high school were boys, and of the 53 students living outside the Samosir area to attend school, 70 percent were males.[3] Nearly three-quarters of those attending school outside the village were in North Sumatran cities and towns, and all but one of the remainder were in Java. Of those in

[3]Two youths and a girl in the 13-to-18-year-old group are not counted in these enumerations because of insufficient information. Data on offspring who had ceased schooling, level attained, and occupation may be found in Sherman (1982:414).

North Sumatra, slightly less than half stayed with close kin; the others boarded at school or in small rooming houses, which are often attached to simple restaurants.

Traveling Outside the Area

Before marrying, if they have not gone for schooling, many young men and, of late, some young women as well take an opportunity to travel, to "see the world," usually looking for paid employment to enable them to subsist and pay their way. This is sometimes done by men who are already married. One may "go on the *ranto*," *laho mangaranto*, or one may settle down "on the *ranto*," *ipangarantoan*, and become an emigrant, a *pangaranto*. The active sense of the word, as in Indonesian *merantau*, has different shades of meaning, depending on the context in which it is used: "to go abroad," "to leave one's home area," "to wander about," "to take a trip," as well as "to emigrate" (Echols and Shadily 1961).

Of 96 village men asked, 70 had gone on the *ranto* before 1977, for periods ranging from one week to forty years, and averaging seven years. Twenty-one had been loggers, thirteen agricultural laborers, ten tea plantation workers, and the rest had run coffee shops, traded, been bus conductors, trishaw drivers, etc.; five had simply been 'wandering,' *maor-aor* (Sherman 1982:415-418). Thus, the phenomenon is by no means limited to the present generation of youth. Judging from the histories of older-generation males, it can be expected that many of the young men absent during this field research will, in fact, later return.

Whereas during much of Dutch rule, many Bataks who emigrated to the East Coast sought to merge into the Malay Muslim majority and adopt new names, that is no longer the case. There has been a birth of ethnic pride. While contemporary Samosir Batak villagers who move to towns and cities outside their home region enter a multi-ethnic society, it is not an unknown social universe. Students, loggers, tailors, or what-not, they usually take up residence with family or in a compound of those from their home area or adjacent territories. They have strong enough ties to their new neighbors to warrant a certain degree of initial aid in learning to get along. Numerous clan associations hold yearly gatherings (along with the wife-receivers of members) in the large cities of Indonesia. Newspapers report thousands at such gatherings in stadiums in Java.

Of those who had not gone "on the *ranto*," six had done agricultural pioneering outside the area. For the Toba, as for the Karo Batak, pioneering is rarely the sort of out-migration we associate with the term, where a family packs all its belongings and moves. As Kipp (1978) points out, Karo make claims and work them for years while maintaining home-village holdings, going back and forth, at most a few hundred kilometers, to take advantage of seasonal differences in crop requirements. Fourteen village men, six of the Sagala clan, had attempted to make a living as pioneers after 1949. The oldest, 55 years old, had made six attempts in two separate locations but, like most of the others, had had problems with flood damage, rats, and other rice pests and claimed he would not return to the East. In addition to those who went to be peddlers, six other men left the village for several months each year during this study to work claims on the East Coast, while their wives tended to village crops.

Life-History Patterns and the Work Force

The occupational history of the sexes puts into relief the parameters of the work force in village agriculture. Both life-history patterns and the parameters of the work force are "social facts," reflecting household developmental cycles as well as postcolonial changes in interaction between local and regional societies.

About 80 percent of the household heads' offspring who are away from the village are males, while 93 percent of those who married out were women. All those who married and settled elsewhere while on the *ranto* were men. For the most part, girls who leave the village elope or go for schooling. The significance of these patterns is evident in considering those remaining in the village, as they view themselves, —as 'workers,' *pangula* (see Table 9.3). Working females outnumber

TABLE 9.3
Age, Sex, and Marital Status of 'Workers' in Huta Ginjang (1976-77)

Age range	Unmarried males	Unmarried females	Husbands & widowers	Wives & widows	Totals Males	Totals Females
13-18	7	25	-	-	7	25
19-24	2	16	5	13	7	29
25-30	4	4	15	22	19	26
31-36	-	-	13	10	13	10
37-42	-	-	18	21	18	21
43-48	-	-	9	14	9	14
49-54	-	-	13	13	13	13
55-60	-	-	11	10	11	10
61+	-	-	12	6	12	6
TOTALS	13	45	96	109	109	154

working males in the village work force by 17 percent, with married women and widows outnumbering married men and widowers by 13 percent. The actual disparity is even greater, since totals include three or four men who are traders and five who are teachers, all of them only part-time farmers.

What is most striking is the preponderance of unmarried females compared to males. Like the disparity between young wives as opposed to husbands, which is also evident, this is a reflection of the tendency for males to go outside the area in search of work and adventure—even as, traditionally, they went courting and were long-distance traders. It may also reflect a tendency to provide for the education of boys when a choice has to be made.

The key point is that Table 9.3 shows the degree to which many boys and men who are out of the village—schooling, traveling, working, pioneering, or trading—have mothers, sisters, or wives who remain at home, raising children and tilling the soil. In most cases, the women provide a good portion of the wherewithal for males who are attending school or engaged in other enterprises. Sisters thus occupied are by no means unconscious dupes. Many view themselves as helping their brothers and their parents. Some seemed to refuse offers of marriage to continue doing so.

Taking Stock of Age and Gender Differentials

While Samosir does support high demographic concentrations, the society, in effect, also feeds a constant flow of out-migrants into the surrounding regions, mainly east, west, and north. Again, this is not an entirely modern phenomenon. Both the cultural ecology and, to some extent, participation in the world economy are traditional.

The process of establishing independence, being a *panjae*, may contribute to the tendency for young men to go on the *ranto*, but 16 village household heads had active fathers, and 11 others had active widowed mothers. Out of 77 Huta Ginjang men who had adult brothers, 52 were resident in the village, born of 22 fathers and 28 mothers (in 6 instances, involving 14 men, they were stepbrothers). Ten men, who were 35 years old on average, had moved to the village on marrying and there were 5 immigrant couples (3 elderly and 2 young). It is thus difficult to make a case that a limit of demographic density has been reached.

Social bonds among villagers play an important part in the maintenance of a high population density. Conversely, it is not entirely as a result of population pressure on limited resources that out-migration occurs. In addition to the conflicts that arise among kin, other factors need to be taken into consideration, not the least of which are the draw of the hustle and bustle of urban life and hopes of "striking it rich" abroad, hopes reinforced by the imported wealth evident to those who travel outside the area and in local markets. The sporadic accessibility of this wealth is known from the examples of kin and neighbors who have succeeded outside.

Transport facilities make it easier than it ever was to 'go on the *ranto*,' and villagers have become accustomed to the relative ease of travel. Visiting kin who live at a distance to attend life-crisis rituals is common and serves as an entertaining diversion for even the poorest.

One last factor is that irrigable land and jobs are more readily available outside the home region, providing additional incentives to those who consider the village too quiet and their work too difficult and insufficiently rewarding.

It is likely that those who remain poor in the cities (many small traders, carters of heavy loads on three-wheeled trishaws, or those in unskilled proletarian occupations) lose touch with their homes, since they lack the wherewithal to commute or to participate when called on to do so. Children of city Batak, whose schooling is in Indonesian, also tend to speak only the national language. This does not entirely alienate them from village kin, for most village men learned to speak Indonesian in school or during their own outside experiences, and village children, likewise, are schooled in the national language. Judging by the constant visits of kin, from city and other outside places of settlement to village, many out-migrants maintain a sufficiently high standard of living to periodically renew ties to their home areas. This allows them or their children to consider returning, if necessary, to the security of village relations of livelihood, finding residence, opening fields, and taking loans of rice to see them through the first harvest.

Chapter 10

Modes of Labor Mobilization

It often seems that all household members living in the village have a penchant for finding work to do. While husbands and wives work in their fields, those barely capable of walking, the very old and the very young, guard drying rice and corn spread on mats in the hamlet courtyards. At night an entire household may clean dried outer leaves off bulbs for market or break the crowns to stimulate new growth in those they are going to plant. As often as not, members of a household undertake separate tasks on a given day. One son herds the cows up the mountain; a girl stays at home to feed and care for younger siblings; their father clears brush; and their mother plants bulbs, joined by two older children when they return from school.

In addition to treating the commoditization of labor—an expected effect of monetization—this chapter focuses on reciprocal labor between members of different households. Sahlins, it will be recalled, considered one consequence of rice export on hinterland society to be that the principal reciprocal relationship between households is closely balanced labor exchange. In order to assess this aspect of labor mobilization, it is useful to consider the young and then proceed to the adults.

The Roles of Children in Agriculture

Since almost one-quarter of work time on village fields was recorded to be by adolescents and about 85 percent of work time is by household members working their own fields, birth is the main means of recruitment or "mobilization" of labor. A common ritual exhortation expresses the value placed on children carrying out assigned chores: "May sons and daughters be born, that there be those to send to [fetch] water, and there be those to order to the fields" (*Tubu ma anak dohot boru, asa adong suruon tu aek adong suruon tu juma*).

To characterize aspects of the duties or relationship of children to parents as "economic" (*ekonomis*) would be insulting to Samosir Batak, for the transliteration is taken to mean "tit for tat"—precisely "balanced" reciprocity—rather than to refer to relations of livelihood. (*Ekonomis* was used pejoratively in debates among household heads, sharing out tasks in preparation for rituals.) Yet, although one can observe a great deal of uncalculated give-and-take among family members, it is also clear that children gain an early awareness of the degree to which satisfaction of their wants hinges on the aid that they provide. Young girls just learning to walk mimic the carting of loads by placing heavy objects on their heads. By the time they are five years old, they begin to make serious efforts to pound rice and corn with older girls and to carry small cans of water as they tag along behind their mothers or older sisters, who headload a bucket at a time for cooking, drinking, and animal feeding. The various techniques of farming and subsistence are learned more by imitation of seniors over time than from deliberate instruction. The games of the young gradually grow from occasional imitations of various chores to their actual accomplishment. The cane-grass stalks with which young boys occasionally target domestic pigs are gradually replaced by the spears used by farmers to protect crops from wild boar or from a domestic pig that has been getting into fields.

By the age of eight or nine, when they are capable of bounding and clambering over the rocky paths of the mountain, boys begin herding. Girls do this as well, at a somewhat later age. After 1 P.M., herding grade-schoolers band together in groups, telling riddles and snacking on wild and domestic edibles from the fields they pass. Other children at this age shoulder lightweight mattocks (worn down to half their original size by adult use) and go off to weed or break up clods in fields previously designated by their parents.

Matching strokes, pounding rice: a mother and daughter; two friends.

A girl works near but at a remove from boys, preparing a short fallow for planting using two-pronged, locally-made tools, the hudali si dua raja, *or* hudali si dua mata.

Those who attend primary school in the morning probably play less but labor as much as children before the present generation. Only about half of those who complete grade school enter "junior high school," commuting to the northern end of Limbong Valley on foot, an hour each way. They get to work in the fields at around 2:30 each weekday afternoon, and thus they may work less than preceding generations of their age. Since most children work after school, one often sees them doing homework at night by the light of a flickering kerosene lamp (while adults engage in conversation around the perimeter of the same room). Teenagers of both sexes work with their age-mates and with their families. Older teens occasionally plant a plot of their own, the proceeds of which help them to raise a bridewealth payment or trousseau or to buy clothes. Likewise, the young sometimes work for wages in the fields of neighbors who need some task done quickly, and they often manage to influence how the money they earn is spent.

Labor and Gender

Except when planting rice, boys and girls work separately in the fields. A sister, for instance, will work near her brother and male cousins but at a remove of about two meters, rather than elbow to elbow, as the boys do, or as she would with sisters or girlfriends. Young girls have rice-pounding teams, made up of sisters or of neighboring friends, though it is not uncommon for a woman to pound rice alone or with her son or daughter, nor is it exceptional for a brother and sister to pound rice jointly, beating time by turns, jabbing the long poles into the tapering hole of the stone pounding block on which they stand.

When groups of men working side by side do the initial turning of sod, the field-holder's wife and any daughters not otherwise engaged may begin breaking up the large clumps of sod that have been drying in the sun the longest, but when husbands and wives are unaccompanied by other adults, they tend to work side by side.

Plowing and harrowing of wet-rice fields is done by men. As with dry fields, tilling after the initial opening may be done by either sex.

Women, usually in groups of six to ten, transplant wet-rice seedlings. In the planting of dry rice, men generally dibble the holes, while women and children of both sexes follow behind and drop in the seed. Weeding of tubers and bulb sections is done by both sexes, and both water bulb sections by plate-splashing from irrigation ditches. Although harvesting is done by young and old of both sexes, men usually stamp rice, while women or girls pass them the bunches, shake out the straw, and winnow the grain.

The rearing of young children is the province of women and their daughters. They also gather brush for cooking fuel, bundling it and head-loading it back to the hamlets. They prepare and cook food (except at feasts, when men do the butchering and help in cooking); and they wash clothes (though many adolescent males wash their own). It is generally women who purchase and carry supplies from the market. These "support services" that women provide for subsistence households account for the fact that on average, women actually do less field labor than men. Gross labor totals for 81 nuclear-family subsistence households in 1977 show that husbands put in 34 percent of household labor time, wives 22 percent, their offspring or children in their care 29 percent, and "others" 15 percent. Women obviously cannot do their other work and match men in the fields.

Table 10.1 makes evident a clear developmental pattern (the stages of which are indicated by the spaces between rows). The table does not purport to show energy expenditure totals but proportions of participation by household and nonhousehold members in growing subsistence and cash crops.[1] Most remarkably, it highlights the usefulness, as well as the arbitrariness, of the framework of six-year age ranging. The divisions indicate statistical similarities. The similarities of the

[1]These figures should not be taken as representing the totals of adult male and female participation in agricultural labor. As can be inferred from the data for widows and on labor in households where the husband is a migrant cloth trader, the statistical difference of adult male versus adult female labor is not as great if all households are included in the age range totals. All men, women, and children participated in labor on their fields in the ratio 32:28:24, with 16 percent participation by "others." My data are, however, a rough approximation, no matter how widespread and long-term the sampling method (see Appendix A). As with respect to measurement of areas, so too for labor; the accuracy or lack thereof is constant throughout.

TABLE 10.1

Mobilization of Labor of 81 Conjugal Families and Others

(Based on number of workdays, equally valued, recorded in 1977)

Age range of husband (number of households in parentheses)	Husbands	Wives	Their offspring or children in their care	Help, cooperative or wage labor, and other extra-household labor in unknown arrangements
19-24 (3)	42.4%	38.6%	-	19.2%
25-30 (13)	46.6	30.2	-	23.2
31-36 (12)	42.2	28.9	7.0%	21.9
37-42 (16)	35.2	21.2	27.8	15.8
43-48 (6)	35.3	23.4	26.4	14.9
49-54 (13)	29.6	19.0	40.5	10.9
55-60 (6)	33.4	18.7	40.4	7.5
61+ (12)	23.0	18.1	47.7	11.2
AVERAGE	34.1%	22.4%	28.7%	14.8%
Widows	-	52.2%	33.0%	14.8%
Teachers	18.0%	19.3	28.6	34.1
Bulb traders	12.3	29.8	44.9	13.0

NOTE: Distribution of Sagalas, their wife-receivers, and their wife-givers in age groups is as follows: 0/2/1; 8/3/2; 5/7/0; 7/6/3; 4/2/0; 6/4/3; 3/1/2; 8/2/2.

numbers suggest that in developmental terms (with only conjugal households included) the youngest couples are, as it were, a group apart; that the next two groups (ages 25-36) are also in a separate category; and that those over age 37 undergo gradual change in a pattern of livelihood seeking in which household productivity increasingly becomes a function of labor supplied by offspring. The youngest group of householders divides field labor almost equally between husband and wife, and, as with the next two groups, about 20 percent of the work on their fields is done by extrahousehold workers. The next two age ranges (25-30 and 31-36) show a marked decrease in relative participation by the wives, who are occupied in rearing children. In the 37-42 and 43-48 age ranges, the work of offspring is added to that of their parents and thus there is a decrease in the proportion of participation by both husbands and wives, although their inputs, relative to each other, remain approximately the same. As the participation of offspring continues to increase with the increasing age of household heads, the relative amount of field labor done by husbands decreases.

Units and Modes of Agricultural Labor

Villagers kept account of the required labor for a number of tasks, particularly for preparing fallow land. Late in the research, I discovered that my data for such tasks, on fields for which I had the most complete records, closely matched the farmers' recollections, elicited by asking "how many people" they had taken to accomplish. If five people worked four days bucking up sod in a field, they say, 'It took twenty people to open this field.' This may be due partly to the need to keep track of obligations incurred in recruiting extra-household labor. The number of person-days of labor is also, in effect, a measure of area (Mayer 1974:88). Perhaps such reckoning of "person-days" was introduced fairly recently, or perhaps, finding themselves under constant observation, farmers came to adopt my paradigm. But a passing remark by an elderly woman suggests otherwise. Returning from a day's weeding of wet rice in the valley, accompanied by her husband, daughter, and son-in-law, she explained that they had all gone together "so that it be finished right away today. Those two parcels of ours are of four days" (*asa torus siup sadari on. Si opat ari, dua inganannami i*). In other words, "it's a four-day job," as we would put it, for one person.

We might now consider the implications of the table with regard to Sahlins' prediction that, because of rice export, the principal reciprocal relationship between hinterland households will tend to be a "closely balanced exchange of labor" that "gives advantage to the family with the most workers." But we will put off addressing the issue until we have more closely examined the three categories of extrahousehold labor distinguished by villagers. These I gloss as "cooperative," "help," and "to work for a return," or wage labor.

Cooperative Labor, "Matching Each Other's Days"

Laboring in a reciprocal arrangement, *marsiadapari*, implies a prior verbal agreement 'to match each other's days,' to "do a day's work" at the behest of one's partner(s) in turn.[2] The participants in this arrangement are called *dongan parsiadapari*, 'companions of matched days,' and they are usually all males or all females. Among younger people and adults, the work need not be the same, nor are the participants the same in each group. If four persons (A, B, C, and D) agree to work in the field of a fifth (Z), the latter owes each of the four a day of work in return. B may ask Z to work on some project without A, C, or D, or B may take Z to the field of P for a day and collect wages paid for both of them. As one informant put it,

> The way they 'match each other's days' is not daily, but if one of them wishes to open land, s/he can invite them all. And it is also possible, if one among them has a need for money s/he can bring his or her companions as wage earners (*gajian*) to the field of another person, and receive the reward (*upa*) of all from the owner of the land.

Generally arrangements are made by informal agreement, with at most a few days' notice, among a varying group of kin, age-mates, and neighbors and with eventual exact reciprocity. In one instance, four adolescent girls were 'hired' (*digaji*) to weed rice. The four—E, F, L, and M—were of two semipermanent groups. The first group, E and F, sought and made the arrangement. Having first agreed to get the field weeded, E had no trouble recruiting her usual companion, F, and the other two girls, L and M, promising that she and F would participate in

[2]The word *marsiadapari*, comprised of the infinitive prefix *marsi-*, indicating mutual or reciprocal action, + *adap* + *ari* (day), is given by Warneck (1977) as *mangadap* or *mangalap ari*, a derivative of *alap*, 'to fetch,' and Lando (1979:121) apparently encountered *marsialap ari*, "(lit[erally, to] 'fetch the day')." I prefer the derivation from Toba Batak *adop* (cognate of Indonesian *hadap*), *marsiadopan ari*, facing, "matching," each other's day. This appears to be borne out by Simalungun *marsialop ari* (Clauss n.d.:16).

a project of their choosing. By the end of the day's weeding, E owed three days' work, one to each of her companions. She worked two days alone with F, and the two spent another day weeding for the parents of L, thus completing E's obligation to both L and M. M was still owed a day by L, and E still owed F one day of work.

As is the case among other peoples of Melanesia, e.g., Tolai (Salisbury 1970:151), and Southeast Asia, e.g., Kachin (Leach 1965:135), cooperative work groups receive midday meals from the field's owner. A pack or two of cheap cigarettes may be provided for men to smoke during breaks, and at least one hot, sweet drink (usually coffee) is served. Women are given betel-chewing ingredients. The Batak owner participates fully in the work, unlike those Kachin described by Leach, among whom the householder "supplies beer and food but does no work himself." In fact, in bucking up sod, the field holder takes upon himself the most difficult position, at the outside of a line of hoeing men and thus has to cut the boundary and hoe a new edge at each stroke. At the end of each row, he moves forward, hoes out the corner of the new row, and takes the inside position again, as his companions line up to the outside of the field.

As can be seen from Table 10.2, intrahousehold labor increases with age of household head. This seems to contradict Sahlins' claim that those with most available labor engage in more interhousehold reciprocal arrangements. Similarly, there is not a significant difference of cooperative labor mobilized between those of the first three age groups and the 37-to-48-year-olds, who presumably have children old enough to work and therefore more available labor. Moreover, those with the most available labor—householders of the three oldest groups—participate in the fewest cooperative 'matching days.'

The size and sexual makeup of cooperative work groups among grassland farming peoples using manual techniques to turn sod (e.g., the Kofyar, the Tolai, the Tiv, the Karo Batak, and the Samosir Batak) vary widely. They are much smaller among Samosir Batak than among Karo Batak (whose groups of up to 20 are mostly women), while the Kofyar groups are large and mostly male. Tiv groups are

TABLE 10.2

Percentages of Household, Cooperative, Help, and Wage Labor on the Fields of the 81 Nuclear Households, by Age-Range of Husbands

Age-range of husband (number of cases in parentheses)	Household	Cooperative	Helping	Wage	Unknown arrange-ments
19-24 (3)	80.8%	5.1%	10.2%	3.9%	-
25-30 (13)	76.8	7.5	7.9	5.2	2.6%
31-36 (12)	78.1	4.0	7.8	6.9	3.2
37-42 (16)	84.2	6.2	1.5	3.7	4.4
43-48 (6)	85.6	6.8	1.9	2.9	3.3
49-54 (13)	89.1	1.0	3.2	4.1	2.6
55-60 (6)	92.5	2.2	2.6	0.8	1.9
61+ (12)	88.8	2.6	4.0	2.0	2.6
AVERAGE	85.2%	4.1%	4.0%	3.7%	3.0%

mixed, including men, women, and young people in a compound-wide cooperative effort for the initial opening of savannah (Bohannan and Bohannan 1968:44). Such differences in the kinds of groups mobilized for a similar task, turning sod, throw doubt on Julian Steward's contention that understanding the organization of work in similar methods of subsistence and similar ecosystems is of fundamental importance for understanding the so-called cultural "core," those aspects of culture concerned with subsistence and economic organization.[3] Wittfogel notes that prehydraulic agriculture involved "little division of labor and no significant cooperation" (1956:155), but it may be more accurate to say 'only periodic' cooperation. This may explain why such differences of organization of labor are found among grass-

[3]As step one of his "method of cultural ecology," Steward called for analysis of "the behavior patterns involved in the exploitation of a particular area by a particular technology" (1955:40). R. F. Murphy has argued cogently that by this Steward was referring to the organization of work, and in referring to "certain economic devices" to 'tools' (Murphy 1970, especially p. 155). I am indebted to R. Griffin Coleman for this reference.

land-cultivating peoples and, indeed, even among people in the same village.

Helping

An absence of express reciprocity characterizes a common form of labor mobilization called simply 'to help' (*mangurupi*). Without reference to kinship and other relationships among villagers, such as proximity or sharing of residence, common age grade, etc., one could assume such help, with no thought of return, to be an expression of sentiment. If a man helps his wife's mother, there is no reason he should refer to his efforts as anything but 'help,' although for analytic purposes, it is of interest to distinguish it from help given to neighbors or more distant kin. To consider the question raised here in its fuller implications, it is necessary to first discuss the position of those whose spouses are village born, those residing intralocally or uxorilocally.

When a couple settles in the village of the wife, the bride's father is expected to provide a house for them; otherwise, their earnings go toward building a house in lieu of any significant bridewealth payment. Women who settle in their natal village with an in-marrying husband do so because of the greater availability of land and with the offer of support from a concerned and affectionate father. It was said that sometimes father-daughter love is so strong that a man will leave a greater part of his inheritance to his son-in-law than to his sons—though no specific cases were cited in support of this assertion. The point was that when a daughter marries someone whose means are so sparse that her father believes she will suffer, the offer to provide for an in-dwelling son-in-law is motivated by a desire to keep the daughter from poverty.

There is perhaps a degree of self-serving in such offers. A man who has a 'spoon-fed son-in-law' may, within limits, call upon this 'wife-receiver from in front of him' (*boru sian jolona*) for aid in a variety of tasks—e.g., pollarding a tree whose boughs endanger the roof of his kitchen, butchering a small offering pig for a household ceremony, or digging the grave of a lineage mate. It needs to be borne in mind, though, that such tasks may, and indeed do, fall to any of the wife-receivers, such as those intralocally married or those who are descended from prior in-dwellers. Indeed, most menial help, except for cooking at larger feasts, falls to wife-receivers of a younger generation grade (who are *panjae*), not to men fully accepted as elders in social ritual. This means that grown sons of in-dwelling wife-receivers are usually the ones called upon in these situations. Still, it remains true that all men in this society are beholden to some other lineage for services. The fact that a man does not live adjacent to his wife-givers in no way puts him above having to render aid when called upon, whether the journey requires hours or days. Any man's wife's mother or father has influence over him by the potential of their involuntary power to affect the well-being of his children. They have more mundane influence in that they may be stingy or generous, or they may deprive him of favors if he does not respond to occasional appeals for help.

Recruitment of 'help' in agriculture may be by informal verbal request or by a letter sent through an intermediary. For instance, a woman's sister and her father's brother wrote from their distant home asking that her husband help them harvest rice. He went without thought of immediate recompense. But by no means all help is done by wife-receivers for their wife-givers. Much of it is done by adolescents for older villagers or young couples, both of whom have a dearth of hands needed for tasks like planting and harvesting.

When a large building project is undertaken, it is common to receive substantial contributions of free labor from co-villagers (*dongan sahuta*, literally, 'companions of one hamlet'). "People just come on their own, [just] like that" (*pasiro be songon i*), it was said—though, of course, they were generally close neighbors or kin. More formal arrangements are made for certain projects. Cement, for example, requires large amounts of sand from the lakeside, so prior to the mixing, an announcement is made of the proposed building schedule and the time of a joint effort to bag it, load horses, and lead them back to the village. This was done, almost incidentally, at the end of the tomb-permission meal referred to in Chapter 3. In such instances, while not so stated, the help given may be viewed as a return for the meal that has been eaten and a preliminary to the meal(s) that will be provided during the progress of the work.

Wage Labor

One of the major questions that a substantivist as well as a Marxian would raise in an analysis of Batak economy is that of the degree to which labor has been "commoditized," and, given our concern with monetization, the amount and distribution of wage labor must be addressed. Here a problem of interpretation comes to the fore.

In addition to traditional help and cooperative labor, there were also what may be construed as forms of wage labor. Long before the Dutch arrived, one who was unknown personally to a craftsman or ritual specialist could engage that person for promised and partially prepaid recompense (an *upa*, 'fee' or 'reward'). We can extrapolate as much from the practice of hiring musicians for rituals described earlier. Agricultural wage labor, mostly hoeing, plowing, or weeding, is also traditional. The term *marsinarea*, which I render "to engage for a return," is, for the most part, used interchangeably with two adaptations of Indonesian words that have related but different referents: *paboronghon* (from *memborong*), 'contracting out a job' for an agreed amount of rice or money, and *mangaji*, 'to employ,' 'hire for cash'—i.e., by the day. For instance, the sharecropper of a field too muddy to be plowed by buffalo 'contracted' to have it hoed for 9 gallons of husked rice. Since it took two men three days, each got rice worth about $1.65 per day, some 40 cents more than the wage for manual labor on dry fields. (At this time, state tea and palm-oil plantation workers in North Sumatra received a wage increase of 20 percent to Rp. 213 [52 cents] per day, not counting their rice ration.)

While the term *mangaji*, 'hire for cash,' is often used to characterize the arrangement whereby a predetermined sum is paid for a day of field labor, it is considered a coarse word. "The rich use it, owners of coffee shops, for domestic servants," as one man put it. *Sinarea* is more generally used. While Warneck's dictionary gives the infinitive, *manarea*, as "to order someone to work," villagers claimed that it is a refined way of saying 'hire for a wage' (*mangaji*), and in the past it designated cooperative labor, 'matching each other's days.' Rather than being 'ordered to work,' 'one would contribute one's strength' (*sumbanganna gogona*).[4] The latter interpretation seems suited to the fact that the term *sinarea* is also used, at least euphemistically, to refer to the wife-receivers who serve as attendants at feasts.

Thus, there is an apparent tradition of what we consider "wage labor" and this characteristic of the mode of labor recruitment involved is openly acknowledged. As one educated young man put it, those who are *sinarea* are "people paid a wage to open land or do other types of work, which is similar to being paid a wage" (*gajian*). Yet the former terminology is preferred. The question is, why are "cooperative" elements and compensatory payments seen as equivalent in such arrangements? It appears that the Batak concept is in many ways similar to "an indigenous concept of wage labour" among the Tolai, described by Salisbury:

> The initiator of a task and his helpers were equals, freely and reciprocally assisting one another. An initiator would acknowledge his indebtedness by feeding those who were helping him and perhaps giving them gifts when the work was finished; he would treat his workers as members of the family or as guests, and would *wapuak* (support) them as he would his children. In practice, the principle of reciprocal help covered, as it still does today, a more asymmetrical relationship in which one person did all the helping, without reciprocity, and the other did all the supporting. (Salisbury 1970:151)

So, too, the Batak had a means of recruiting labor without any reciprocity in kind, by payment of rice, the subsistence staple and general medium of exchange, all the while maintaining (even to the present) that the underlying basis of so doing is one of reciprocity, of essentially the same character as the cooperative 'matching each other's days.' Their analogy appears to rest on the fact that the feeding of workers, which is found in all forms of labor recruitment in village agriculture, introduces an element of "support." Further, the tradi-

[4]*Sinarea*, from the root *sarea*, is the reflexive form of *manarea*.

tional transfer of subsistence resources (rice) to workers who 'contributed their strength' was an additional concrete manifestation of support.

Variation in Modes of Labor Mobilization in the Agricultural Cycle

The relative monthly occurrence of the three modes of mobilizing extra-household labor is shown by means of a graph in Figure 10.1. In contrast to Sahlins' prediction of closely balanced reciprocity in labor as the principal reciprocal relationship between households, there is not in fact a great deal of reciprocal labor. What is shown in the graph—help, wage, and cooperative labor—amounts to about 12 percent of all recorded agricultural labor, and, of that, by no means all is reciprocal. Wage labor is paid. Help is often neither directly recompensed nor returned. Furthermore, while the high and low concentrations parallel the key steps of the agricultural cycle, not all reciprocal labor is marshaled for growing rice.

As can be seen, in March and April a shift occurred from a preponderance of arrangements involving wage labor (devoted mainly to field preparation for the largest bulb plantings of the year during the second half of the rainy season) to a preponderance involving help. The latter coincide with the time at which the greatest number of dry-rice fields are harvested. For the most part, help was by young people to aid in stamping rice. The rise and fall between points A and B—i.e., for the month of May—might be the result of a break in data gathering of some ten days at the end of May. While the amounts of both help and wage labor were declining at that time, cooperative 'matching days' arrangements might have begun to show a rise during May if fuller data had been collected. In June, when the initial effort to open new grassland fields was undertaken, cooperative labor was at its peak for the year, and that was for dry-rice field labor. In October, with the coming of the rains, help again increased markedly as the dry-rice planting was accomplished, a month later than in the previous year of normal rains.

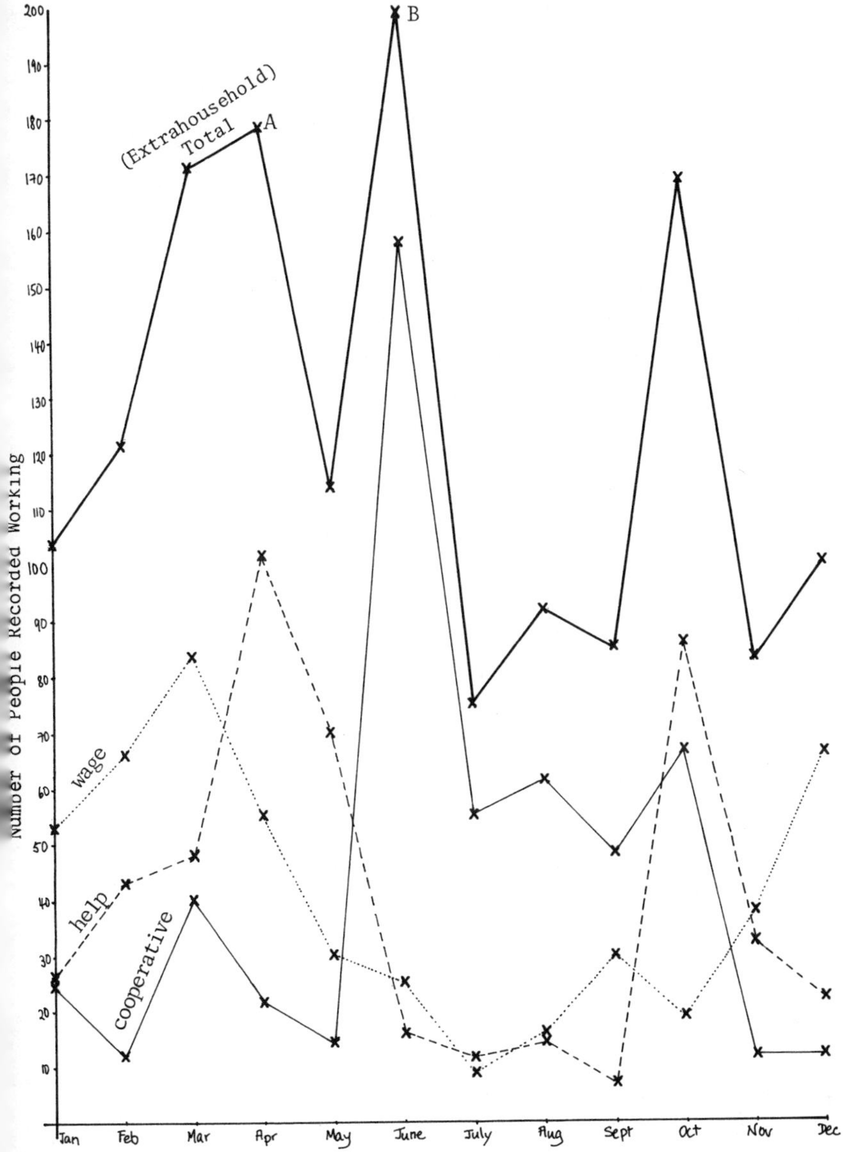

Figure 10.1. Relative monthly occurrence of extrahousehold labor

Ratios of Household and Extrahousehold Labor

It would be a mistake to take these data as support for Sahlins' claim that closely calculated exchange of labor between households is the primary reciprocal relationship. Not only is a good portion neither reciprocal nor "closely calculated," but the degree of participation also depends on the stage of household development. As was seen in Table 10.2, extrahousehold labor makes up between 15 and 20 percent of agricultural endeavors of the first three age-range groupings, and there is a drop to barely half as much in the last three age ranges. Also notable is that the younger age-range groups engaged labor for wages and got help to a greater extent than older groups. These findings contradict Sahlins' claim that more available labor gives the advantage in engaging in extrahousehold labor to families with the most workers. In fact, the latter generally have enough children to maintain a high level of production without engaging an inordinate number of wage workers or doing much cooperating. Most need their cash income for schooling, an expense foregone by younger couples.

For comparative purposes, the figures for households headed by widows and the averages for teachers, bulb traders, and the *panjae* (those in the process of establishing independence) are shown in Table 10.3.

TABLE 10.3
Extrahousehold Labor Recruitment by Widows and Others

Recruiters	Intra-household	Cooperative	Helping	Wage labor	Unknown arrange-ments
Village average	85.2%	4.1%	4.0%	3.7%	3.0%
Widows	85.2	3.9	7.0	3.9	-
Teachers	65.9	0.5	7.8	18.4	7.4
Bulb traders	87.0	1.2	3.2	8.6	-
The *panjae*	77.6	7.1	6.9	5.3	3.1

TABLE 10.4
Modes of Labor Mobilization by Sagalas and Their Affines

Mode of mobilization	Sagalas	Their wife-receivers	Their wife-givers
Intrahousehold	85.4%	84.6%	84.0%
Cooperative	4.2	4.1	2.6
Help	3.9	3.7	3.9
Wage labor	4.3	3.4	3.1
Extrahousehold total	12.4	11.2	9.6

NOTE: Not including unknown arrangements.

Note that it is those who receive a guaranteed monthly wage, teachers, who are also occupied in school for half a day, who pay wages for the highest percentage of their field labor. The households of both teachers and bulb traders are also notable for their low degree of participation in cooperative work.

There are no great disparities on the basis of clan groupings with respect to degree of participation in intrahousehold labor. Table 10.4 shows the degree of participation of household members, which are nearly identical, and the relative contributions of each mode of extra-household labor, also nearly identical, for the 81 nuclear family households by clan groupings.

The most striking difference among the three clan-based groupings

TABLE 10.5.
Degrees of Participation in Household Labor by Sagalas and Affines

Participants	Sagalas	Their wife-receivers	Their wife-givers
Husbands	28.2%	37.3%	44.5%
Wives	21.2	24.5	22.8
Their children or children in their care	36.0	22.8	16.7
Intrahousehold total	85.4	84.6	84.0

is seen in Table 10.5, where a breakdown by husbands, wives, and children is given. Sagala children appear to do significantly more work in household fields than children of either wife-receiving or wife-giving affines, while the men of both wife-receiving and wife-giving households do proportionately more of their households' field labor than do Sagala men.

Yet totals of extrahousehold modes of mobilizing field labor are marked by insignificant differences among the three groups.

The proportionally greater contributions of children of Sagala parents is attributable to the relative differences of available household labor among the three groups. The following arbitrary scale of "labor power," according to criteria of gender and maturity (and, for those attending school, available time), was used to determine available labor of the conjugal households:

Adult male	10	Female teenager	7
Adult female	9	Junior-high student	4
Male teenager	8	Grade-schooler	3

Using this scale, it turns out that the average nuclear household of each of the three groups has the following "labor-availability quotient":

Sagala:	30.5	(Average of 41 households)
Wife-receivers:	26.5	(Average of 27 households)
Wife-givers:	23.1	(Average of 13 households)

These figures indicate what first-hand impressions did not: that the Sagalas have about 13 percent more help available from children than their wife-receivers and 25 percent more than their wife-givers. These differences, in turn, entirely account for the percentage differences of labor contributed by dependents, which were noted in Table 10.5. They also explain the greater proportion of labor contributed by husbands who are wife-givers and wife-receivers of Sagala.

There do not appear to be absolute disparities along the lines of clan affiliation in terms of who works for whom and by what arrangements. Taking affinal relationship to Sagalas as the basis of categories of "field owners" and "extrahousehold workers," the ratios of partici-

TABLE 10.6
Combinations of Owners and Workers in Extrahousehold Labor

Clan of owner + Clan of worker(s)	Cooperative	Help	Wage labor
Sagala + Sagala	42.6%	18.7%	28.4%
Sagala + Sigiro	5.7	4.7	12.4
Sagala + other wife-receivers	10.2	15.0	22.4
Sagala + wife-givers	3.4	3.9	4.1
Sigiro + Sigiro	11.8	17.8	2.9
Sigiro + Sagala	5.7	3.0	3.9
Other wife-receivers + Sagala	7.7	9.7	12.1
Other wife-receivers + others	7.3	14.2	6.5
Wife-givers + Sagala	2.6	4.9	3.1
Other combinations	3.0	8.1	4.2

pation in modes of extrahousehold labor are shown in Table 10.6. Sagalas, who make up half the households and slightly more than half the work force, join each other in about 40 percent of all cooperative labor recorded. One might have expected they would do so in half, but the disparity is not great. A similar disparity is found in the hiring done by Sagalas. Two-thirds of all wage labor is hired by Sagala households. Over 40 percent of all wage labor is done by non-Sagalas hired by Sagala households. Sagalas hire their clansmen in less than 30 percent of all cases of wage labor. However, some 40 percent of those hired by Sagalas are other Sagalas. Households affiliated with other clans hired Sagala workers approximately 20 percent of the time. There is, then, no absolute clan-based division of labor. From the high degree of interclan participation in all extrahousehold labor, it is arguable that these disparities are not in the first instance the result of a class structure based on clan affiliation, as Leach would have it of the Kachin, whose clans also relate in terms of the direction of marriage (1965:78, 257). Indeed, no overt form of class, particularly no serfdom or debt-bondage is found in Samosir Batak village social organization. I saw none of the half-dozen debtors for rice or cash loans work in the fields of their creditors during my two-year stay in the village.

In the early 1930s, Vergouwen predicted that "[h]ired labour will continue to rise in importance as the supply of money and its free movement increases" (1964:328). This was certainly accurate with respect to Batak wage migration to the cities, towns, and plantations, but it has not occurred in village agriculture, as is clear from Table 10.2. (Even if the "unknown" category is added to wage labor, the latter makes up less than 7 percent of village agricultural labor.) Most villagers who earn money do not use it to hire others. Among other things, they take wet-rice fields in pawn, buy livestock, roof their houses with corrugated zinced-iron sheeting, and buy furniture, food, tools, mats, clothes, and cassette tape decks. Many spend it on the educational expenses of their children.

Those who have an income from teaching, trading, carpentry, or other endeavors do spend more than most other households to engage wage labor. At the other extreme are households that have neither sufficient cash income from produce nor enough surplus rice to hire labor. Insufficient rice stocks even make it beyond their means to engage in reciprocal cooperative labor arrangements: just as they would need to feed wage workers, it is necessary to feed cooperative workers, and this may involve unmanageable expenses of rice and incidentals. The members of a low-income, poor-harvest household might subsist largely on mixed rice and corn; they would be forced to serve laborers unmixed rice and fresh fish (as opposed to dried). Thus, in explaining why they had not engaged in reciprocal work arrangements, such householders would say, simply, "There was no 'food' (literally, 'cooked rice')" (*Ndang adong indahan*). (Those who did the most wage labor themselves cooperated in opening each other's fields.) This explains the anomaly, noted in Chapter 6, that those who grow irrigated rice also grow ten percent greater area of dry rice than do those who only grow dry rice. Apparently, the guarantee of sufficient stocks of rice to feed one's household and one's cooperative or wage workers makes it possible for those who have irrigated rice to cultivate greater areas of dry rice than those whose stocks are more subject to the vagaries of drought and winds.

Lest it be assumed that this bears out Sahlins' views, it should be noted that the ability to engage in more cooperative labor and to hire more wage workers has nothing to do with rice hoarding for export. Rather, it is a function of the ability to "redistribute" a greater amount of rice by feeding workers and it results partly from differential access to irrigable land. It is true, then, that different households accumulate different amounts of rice. But it is not true that rice stocks are not liquidated in favor of need—at least to some extent they are, since those who hire out as workers often do so for rice.

As to whether monetization has led to the commoditization of labor, given the relatively small amount of wage labor found in village agriculture and given the care that people take to retain a notion of 'support' rather than 'payment,' it seems justified to argue that such commoditization has not occurred to a significant degree.

The above comments speak to the relevant aspects of Sahlins' analysis of the consequences of hinterland rice export (1972:224), as well as to Leach's feudal analogy. They are also germane to several other facets of the question of the commoditization of labor. These are interrelated, both arising in regard to rituals of contract for "skilled" services and the labor of feast workers.

In Chapter 5, I showed that rituals of contract involve haggling that rivals any in the market. A question that can legitimately be raised in concluding this chapter is whether having such traditional rituals of contract for skilled services in effect constituted commoditization of labor. Second, we have seen that rice was traditionally used as a "wage," though this was denied by a "fiction" of reciprocity—i.e., a "fiction" in terms of *our* model. Thus, we may ask whether such commoditization of labor results either, as Sahlins might suggest, from the traditional export of hinterland rice; or, as Polanyi might, from the "market principle" entering and perverting a householding economy, or, as Boeke might, from cash doing so to a formerly pristine communal ethic.

To answer these questions, we need to reconsider the usages of the root *ula* for both feasting and labor. It will be recalled that the best explanation for that and for the parallel Indonesian usages of *kerja* and Tikopian of *fekau* is that both kinds of activity are seen as "endeavors" involving stated or taken-for-granted relations of reciprocity either between humans or between humans and spirits. In recalling this, I want to emphasize the way that an attitude that takes Batak models seriously might approach the question of "contracts" for skilled services. Indeed, what is involved there, too, is a reciprocal relationship. The haggling with orchestra members (as with carpenters) has nothing to do with rice export, or market exchange as a principle supplanting householding, or monetization destroying a communal ethic. Rather, it has to do with a concept of "skill," and indeed, special skill, *pandai*, which has a connotation of tapping into supernatural sources of power. It is perhaps more for that than for their "labor" that these practitioners, as well as midwives, shamans, and other specialists, are recompensed. This would explain why they have to give blessings at the end as well.

The similarity of what the Batak call the *adat*, the ritual of contract, in such dissimilar enterprises is, I would argue, attributable to the need in each case to make explicit or "public" the fact that those who serve a mediating role between the principals and the respective spirits (e.g., the 'house-dwelling ghost' or the spirit that demanded a given offering) have done so with only the best of intentions. As Firth pointed out (1979), in non-Western societies people distinguish skilled from simple labor—they do not conceive of labor as undifferentiated. In the recompense for the work of 'skilled ones,' as in market trade, what we find is an economic model that assumes some people have abilities to tap sources of special efficacy.

Chapter 11

Ownership, Care, and Values of Livestock

This chapter briefly treats modes of ownership and transfer of livestock. It is a complement to the preceding account of correlations of clan, age, and available household labor with modes of labor mobilization and to an account of the correlations of the same three variables with landholding, in the following chapter. As will be seen, a number of discernible patterns in the distribution of livestock are also found in the distribution of land.

Husbandry

While many villagers claimed that they or their fathers formerly owned much more extensive herds of cattle and buffalo, no one claimed to have had large numbers of pigs, and households generally raise only a few pigs at a time. Unlike many Melanesian peoples, the Batak do not engage in large-scale tuber production for pig feed. Pigs are nevertheless valuable as marketable commodities, for special meals, feasting, and, divided in portions, for "obligatory gifts" in ritual.

Since Samosir has much pasture, it is reasonable to assume the prices that came into being in the traditional economy were primarily for cattle exported to other, more heavily forested areas where a similar ritual system prevailed. In addition to the market prices of livestock reported by Controleur Middendorp (1913:27f.), I have also noted the amount of export, given in guilder totals by his successor, Haibach (1927:23) (v.s., Chap. 7, n. 5). In 1926, 63 percent of more than 170,000 guilders worth of exports was received for buffalo, cattle, and horses, 25 percent was for agricultural produce and fish, and 12.5 percent for blessing shawls. Presumably, this reflected the increasing demand for meat that came with the growth of East Coast cities and plantations before the Depression. Oerlemans' (1937) table of livestock population from 1933 to 1936 shows a steady decline for all types, a decline he attributed to the need for cash. The number of buffalo, for example, declined from 13,451 to 9,767.

Modes of Ownership and Sharing of Caretaking

There are essentially three modes of ownership of livestock: they may belong to an individual or members of one household; be jointly owned by members of two or more households; or be held by a caretaker. Vergouwen (1964:319) described these modes in 1933 much as they are found today. He had the impression that joint ownership of goods was "gradually disappearing."

The caretaking of animals in return for a portion of the offspring resembles the sharecropping of wet-rice fields for a portion of the crop (cf. Bohannan and Bohannan 1968:122; Stevenson 1943:51). Several such arrangements are made in Huta Ginjang: goats are divided equally, such that if three kids are born, both owner and tender are entitled to one and a half; pigs are also divided equally ('in two') between the owner of the sow and the raiser, and if an odd number is born, the tender gets one more than the owner. Where there is a choice, males go to the tender and females to the owner—i.e., maternal and productive attributes are the prerogative of the initial owner. For cattle and buffalo, three-quarters of each calf belongs to its mother's owner, one-quarter to the custodian. Offspring of cattle held in joint ownership are divided in the same proportion as ownership of the mother. There are also a few instances of caretaking in which the tender "borrows" the stock (generally cattle) for a month or so, only to acquire manure.

Those who own parts of cattle may have a diverse set of shared-ownership relationships with different partners. They generally take turns in caring for the animals so that they get the entire herd at one time for a given period, conserving the effort needed to pasture one or two stock at a time without respite. The periods may run from one month to a year at a time but are generally of intermediate length. (Another mode of rotation of caretaking buffalo, near Pangururan, was based on turns of four days per quarter-buffalo owned.)

On the surface, we find an institution that involves a great deal of reciprocity in caretaking arrangements. It would be difficult to argue that they are more or less important than those involving labor, which Sahlins predicted would be the "principal reciprocal relation between households" as a result of hinterland rice export. There is no need to discuss the degree to which sharing of ownership and caretaking involve balanced labor reciprocity; I raise the issue as an instance of oversimplification in Sahlins' analysis. With that caveat, let us turn to social and other parameters of the distribution of livestock.

Distribution of Ownership in the Village

Van Bemmelen (1931:16) and other Controleurs of Samosir maintained that the "chiefs" (Dutch, *hoofden*) owned most of the livestock. The veracity of such statements is as difficult to judge as claims of former herds numbering hundreds of cattle. The Dutch may have been deceived by exaggeration on the part of their appointees. Currently distribution is not equitable, but ownership is not restricted to a small proportion of households either. The ownership of bovine stock by Sagalas and their affines is shown (for nuclear households) in Table 11.1.

Over half the households were at least part owners of cattle or buffalo. Looking only at nuclear households, 18 percent more Sagalas own some bovine stock than their wife-receivers, and 8 percent more Sagalas than their wife-givers. Considering *all* households (not shown), 32 percent of the Sagala households own 61 percent of the buffalo, and slightly less than 40 percent of the Sagala households own

TABLE 11.1
Ownership and Non-Ownership of Bovine Stock
(81 nuclear households)

Stock and ownership	Sagala (41 households)	Their wife-receivers (27 households)	Their wife-givers (13 households)
	BUFFALO		
Households owning some	15	8	4
Percent of total buffalo owned	55%	16%	29%
Percent of households owning none	63%	70%	69%
	CATTLE		
Households owning some	17	10	6
Percent of total cattle owned	71%	18%	11%
Percent of households owning none	59%	63%	54%
	CATTLE AND BUFFALO		
Households owning both	5	5	3
Percent owning both	12%	19%	23%
Households owning neither	14	14	6
Percent of households owning neither	34%	52%	46%

71 percent of the cattle. Since Sagalas comprise only 50 percent of the households, it is clear that some have disproportionate numbers of cattle or buffalo. Their wife-receivers, who comprise 35 percent of the subsistence households, own only 14 percent of the buffalo and 18 percent of the cows. Considered as a group, their wife-givers, com-

prising 15 percent of the households, own 25 percent of the buffalo and 11 percent of the cattle. There are thus clan-based differentials.

When we examine the distribution by age and by available labor, we find that older householders generally own more livestock than younger householders do. Of the 54 household heads aged 19-42, 24 percent own some buffalo, and 29 percent own some cattle, while of the 58 households headed by men or women older than 42, 34 percent have some buffalo and 48 percent some cattle. However, the correlations are not precise (see Table 11.2, which shows nuclear households only): the figures for six-year age ranges of household heads show many exceptions to the pattern.

A slightly better correlation is found between the average available labor quotient of households and bovine stock owned. In other words, the absolute number of children who are capable of herding correlates to some degree with ownership of cattle and buffalo. Again, however, as is apparent from Table 11.3, the correlation is not entirely consistent.

TABLE 11.2

Distribution of Bovine Stock by Age of Household Heads

(81 nuclear households)

Ages	19-24	25-30	31-36	37-42	43-48	49-54	55-60	61+
Household heads	3	13	12	16	6	13	6	12
Percent owners of age group	0	8%	25%	38%	50%	54%	33%	42%
who own [%] of all buffalo	0	[0.5%]	[10%]	[33%]	[16%]	[19.5%]	[8%]	[13%]
% owners of age group	0	31%	33%	31%	33%	85%	50%	33%
who own [%] of all cattle	0	[7%]	[8%]	[14%]	[2%]	[46%]	[7%]	[16%]

TABLE 11.3
Distribution of Bovine Stock According to Available Labor
(81 nuclear households)

Average available labor quotient (number of house-holds in parentheses)	Average number of children age 7-18 yrs. in village (excluding junior-high students)	Average number of *kae* (quarters) of cattle and buffalo, combined
9-19 (25)	0.1	1.4
20-26 (9)	1.8	6.4
27-30 (15)	2.1	8.7
31-33 (10)	2.6	6.0
34-38 (9)	2.4	7.1
39-48 (13)	3.3	12.7

A more marked correlation shows when the observed optimum age range of herders, 10 to 13 years old, is used as the criterion of comparison among households, as is clear in Table 11.4. Households that have neither grandchildren nor children between the ages of 10 and 13 (excluding children attending junior high school in Limbong) own an average of two "quarters" of cattle and buffalo combined. Those that have one child in the 10 to 13 age range own an average of 8.4 "quarters," and those with two children of optimum herding age own

TABLE 11.4
Distribution of Bovine Stock in Relation to Herding-Age Children
(all households)

Number of children of ages 10-13 excluding those in junior high school (number of households in parentheses)	Number of "quarters" (*kae*) of cattle and buffalo owned by the average household
0 (55)	2
1 (36)	8.4
2 (21)	9.9

A group of herders, separated from their charges.

Herd boys and water buffalo; in the dry-rice field behind and below them there is a bird-frightening construction of rattan lines tied to a center pole that is visible.

an average of ten "quarters" or ten 'legs.' There is a palpable difference between having at least one child of age 10 to 13 and having none, as concerns the evident desirability of keeping bovine stock. Moreover, 41 of the 55 households that have no children of optimum herding age own no bovine stock, a statistically significant finding, given that only eight of the 36 with one child have no stock, and only 3 of the 21 with two herding-age children have no stock.

Significantly, the Sagala household heads, taken as a group, average almost three years older than non-Sagalas. This partly accounts for the fact that while 33 (58 percent) of the Sagala households have children of optimum herding age, only 17 (44 percent) of their wife-receivers and 7 (41 percent) of their wife-givers have such children. In this perspective, the preponderance of ownership by Sagalas appears much less striking than it did at first (see Table 11.1). Although the differences with respect to clan membership may not be entirely obviated by correlations with age of household heads and observed "ideal age" in herding—perhaps only a multivariate analysis with data from many more villages could settle the issue—they do indicate that ownership of livestock is in large part determined by considerations of time budgeting. Those who have children in this age range are predisposed to keep bovine stock. Though some may not have the means of acquiring livestock, others who have the stock or the means to acquire it may not have children to herd. Presumably, even in precolonial times before people needed to sell livestock to fund education, as they now often do, this led to the modes of shared ownership and caretaking described earlier.

Clan affiliation of those who share ownership may also contribute to the disproportionate share of bovine stock owned by Sagalas. The combinations of clan affiliations for 49 partnerships involving cattle and 43 involving buffalo are shown in Table 11.5. Only four partnerships among Sagalas involving buffalo and five involving cattle were of lineage mates—four of brothers and two of fathers and sons. There are almost the same number between Sagala households and their wife-receivers as among Sagala clanmates. The variety of partnerships in-

TABLE 11.5
Clan Affiliation of Partners Sharing Ownership of Cattle

Clans of partners	Numbers and percent of partnerships for stock type: Cattle		Buffalo	
Sagala + Sagala	17	34.7%	12	27.9%
Sagala + wife-receivers	16	32.6	14	32.5
Sagala + wife-givers	4	8.2	10	23.3
Other co-clansmen	5	10.2	3	7.0
Others of different clans (other affines)	1	2.1	1	2.3
Unknowns (extra-village)	6	12.2	3	7.0

dicates that the primary concern of those seeking partners or caretakers is to find someone willing and able. Most of the partnerships with wife-receivers appear to have been initiated by caretaking arrangements, since, generally, Sagalas own three quarters for every quarter owned by a wife-receiving partner.

Distribution of Pigs, Goats, and Horses

Pigs. Most of those who own cattle also own pigs, and some 60 percent of those who do not own cattle raise pigs. About half of the latter are young couples, and the rest are evenly divided among age groups. About 85 percent of the households tend pigs at any given time. The most that a single household tended was six, of which three were slaughtered for a feast before they reached two-thirds of full size (full size is about 80 kilos). Those with no pigs generally had lost one to disease or had sold one that was getting too big to feed and were awaiting half the litter of another, previously given out for caretaking. At the time of the survey, twelve households were caring for young sows (of which five were arrangements of Sagalas of differing lineages and two of men of the same clan). Nine, mostly elderly, householders said they did not raise pigs. The average number kept by Sagalas was two and by their affines one-and-a-half.

Since sows average three litters in two years, the pig population would increase enormously over time if it were not for the need to feed them and the fact that suckling pigs are essential to ritual. I observed only occasional instances of sales, gifts, and sacrificial offerings of pigs or piglets, but such attrition is attested by the median numbers tended at one time. I documented a large variety of "special meals" such as the thanksgiving gathering held by a teaching-school graduate on landing his first job, at which a piglet served for meat.

Goats. Half of the 30 percent of households that raised goats did so in caretaking arrangements, many with kin or acquaintances from other villages in the area. Very few households that raise neither cattle nor pigs keep goats.

Horses. Horses are the main means of cartage for crops, manure, cement ingredients, and even lumber. Ownership of horses is rather evenly distributed in the age groups, with only a small majority of the 34 full owners and 16 joint owners being in the half of the households headed by men and women over 42 years of age. No household keeps more than one horse. There is, again, a disproportionally greater number of Sagala than non-Sagala owners (with 56 percent of horses or shares of horses owned by Sagalas, 28 percent by their wife-receivers, and 16 percent by their wife-givers). The relatively slight difference can be partly accounted for by the fact that all but one of the eight jointly owned horses belong to brothers or to fathers and sons, relationships that are more likely to occur among Sagalas, since none have moved to the village.

Of those who do not own horses, 42 households have close agnates (14 brothers, 12 fathers, 9 sons, 4 father's brothers, and 3 brother's sons), and 7 have close affines (5 wife's fathers and 2 daughter's husbands), who are horse owners. Because harvests and plantings are staggered, almost all households have access to a horse when needed. Borrowing of horses is, in fact, not always from one's closest kin. For instance, one descendant of the founder preferred to borrow from a distantly related lineage mate, from two Sagalas of other lineages, or from a neighboring wife-giver of a distant lineage mate rather than from his brother. Personal disposition and the degree of other involvement play parts in such avoidance.

Culturally Figured Values of Livestock

The use of livestock in a graded series of feasts has been described, in one ideal progression, in Chapter 5. It was said to have its inception in a set of caretaking arrangements—the loan of a pig from wife-givers and a chicken from wife-receivers. Although I learned of only seven formal caretaking arrangements involving cattle during the month I was actively inquiring on the subject, I did note that they were mostly with wife-givers from other villages in the region. This is part of a meaningful pattern.

Wife-givers, as has been explained, exercise an uncontrolled mystical influence on wife-receivers, but wife-receivers are also important to wife-givers, and people are very conscious of that and often express it. One way is by giving an animal into a caretaking arrangement. On one occasion I met a man from Pangururan leading a goat to leave in the care of a villager. He would not, I suspect, have undertaken the arduous climb if he did not think it would yield returns. Indeed, a church elder explained, "In the past, [it was] to take good fortune from another person that one would tend livestock for a share of the offspring" (*Dulu, mambuat nasib dari orang lain maka dia mamahani*). Vergouwen wrote much the same thing—namely, that joint ownership (*ripe-ripean*)

> can be a means whereby one may acquire some part of the prosperity of one's companion, *mambuat tua ni donganna,* and . . . people see in joint ownership a means of participating mutually in each other's prosperity. . . . This applies especially to cattle which . . . grow and increase, particularly in the hands of someone who seems to be destined to be prosperous. (Vergouwen 1964:320)

In spite of the church elder's caveat—"In the past . . ."—this must still be a consideration. It is not only the caretaker who hopes to benefit from the arrangement. In caretaking and in joint ownership, each party is the potential recipient of benefits of more than material character, because any increase of one's stock may serve a ritual use (Firth 1963b). Examples of this, both as offering and as consecrated food, have been described earlier. To conclude this chapter, it is appropriate to recount a ritual prestation of livestock—or, in this instance, of a portion.

Ritual Prestation of Livestock

The following demand, by a bride's father's younger brother at a city wedding, is typical of one for bridewealth.

> Well, our sisters' husbands, men of Simanjorang. . . . It happens that I am myself [like you] from the homeland. I know well that I get betel-nut, I get the chopping block, I get [fulfillment of] law, I get [fulfillment of] oaths. Since this *adat* ceremony is being held in [the city of] Medan . . . , you men of wife-receivers, I feel lost. But you know . . . I follow what was done by my father. Like those beside me, when I am called on later, what I will present is a *batangan* shawl. That will be paid by me (*gararonghu*). As long as you are generous, I will be generous. So, as for the portion [due to me], add a lot at once; reciprocate well (*denggan balosi hamu*).
>
> Let me remind you of just one thing: I am the one who is called, 'Long is not enough, short is all wound up.' Most importantly, keep in mind, prestige is what I am fetching, prestige is what is brought [by me] (*iang na hualap, iang na tinaruhon*). Make it proper, sisters' husbands. Let me be conveyed a 'ruminant' (*na mangagat*) that exists in Huta Ginjang.

Others chime in, "Deliver a buffalo! Deliver a buffalo!" But the speaker for the wife-receivers answers, "As for the bridewealth that you request, the rope of a ruminant is what we will give" (i.e., a token cash payment).

To this, the uncle of the bride responds:

> Men of wife-receivers (*Raja ni boru*), I'll say thank you, but no rope to me. I am the one who receives fame (*Sijalo barita do ahu*). All you have to say is, 'So-and-so-much is your portion, brother-in-law,' [and I will accept and say,] 'Prosper [and may your soul] grow staunch' (. . . *Gabe horas*).

With this assurance, the groom's father's younger brother—a

teacher and a lay preacher—takes up the challenge:

> Prosperity and staunchness [of soul to you]. . . . [As for] that which you requested a moment ago, if [we] your wife-receivers have any, [it is because] you are the well, we are the net. As you said, prestige is what is fetched, prestige is what is delivered. As for what you have requested, we will give it: one leg of a cow!

When another speaker for the bride's father asks for an additional payment of a 'rope,' the groom's uncle replies,

> Sirs, you requested the one that chews grass, and we have already given it. I request that [you] come view it. We, your wife-receivers are prepared [to receive you].

That ended the episode, though the bridewealth session continued for hours.

People say that many recipients of bridewealth prefer to 'receive' part of a cow or buffalo, rather than a large cash payment, because of the cow's potential progeny. For each calf born to a cow of which one owns a quarter, one is also entitled to a quarter, so that if good fortune prevails, in four years one may possess four quarters from the initial gift of one. The ritual gift of livestock is thus thought to result in prosperity increasing and in prestige accruing. Although it is left unsaid, such bridewealth is not conveyed immediately. Only if the cow were to die in a mishap and be divided among the village owners with the excess being sold would the wife-giver receive his 'portion' and his wife-receiver be deprived of access to the fertilizing by-product. For the time being, nothing is actually given, but a debt is undertaken.

Of course, it is through just such prestations, as well as through caretaking arranged in more mundane fashion, that the complex web of shared ownership of livestock in the village has developed. I will analyze their significance after the following account of landholding.

Chapter 12

Landholding and Transference

The different amounts of rice and other crops produced by various households are, in part, the result of available labor, but they are also partly the result of access to land. Here we examine what determines access. Landholding and transference of land in Samosir are not simply matters of ownership and sale of "real estate," although the Batak sometimes talk as if that were the case. I will show that the cultural values that define people's identities are bound up in distribution of land.

It should be kept in mind that we are concerned with land as a means of producing rice and the question of commoditization of land. Is land a commodity? If so, did it become one as a result of monetization? Both social and ideological aspects of its distribution and transference must be taken into account in assessing whether land has been "commoditized," and if so whether it can be considered "real estate." After briefly confronting the cultural biases inherent in the very subject of "landholding," I will show how deeply held spiritual values concerning land or territory are intertwined with the utilitarian values that it has for villagers.

Cultural Biases in Analyzing Landholding

Drawing on themes in the work of Malinowski and of Maine, P. Bohannan argues that the notion of "tenure" assumes an idea of "land" divisible into measurable parcels. Thus, he maintains, the assumption that a land system is always a property system—

> even if land does not enter the market—has led to the continued life of a silly concept called 'communal ownership'. . . . Notions of 'communal ownership,' manipulated by people who assume property and market as the basis of human society, have made the land the basis of grouping in [African systems] in which spatial extension and concomitant rights to exploit the environment are mere aspects of the social group. (Bohannan 1960:446)

Bohannan pursues this point in his analysis of the Yoruba lineage group called the *ebi*:

> The Europeans, in the legal system they fostered, gave the *ebi* a legal reality which it formerly had not possessed. From being only a social group, it now became a legal entity. . . . [I]n the indigenous system, the *ebi* did not 'own' land communally or any other way. Rather it was a social group with a spatial dimension. (Bohannan 1960:448-449)

There is a sense in which Bohannan's observations apply very well to the Batak *marga* ('clan'), each with its traditional *golat* (ancestral home area), and they seem to apply particularly in the Toba Batak confrontation with Dutch theory and policy. L. Castles has argued that evidence, from records of a debate concerning whether plantation concessions should be granted to European companies to exploit Toba Batak areas, shows that missionaries—fearing a corrupting influence on their Batak converts—were able to secretly prompt Toba leaders to protest when survey work was begun and to put forward successful claims to the central government in Batavia (now Jakarta) regarding clan ownership of land (Castles 1972:129-137). Even though their claims ran contrary to colonial government decrees with respect to so-called waste land, the decision from Batavia favored the Batak. This may have been because Dutch predispositions, like those of British administrators, made them amenable to claims that appeared consonant with a notion that clans (*marga*) were landholding corporations rather than groups which viewed their spatial extensions and rights of exploitation as aspects of their descent or group identities and interrelationships. The latter view is pursued below.

Rights of Clans, of Descendants of Hamlet Founders, and Access by Others

All male members of the Ruma Pintu branch of the Sagala clan consider themselves 'of one land' (*sisada tano*); all are landholders (*partano*) and 'have *golat*' (*margolat*), as do the Sigiro wife-receivers of the land. *Golat* may have a number of referents, perhaps best glossed as 'ancestral home area.' Some *golat* are established by pioneering unclaimed land, *manombang* (this verb was used in reference to the cutting of forest and building of wet-rice terraces on the East Coast of Sumatra or to opening grassland for dry fields on the outskirts of village territory). The founder of the first hamlet was the first 'to come pioneer the land of Huta Ginjang' (*na ro manombang tano Huta Ginjang*). Similar "rights in land brought under cultivation" are inherent in the status of *boru tano* (wife-receivers of the land) of descendants of the first in-dwelling affines.

As was brought out in Chapter 3, male descendants of the founder of the first hamlet in Huta Ginjang retained ritual perquisites with respect to enterprises 'of the land,' including the building of new hamlets and tombs (privileges referred to as *harajaon tano*). Theoretically, it is with their leave that agricultural enterprises are pursued by immigrants to the village. It is said that only informal permission is requested. Although in the past a small meal may have been served to one or another hamlet headman for the privilege of staking a claim, immigrants now only need seek permission to cultivate from those who have a prior claim to particular plots.

Several men who had moved to Huta Ginjang used the verb "to pioneer" (*manombang*) to refer to opening fields in long-term fallows near the hamlet cluster, to which they had since maintained usufruct. One immigrant said that two such fields in separate areas had been 'supplied by their owners' (*itogihon nampuna i*) and that he had pioneered them. Thus, the unitary blocks of *clan-owned* land we tend to imagine and depict on maps, such as that appended to Ypes (1932), of huge clan-specific parcels, are in fact only one level of abstraction of the Samosirese "tenure relationship to land," one sometimes referred to by the people themselves.

Straight lines (walls, hedges) are indigenous demarcations between some areas. But many of the ancestral *golat* are divided and held by lineages or clans descended from other hamlet founders. Far from jealously guarding the area surrounding the hamlet founded by the first man to pioneer Huta Ginjang, the founder and his descendants welcomed new settlers because, as was reiterated by a number of them, "we like to be many" (i.e., safety lay in numbers). In other words, within "sub-clan-*golat*" are "localized-lineage-*golat*" whose boundaries are known but not necessarily clearly demarcated. They may be more subject to change than larger *golat* because the fortunes of minimal lineages are much more subject to change than those of larger groups.

In Huta Ginjang, with the exception of traditional areas of pasture above the hamlets, the lands were almost entirely brought under cultivation in the past. Most of the parcels are inherited, 'opened by an ancestor.' Aside from a few steep slopes, every patch has an owner, *nampunasa*, much as every house and tool has.

Thus, in settled areas, all land came to be considered the *golat* (ancestral home area) of one lineage or another. Except as the result of gifts of land, its forcible seizure, or the extinction of its inheritors, the *golat* were permanent. Therefore the Samosir Batak tenure relationship to land cannot simply be viewed as analogous to African systems in which "the social organization . . . is only incidentally linked with the physical environment for comparatively short periods of time by activities such as farming," as P. and L. Bohannan write of the Tiv (1968:80). In part, this is because physical alteration of terrain in building both irrigable and dry-field terraces gives the builder and his descendants permanent tenure, and this is reinforced by the sedentism encouraged by an assured rice supply, which is in turn made possible by the feats of landscaping.

There is no rule, as that of the Tiv, that every male of a lineage has a right to "sufficient land" for the subsistence needs of his household.

There is, rather, a well-developed set of notions and precedents providing for selective inheritance of land and for out-migration by individuals and small, closely related groups of affines. As a result, there are enclaves of Sagalas, for instance, in locales south of the lake (e.g., they are *boru tano* of the Siregars of Sipirok), as well as in Dairiland and the East Coast lowlands (visits to out-married sisters, courting, and trading may have facilitated such moves, as they do now).

So, while in one sense spatial extension and "concomitant rights to exploit the environment are mere aspects" of the Batak social group, the relative permanence of *golat* gives these rights a different set of referents. On the one hand, the local territory can be viewed as a sacralized topography in which ancestral hamlets, ancestral tombs of carved stone, and geographical landmarks such as outcroppings of rock or springs of water (the abodes of spirits) have special significance for groups of people at varying levels of conceptually distinguished ties of coalescence. But the fact that prayers to earth and water spirits, which accompany a variety of household offerings, are not directed exclusively to those within the village *golat* or even within the Sagala clan *golat* indicates that the ancestral spirit power that is significant for any given lineage comes from other clans' spirits as well.

Further appreciation of the conceptual underpinning of Batak landholding can be gained from analogy with A. Strathern's analysis of certain New Guinea peoples, among whom "the notion of 'growth from soil' is important in establishing identity." "Food," Strathern suggests, "is a mediator between locality and kinship." He reasons that

> clansmen are felt to share identity. One way of symbolising this is in terms of descent-constructs [which] posit that clansmen share substance in some way through their descent from an ancestor. Another way in which they share substance is through consumption of food grown on clan land. . . .
>
> . . . Salisbury [1965] refers to Siane clans as 'corporate groups possessing a stock of land and of ancestral spirit' [*korova*]. . . . Ancestral *korova* are also identified 'with the land from which they originally emerged and to which they are relinked by mortuary rites. They make the land fertile and in return receive portions of all crops.' . . .

> . . . Food grown on the land is thus impregnated with ancestral spirit. Locality and descent are in this set of ideas exactly fused. (Strathern 1973:28-31)

The Batak notion of 'spirit power' or 'soul force' (*sahala*), which may be concentrated at points in the environment and may pass between people as well as between ancestors and their descendants, roughly resembles Siane *korova*. There is, likewise, a clear link in the Batak beliefs and practices of sacrificial feasting between the bounty of crops, the fruitfulness of people and livestock, and the beneficence of paternal and maternal spirit power.

Food is frequently used as a medium of blessing by the Batak. Offerings (including rice and meat or fish) made to ancestral spirits and to wife-givers are accompanied by prayers beseeching what is essentially reciprocity in the form of bounteous crops and fecundity. Ritual prestations of food like those made by wife-receivers to wife-givers and by children to dying parents invoke the ancestral spirit power that is disposed of by the living. Among affines, food is used to elicit a ritual response and—from wife-givers to wife-receivers—as a medium of transferring 'blessings' or 'spirit power.' Although this does not demonstrate conclusively that food serves as a mediator between descent and shared locality, such appears to be the case, though it serves this role differently than in Strathern's example.

On the occasion of a tomb-permission feast (Chapter 3), when the special 'showing parts of the food' were divided by the descendants of the village founder, the Sagalas and all adult males of the village received some portion of the 'showing parts,' and all male elders (not just hamlet heads and *bius* heads) pronounced blessings at the end of the gathering. Hence, when land is the subject of specific ritual action, food serves as a mediator between descent and shared locality. The division of special portions was based on a pioneering compact with earth spirits and was made in the idioms of descent and affinity.[1] But

[1]There was no support for the argument put forward by a man of Sagala lineage VII that the division of the tail section ought to be based on ancestrally shared trials and tribulations—i.e., locality, not descent (see Sherman 1982, app. 9.1).

this does not appear to be as much a matter of shared locality being equated with or transmuted into shared descent—based on a notion of food bearing ancestral spirit power from the earth being absorbed by the living—as Strathern suggests is the case in certain New Guinean cultures. Rather, consecrated food assumes its usual Batak role of power-bearing substance, shared among those 'of one land/one territory' (*sisada tano*), as it also serves among those of different territories. And people share food in a situation 'relating to the land' because they are of one locality and despite the fact that they are not of common descent but of different clans. Only the division of the food is according to a descent idiom. Descent and locality are not "exactly fused"; they are integrated into extralineage ritual by the medium of shared food. This gives us a purchase for grasping Batak concepts of landholding.

Returning to our point of departure, the alacrity with which some Bataks were able to adapt to Dutch notions of clans as landholding corporations—in order to resist the granting of land for plantation concessions—reveals a degree of correspondence between their notions of landholding and those of the Dutch. That is to say, the traditional concept of *golat* appears in some measure to correspond to Western notions of land tenure. What is different is the basis for the tenure, which for the Batak is based on pioneering, compacts with localized spirits of the earth, and subsequent gifts of land to others.

According to Vergouwen, for those who are not of what he calls "the ruling *marga*" (which is in fact the *raja tano*, a clan or subclan exercising ritual perquisites with respect to land), "any right . . . to land for cultivation is a derived right . . . [though it is] stronger than a mere right of usufruct resting on terminable contract" (1964:113-114). However, this "right of use," as he puts it, "becomes stronger as the period of time during which an in-dwelling *marga* stays with another *marga* increases, because, as a rule, many-sided relationships result from the marriages which take place." This is how it happens that the tenure relationship to land of those not members of lineages descended from a settlement founder comes, over time, to be as strong as though they were in direct line of descent from the original pioneer. Although in-dwellers are not *pargolat* ("owners"), they attain permanence of tenure because dispossessing them would involve an unraveling of the "many-sided relationships" that have been built up over time.

This gives insight into an important characteristic of Toba Batak tenure relationships to land. For, as a result, a point is eventually reached at which the proliferating descendants of any given founder are forced to cultivate less-than-optimum fields or to leave the area. Indeed, this was probably the situation that led to the founding of Huta Ginjang. Even its irrigable land is less desirable than the valley *sawah*, since it gets colder and water is far scarcer. Yet the prior tenure of irrigable valley fields by affines of more senior Sagala lines pre-empted the descendants of Sagala Huta Ruar from securing an adequate livelihood there. The same process is at work in the present village with respect to descendants of the founding pioneer. Let us examine more closely how this process occurs.

Grants of Fields to Wife-Receivers

When an intralocal or an uxorilocal marriage takes place, the wife-receiver generally requests a field as a 'path of life,' a 'blessing-shawl field' (*juma parulos*). As a Sagala man put it, "if the wife-giver has, he cannot refuse; he must give, even if only a little." Some say that in the past such a field could not be taken back under any circumstances—that they were all 'shawl fields that cannot rot' (*ulos na so ra buruk*) (the epitome of the latter is the land of in-dwelling wife-receivers of the village founder's line). Whatever the truth of such assertions, some shawl fields are not automatically heritable. The son of a marriage may continue to use the field with the permission of its giver or his male heir; but permission need not be granted, and the field can be "taken back" (*sinusat*), particularly if there is an eligible daughter in one's mother's brothers' lineage and one does not marry her. In one instance, a field given to a married sister (of Sagala IV) and her husband was taken back after both died and her emigrant son pawned the field to his own sister's husband of a third clan. As another man put it, the giver (or his heir) says to himself, "'It's not my daughter eating that,' and he plucks it" ('*Ndang borungku mangallang i,' jala icabut*).

Leach treats the access to land by in-dwelling wife-receivers among the Kachin as indicating a landlord-tenant relationship (1966a; 1965:218). It is true that the relationships (of which access to land through gift is an integral component) have numerous expressions that bespeak not parity but, as Lehman indicates, an asymmetric reciprocity (1963:123-125). But if a descendant of the first marriage for which a field was given marries one of his mother's brother's daughters, the tenure of the 'shawl field' becomes permanent for the descendants of this second marriage. This kind of "marrying into land" gets beyond a landlord-tenant relationship. There is, after all, no rent in cash or produce either asked or paid. Rather, it represents a situation of land linking people as affinal kinsmen and providing the basis for an unending progression. The right of a user to dispose of a field has often been taken as a measure of "fullness of ownership" (Hill 1963:111). It might be more appropriate to compare the position of first-generation immigrants to the village—whose wives are also immigrants, especially those few whose sisters married non-Sagalas—to that of tenants, insofar as they cannot sell, pawn, or bequeath the land they have "borrowed." Not even they, however, pay for the use of land they open; and for those who marry Sagala women, and on whose sons there seems to be a "lien" to marry maternal uncles' daughters (Lehman 1963:126), there is a sense in which, rather than there being a notion of tenancy, land serves as "groomwealth" (Sherman 1987:876-877).

Inheritance

Fields are not only granted to wife-receivers. The patrilocal residence of 75 percent of village couples also gives rise to the transfer of rights to land in the majority of cases. Fifty-eight village household heads received a dry field or valley *sawah* from their fathers as a *panjaean* to establish independence. Sixteen, all wife-givers or wife-receivers of Sagala lineages, did not receive such a gift. Eight others had "pioneered" unclaimed fields. Six household heads did not receive the gift of land formally because they had lived with and supported their parents. Five households of wife-receivers received "shawl fields."

Overall, whereas half the households are Sagalas, two-thirds of the Sagalas received such gifts of land, while slightly less than one-third of the others did. This reflects the stronger rights to prime land of Sagala households, but it also makes clear that the rights are not absolute, and it highlights the importance of other means of access.

Although eldest and youngest sons are favored in inheritance, because of their positions in the social developmental process of households, middle siblings are not entirely excluded. As Vergouwen notes (1964:282), some fields of great value are kept intact from generation to generation and cannot be given to wife-receivers; these fields are, for preference, passed from oldest son to oldest son. Again, it is generally the case that "if the deceased had several fields lying along an irrigation canal or rivulet, the eldest son gets the one lying upstream" (ibid.:284). In most instances of irrigable holdings in the village, the eldest brother held title to the field closest to the stream-bed and upstream from fields of younger brothers (i.e., closest to the source of valuable water). The oldest man of the most senior Sagala lineage owned the largest set of irrigable terraces, the embankment just below the spring, on the eastern side of the brook. He was not a descendant of the founder.

There is some leeway for adjusting the landholdings of individual households within areas held by any given one-father descent group in response to demographic changes. If an older brother dies with no heirs, his fields pass to his younger brothers, and some fields may be used by the latter if a deceased man's sons are absent or too young to work them. In such situations, a widow's needs are considered but not always to her satisfaction.

Wet-rice terraces and dry, terraced fields are, then, held or owned as property. (Some additional means by which they are alienable within the bounds of local society will be shown in more detail below.) Tenure is by means of inheritance, grants, or claims on pioneered land designated as 'never having been worked.' Inherited fields, of course, had also been pioneered and bequeathed.

Since land was not mapped or set down in deeds, there is no way of ascertaining how demographic change may have mitigated the supposed permanence of tenure. The degree to which land is passed in patrilineal lines and serves as a link between ancestors and their descendants was brought out pointedly in feast-dancing instances of spirit possession. Crowding around the possessed subject (generally a woman who had "married in"), people badger the spirit with questions. One of the prime tests of its identity in such a situation is a demand that the spirit specify what fields have been pawned since its passage from among the living. Appropriate answers constitute a public reminder of the ancestral rights the feast-givers hold and are, perhaps, a goad for them to redeem the fields.

Villagers indicate their intention to farm a long-fallow field by digging up a few scattered squares, a foot or so on a side, and leaving the sod upside-down next to the bare spots. These are called *tallik* ('cut'), and there is no limit on the practice (cf. Ypes 1932:153, 206). They may be renewed every few years indefinitely. Having a few squares dug up, the whole field is considered to show "traces of work" and is reserved. A *tallik* is thus a public sign of ownership that says "open for grazing only," so to speak.

It is instructive to look at Dutch attitudes toward Batak practices, given the colonists' claims of eminent domain over so-called 'waste land' (Indonesian, *tanah kosong*, i.e., grassland). Ypes (1932:202-203) writes that once a dry field is bequeathed by the developer to a son, the rights of the son "become fixed—*golat*—and cannot be lost even if the land is left in long fallow." Anyone who wants to use it has to ask permission, but if refused, he claims, permission may be granted by the *raja doli*, a *bius* official, after three more years of fallow.

No such time limits on maintaining rights of disposal over the use of dry fields were hinted at or appeared to be operative at the time of my research. Rather, the same set of prescriptions applied to dry and irrigable fields:

> A cultivator who is a *partano* never loses the rights over a wet-rice field he has developed, not even by long fallow. . . . If someone else wants to work it he always needs the permission of the owner of the field. . . . If the owner refuses, the *raja doli* must also accept it. (Ypes 1932:203-204)

Loss of "tenure" after a five-year fallow occurs only in traditionally-contested areas between territories. I suspect that Ypes' claim with regard to dry fields is evidence of a Dutch tendency to see to it that land be productively used and be redistributed if it was not.[2]

Ypes also claims that a *parripe* (by which he means one who has "married in") has only rights of usufruct.

> If a *parripe* in Samosir leaves a piece of ground that has been vested to him for opening, then he loses his right to the land at once, even if it is a *sawah*. The same happens when a *parripe* continues working a field developed by his father if he later leaves it fallow. (Ypes 1932:204)

Everything hinges on the phrase "vested to him for opening," for these strictures would apply only to a *juma parulos*, the 'shawl field' just discussed. In effect, there is inequality among wife-receivers, both on the basis that those 'of the land' have guaranteed rights and also on the basis of length of settlement. What intervenes are the "many-sided relationships" formed over time. Thus, a good number of long-fallowed irrigable and dry fields in areas throughout Huta Ginjang were indicated by Sagala men as belonging to men of other clans, both wife-givers and wife-receivers of Sagala. When I asked those named how they had gotten possession, the answer was, invariably, "It was opened by [my] ancestor" (*Pinungka ni ompu*).

[2]See Kahn (1976:86-87) for discussion of similar scholarly Dutch claims in Minangkabau, "to preserve a subsistence economy. . . ."

Patterns of Descent and Affinity in Landholding

To give body to the above generalizations, it is useful to examine patterns of landholding in Huta Ginjang. They are not easy to represent statistically, pictorially, or in prose, but the effort is repaid because differences among lineages do reflect social and ideological norms. Perhaps most unsatisfactory, subject to field error and later misinterpretation, is Table 12.1, which lists fields in approximate descending order of desirability, from left to right. It represents only what I happened to learn during a particular interval, and should in no way be read as binding or fixed. Even the Sagala genealogy is subject to debate and disagreement, by both villagers and their Valley kin.

The availability of water can make the difference between a successful crop and a ruined one, so irrigable fields are given first rank. A number of households of Sagala lineages hold parcels in the most desirable, broad, irrigable fields, while others have parcels on the steep hillside adjacent to the brook—irrigable, but with greater difficulty. A number have neither. (Brothers who are close in age generally have comparable holdings.) As a second criterion of desirability, I adopt B. DeWalt's "weighting" of distance, for, as he notes, those "who live further away from their lands might be less able to care for their fields" (1979:97). To the factor of distance, however, must be added that of altitude; since crops grown at lower altitudes mature faster, a food shortage can be made up more quickly, and more crops can be grown in the same field in a year.

In Table 12.1, some two dozen areas of fields have been grouped in order of increasing distance and increasing altitude: (1) valley *sawah*; (2) village irrigable (including some non-irrigable fields next to the hamlets); (3) non-irrigated fields below the hamlets near the streambed; (4) fields at a distance from the streambed and at higher altitudes; (5) those above the village; and (6) the distant, high, dry fields. The last yield almost the same rate per hectare as valley *sawah*; their difference lies in the time and labor it takes to grow the crop and in the fact that yields are more certain from year to year in irrigable fields than in dry.

The table shows percentages for the primary named areas in use during this field research by genealogical group. As we have seen, a little more than half (65 of 112) the households own or have taken in pledge for a loan some irrigable land. A plurality of villagers work one parcel, somewhat fewer work two parcels, and a handful work three or more in irrigable areas of the village proper. The question is, to what degree are these inequities—whereby some households tend to use more desirable (irrigable or nearby) fields and others only non-irrigable, distant fields—clan or lineage linked? Judging by the preponderance of irrigable holdings and of nearby dry fields belonging to Sagala lineages of the same father and mother as the founder (V), such inequities do indeed exist and they are not insignificant. They stem from the vagaries of precedence and demography, but they are mitigated by holdings of other lineages both in the village and in the valley. The table shows that descendants of the founder and their 'brother' lineages have relinquished whatever control they once had over a great portion of the most desirable holdings. A number of men of the founder's and closely related lineages lack irrigable fields entirely, and were said to have pawned those they once had.

It is notable that holdings of lineages descended from 'one father' (Sagala lineages II-VIII) are generally concentrated, as are those of lineages I, IX, X, and XI. Likewise, holdings of lineages II and III contrast with those of IV-VII, reflecting descent from two different 'mothers.' Such concentrations (compare the holdings of lineage I and lineage V, for instance) are attributable to dividing up inherited fields among the brothers of one father. The pattern is somewhat attenuated in the most distant fields, where are found the most small holdings of the greatest number of different lineage groupings.

Patterns that result from the tendency to group fields of related patrilines are not precise, two-dimensional, bifurcating genealogies "on the ground," since they are crosscut by a variety of holdings of affinally related in-dwellers. The drawings of terraced, dry fields in Figures 12.1a, b, and c (180-degree, bird's eye views from higher ground) demonstrate some of the patterns that develop. (Individual household fields are separated by darker lines, which belies the actual

TABLE 12.1

Percentages of Different Areas Held by Sagala Lineages and Others

Type of field:	Valley *sawah*	Irrigable relatively level			Unirrigable low - lying				
Code of field	A	B	C	D	E	F	G	H	J
No. of holdings	107	32	37	17	14	24	17	17	28
No. of households with holdings	46	28	33	16	14	21	17	17	28
Lineages/ Clans									
Sagala I	17.4	2.2	2.6	45.9	18.1	-	-	5.3	-
II	12.3	4.7	-	-	-	9.0	1.9	28.4	-
III	7.1	9.2	16.6	-	-	20.2	-	10.5	-
IV	2.0	2.2	7.5	-	-	-	-	-	12.0
V	11.2	19.7	28.5	-	61.7	29.8	7.1	-	30.4
VI	1.4	7.9	17.0	-	-	16.4	12.9	4.2	16.6
VII	0.9	14.7	1.3	-	-	10.6	-	2.6	3.8
VIII	8.1	7.2	-	-	-	-	-	4.4	-
IX	0.9	-	-	-	-	-	-	-	-
X	2.0	-	-	5.2	-	3.8	-	-	-
XI	0.5	-	-	12.2	-	-	-	-	-
Other Sagala	-	-	4.5	-	-	-	-	-	-
Sigiro *boru tano*	10.9	21.5	2.6	-	-	-	33.5	15.7	8.7
Simanjorang	11.5	-	2.7	8.2	5.5	-	-	23.6	13.5
Limbong	-	2.0	2.7	-	7.7	-	17.7	-	-
Other wife-receivers	2.3	-	7.9	6.1	3.1	10.2	6.5	5.3	7.7
Simarmata	0.6	8.7	2.5	-	-	-	-	-	5.8
Simbolon	8.6	-	-	11.2	-	-	17.2	-	1.5
Other wife-givers	2.3	-	3.6	11.2	3.9	-	3.2	-	-

(Continued)

TABLE 12.1 - cont'd

Dry fields, separate from stream					Dry fields above the village				Distant, dry higher fields		
K	L	M	N	P	Q	R	S	T	U	V	W
10	28	17	34	7	42	6	3	8	44	16	21
10	26	15	32	7	41	6	3	7	42	16	21
-	22.2	32.9	6.4	-	-	-	-	66.4	2.5	8.4	-
-	-	-	17.0	-	2.2	-	-	-	1.0	-	21.8
-	-	-	2.8	30.8	-	-	-	-	-	-	4.7
-	6.6	-	8.6	-	3.8	-	-	-	4.1	-	3.6
-	-	-	4.2	-	21.7	-	-	-	7.6	-	5.4
-	-	-	2.0	-	18.0	7.3	-	-	1.3	5.9	10.7
-	-	-	-	15.4	1.7	-	-	-	-	22.8	-
-	-	8.4	5.6	-	-	-	-	-	-	4.2	-
-	13.7	-	12.3	-	-	-	-	-	2.5	9.7	-
-	17.5	-	1.7	-	-	-	-	-	8.9	-	-
-	4.2	-	4.2	7.7	-	-	13.2	-	6.3	-	-
-	-	-	-	-	-	-	-	-	3.8	-	-
65.0	-	12.3	1.9	7.7	26.8	22.0	-	-	9.6	2.9	21.1
15.5	7.8	15.9	-	38.4	4.2	-	75.5	16.1	12.3	8.4	-
-	-	5.0	2.5	-	8.4	70.7	-	-	3.8	6.3	-
-	12.9	13.2	4.7	-	3.5	-	-	-	11.8	8.4	15.8
19.5	-	-	-	-	8.0	-	-	-	0.9	4.6	1.8
-	6.8	-	14.1	-	1.7	-	-	-	7.0	2.9	4.3
-	8.3	12.3	12.0	-	-	-	11.3	17.5	16.6	15.5	10.8

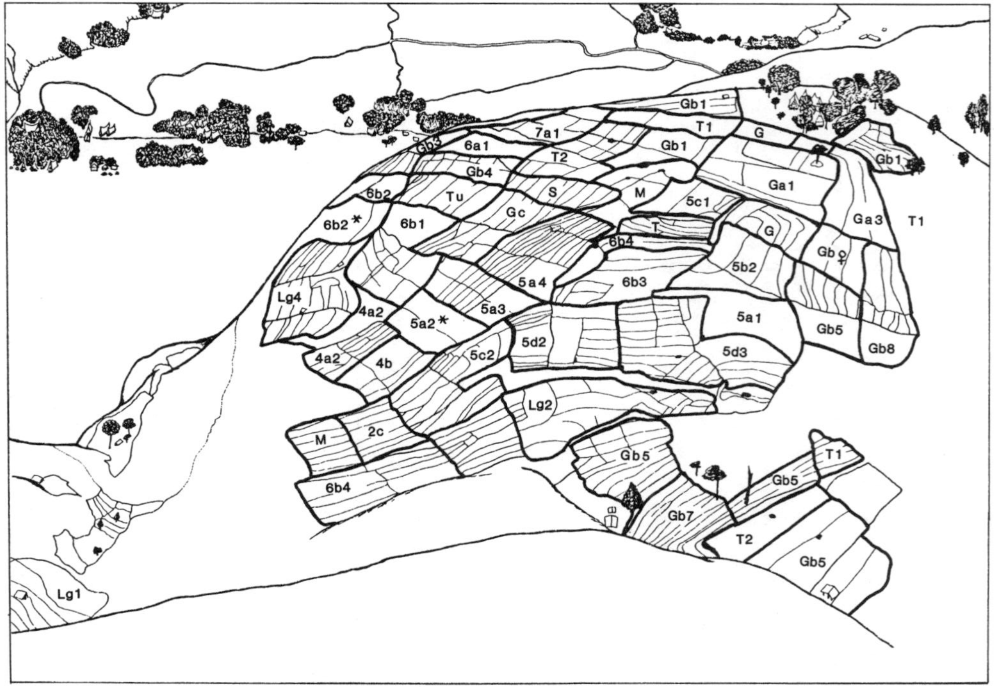

Figure 12.1a. Distribution of landholding (180° view; not to scale).

numerals = Sagala lineages
G = Sigiro *boru tano*
Lg = Limbong
T = Simarmata
M = Simanjorang
S = Simbolon
Tu = Situngkir

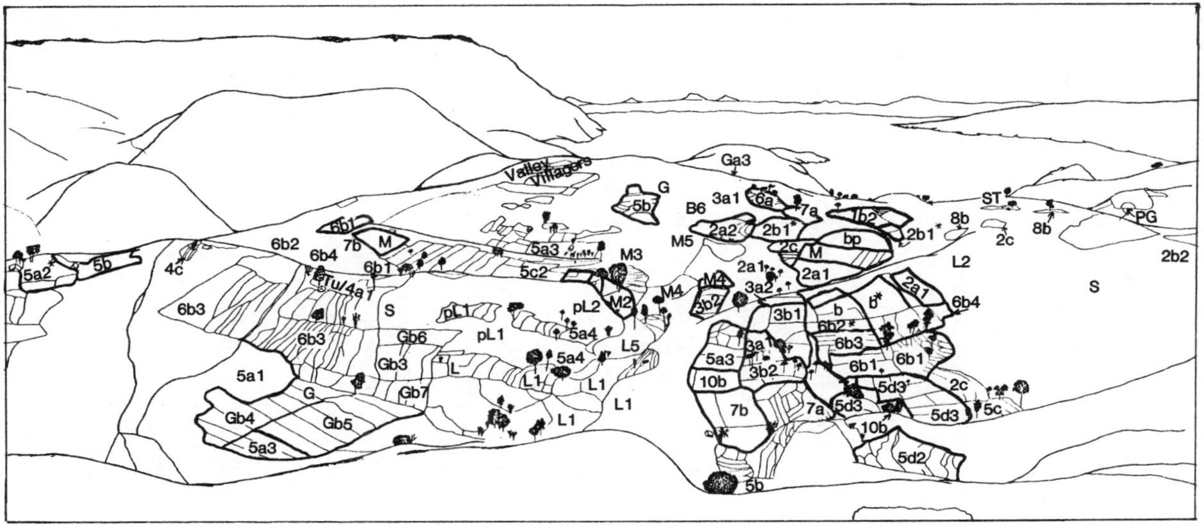

Figure 12.1b. Distribution of landholding (180° view; not to scale).

numerals = Sagala lineages	G = Sigiro *boru tano*
PG = Sigiro wife-givers	b = Sigiro wife-receivers (other than *boru tano*)
pL = Simalango	M = Simanjorang
ST = Sitanggang	L = Limbong
Tu = Situngkir	S = Simbolon

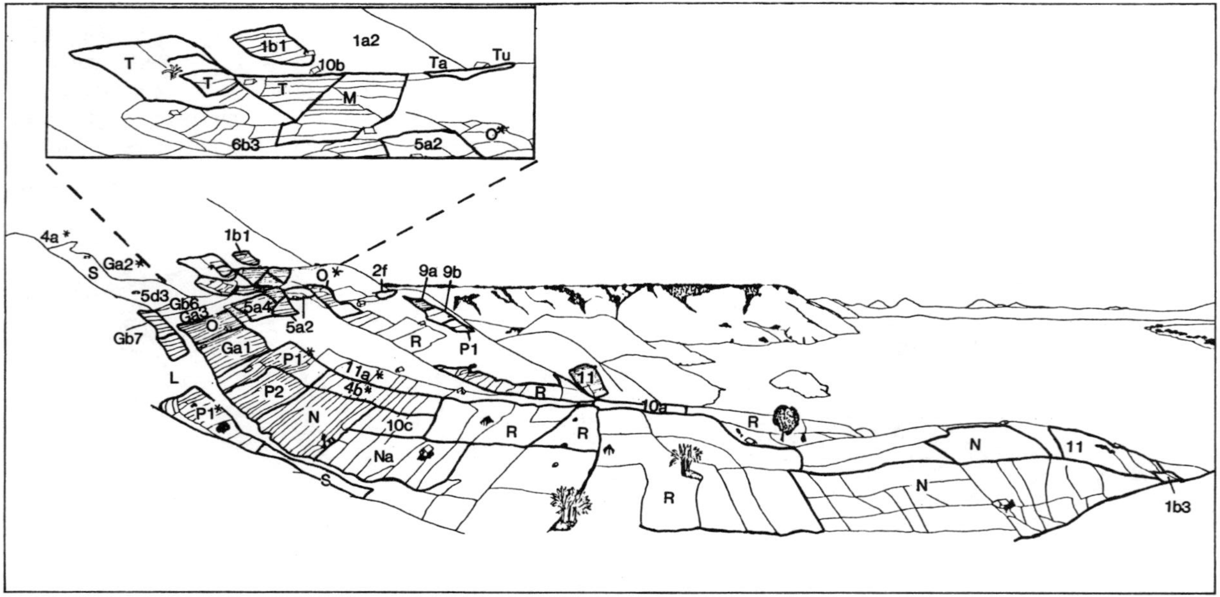

Figure 12.1c. Distribution of landholding (180° view; not to scale).

numerals = Sagala lineages	R = Saragi	Ta = Sitanggang
S = Simbolon	N = Naibaho	L = Limbong
T = Simarmata	Na = Sinaga	Tu = Situngkir
G = Sigiro *boru tano*	O = Other Sagala subclan	M = Simanjorang
P = Sigiro wife-givers to Sagala		

appearance of the areas. Those marked with numbers first are of Sagala households whose lineage is indicated with Arabic rather than Roman numerals in the drawings, to reduce the number of lines; sublineages are indicated by lowercase letters and birth order by subscript Arabic numbers.)

In addition to overt concentrations of holdings by some lineages and the lack of same by others, some further patterns emerge. The bottom left-hand corner of Figure 12.1a shows one of the fields closest to Limbong, where there is a Limbong clan household farming a field that may be said to "guard" the approach from the territory of Limbong. On the right side of Figure 12.1c are Naibaho household fields, which likewise "guard" an approach from their home territory of Pangururan. In both cases, the household heads are of lines that have long inhabited Huta Ginjang. It appears more than coincidental that these Sagala affines came to hold the fields in question—i.e., those who initially did so were perhaps motivated by prior acquaintance with potentially threatening neighbors at the periphery of village fields. The same pattern for the Sagalas is exemplified in Figure 12.1b, in which the perimeter fields of this low-lying area, those closest to the north end of Sagala Valley (at the upper left side), belong primarily to members of Sagala lineages.

Recent Pioneering in the Vicinity of the Village

Differences between Sagalas and non-Sagalas are also reflected in recent pioneering activities near the village. At the perimeter of the inherited fields on the eastern extreme of village lands, where during Dutch times and earlier, canoe-commuting and other inhabitants of Samosir peninsula (mainly SiTanggang clan) farmed the northeast slopes of Mt. Pusuk Buhit, there are ample long-fallow fields that are increasingly farmed by Huta Ginjang households. Until 1949, some 40 Pangururan households had lived in one such area, using the Huta Ginjang spring for bathing and a source of water. During my stay, eighty-nine households (79.5 percent of the village) had fields on this eastern flank of the mountain, while 16 (18 percent) had relinquished prior holdings and seven of them had taken new fields there. Of the 56 Sagalas, 14 had not farmed in these areas; 8 (including 2 widows), or 35 percent of those who had not, were of the founder's lineage (Sagala V). The nine other households that had not farmed these areas were wife-receivers (of numerous Sagala lineages). Thus, only 9 percent more non-Sagalas than Sagalas had found it practical to open fields there.

Some villagers claimed they had been moved to open fields in these areas by a government regulation that held that fallow land could be worked by anyone. Since many had opened fields there before 1957, when Indonesia nationalized foreign plantation holdings and allowed squatting on them, and since the rule was not applied within the village except to unclaimed parcels, it might appear that their statements were after-the-fact rationalizations. But that may not necessarily be so. Ypes wrote of the area in question, rejecting claims of a previous researcher that the area between Sagala and Pangururan was a no-man's-land: both territories disputed the area, said Ypes, and, "for some few years it has gone over to the *bius* of Pangururan" (1932:196). The Dutch had thus apparently supported the Pangururan claim.

In such previously contested areas, the rules of "permanent" tenure that apply to traditional Huta Ginjang lands are not observed. If a field is left fallow for five years, there is no need to ask permission to reopen it. Informants agreed that this was because the area had been the *golat* of the Pangururan people under the Dutch. There was at least one parcel in dispute: a newly-married Sagala (VI) let a crop in a pioneered field go to the birds and rats rather than agree to pay a tithe to a Pangururan man who appeared and made a claim after the first weeding.

The Lending of Land

The incidence of loan of fields is shown in Table 12.2. They were mostly loaned by those over 40, evenly spread from a genealogical standpoint and mostly to younger men.

TABLE 12.2
Lending of Fields

Fields lent to:	Fields lent by: Sagala	Wife-receivers of Sagala	Wife-givers of Sagala
Agnates	18	16	0
Own wife-givers	1	3	1
Own wife-receivers	14	3	4

Although the rules cited by Ypes for gaining access to fields were never referred to by villagers, it was made explicit that "here a man bears a grudge if he requests [to borrow] a field and it is not given."[3] How can Sahlins' claim that the "intensity of sharing is low" in Southeast Asian hinterland societies be assessed in the light of such a statement and the data on loan of fields? It could be countered that there are tangible rewards for generosity in "sharing" fields. For example, in one instance a man got the loan of an irrigable field from a neighbor with the promise that he would take it in pawn if the owner needed money (if his son was accepted at a city school). This was mutually beneficial, giving the borrower use of an irrigable field in the dry season and the lender a cash loan if he needed it; if not, the lender would get his field back the following season. Borrowing is usually of small parcels, generally for one crop of bulbs, whereas pioneering is of larger parcels, and the first crop planted is generally rice. Since the borrower often has the job of opening the field from fallow and leaves it to the owner in an easily worked state, loaning a field is not a one-

[3]Note that even among the "migratory" primary forest-cutting Iban, for whom land tenure is much less "stable" than for sedentary Batak, "token rental" (*tase damun*) is proffered as a means of shaming the recalcitrant to "lend" clearings for use of which, having felled the forest, they hold precedence (Freeman 1970:147-148). Likewise, among Kachin swiddeners, Leach notes (1965: 155) that "when [jungle land] is cleared the second time . . . some other lineage may use it, sometimes just by 'borrowing' it, sometimes on payment of a token rent."

sided act of generosity. This may explain why opening unclaimed fallow land is more extensively practiced than borrowing (see Table 6.2). While sharing of fields does not entirely benefit the one in need, the number of cases does not bear out the claim that intensity of sharing is low.

Sharecropping

Giving out irrigable fields to grow rice in return for a share of the crop is also common. For Huta Ginjang villagers, such sharecropping arrangements are a means of access to valley *sawah* and not to mountain dry fields. The practice is referred to as "splitting betel nut," *mamola pinang*. Landholders in this area demand one-third of the yield. They make no input of seed, fertilizer, or labor, but some help stamp the rice when invited to pick up their shares.

As was noted earlier, of 46 households that held one or more *sawah* (of whom 21 had taken one or more fields in pawn), over half gave out fields for sharecropping. Sixteen gave all their *sawah,* while nine others worked some themselves. About two-thirds of the owners of valley *sawah* living in Huta Ginjang, therefore, work some fields themselves, while slightly less than half work all that they hold. Many of those who gave fields to be sharecropped expressed some dissatisfaction, usually because their share was not a third but a quarter of what they were used to reaping. Most, however, did not intend to seek other sharecroppers because "no matter who, it is always that way" or because they did not want to cause a rift with kin by withdrawing permission to farm a field. Thus, although the agreed rate is one-third of the harvest, most field owners will accept a quarter.

Sharecropping has long been looked on as a feature of feudal-type social systems, as signaling the existence of a class of landlords with interests opposed to those of a class of tenants. Bray and Robertson (1980:211) point out that this view is common to traditional economic thinkers of several theoretical persuasions. Considered in these terms, its existence in Samosir would clearly tend to bear out Leach's landlord-tenant, feudal lord-vassal analogy. But Bray and Robertson make the case that the interests of both sharecropper and landowner are often complementary and that the existence of contraposed classes is called into question by charting the developmental cycle of the domestic group in relation to sharecropping. To take the example of Huta Ginjang, the first year all five household heads that sharecropped valley fields were under 27. The second year, two of these young men quit sharecropping, but two other men in their early forties began. One had pawned his own *sawah* to get a bridewealth payment together, and the other had moved to the valley to take a teaching post. As Bray and Robertson put it, sharecropping has an "episodic nature" in the life of households in Kelantan. So, too, in Samosir.

Pawning and the Question of Commoditization

The subject of pawning is germane to the question of whether commoditization of land has resulted from monetization. Landholders who emigrate may pawn some or all of their holdings or entrust them to the care of close kin. If this is done with wet-rice fields and the fields are used, the arrangement is typical of sharecropping, although not referred to as such. Only a few such arrangements were encountered. More frequently, an emigrant's fields are pawned to gather a sum of "capital" (*pongkot*; Indonesian, *pokok*) to set up an enterprise outside the village, usually farming or trading.

Others pawn fields to pay gambling debts, stage curing rites, or fund education. Vergouwen (1964:294) maintained that pledging of land by those going abroad was of recent provenance; yet, given the large indigenous lexicon on pawning, there is no reason to believe that precolonial emigration and trading ventures, even if undertaken by prominent hamlet headmen, were not, to some degree, financed by pawning land. Fields are pawned, given in pledge (*manggadehon*), or as security for loans of rice, gold, or money for a period (*janji*) averaging six to seven years. The minimum had, in fact, passed for most fields held in pawn, but there is no limit beyond which the right of redemption is lost. If the debt is never repaid, the field 'sticks fast' (to the one to whom it was given as security).

There is, then, a system of pawning "which may approximate sale," as Leach (1965:116) found among the Kachin. Nevertheless, land is not treated as real estate. It is not part of a factor market, and it has not become commoditized except insofar as it was already treated as a very special commodity, an aspect to which I will return in the next chapter.

The most frequent pawning arrangements in Huta Ginjang, as can be seen in Table 12.3, were between agnates of Sagala lineages. Clearly an effort is made to keep the tenure of land within a restricted circle. Among the 12 wife-givers to whom Sagalas pawned irrigable fields were father's mother's brother's sons and mother's father's brother's sons, as well as a brother's wife's brother. The wife-receivers who took fields in pawn from Sagala households included a son-in-law and two sister's husbands. The table also indicates that land is not inalienable lineage property, since fields are pawned to nonlineage mates and there is a possibility that one will not be redeemed. Indeed, pawning provides a way of denying access to land to close kin if they are unwilling to provide commensurate favors.

TABLE 12.3
Categories of Kin to Whom Fields Were Pawned

	Fields pawned by:		
Fields	Sagala	Wife-receivers of Sagala	Wife-givers of Sagala
Irrigable, pawned to:			
Agnates of same lineage	8	1	-
Other agnates	10	-	1
Own wife-givers	12	5	1
Own wife-receivers	5	-	1
Dry, pawned to:			
Agnates of same lineage	1	-	-
Other agnates	7	1	-
Own wife-givers	3	3	-
Own wife-receivers	7	-	-

During the time of the pledge, the creditor may have the field (a set of terraces) sharecropped or may pawn it to a third party,[4] though if the field is left for so long that the original creditor dies, problems may arise. Contracts written in Indonesian on a model introduced by the Dutch and revised in use typically make no stipulation of area, dimension, or amount of seed of particular terraced fields. They only list the owners of adjacent fields at the boundaries in the four cardinal directions, either by given name and clan, teknonym (e.g., father of X), or by using one type of name for some neighbors and a different type for others. One dispute involved a wet-rice terrace in Sagala Valley that had been pledged during the Japanese occupation (in 1944) for '500 stone money' (specie), which had been used to redeem a rice debt at the rate of 10 [pieces] per *kaleng* (20 liters). Thus, the amount of rice was supposed to have been 50 *kaleng*, but the son of the deceased creditor insisted that the rate had been 1.5 per *kaleng*—i.e., the loan could have purchased over 330 *kaleng* of rice. The deceased man who made the loan had, according to his son, allowed the field to be divided, so the indebted owner could use half because they were close friends. The owner claimed that he had repaid half the debt for that privilege and thus owed only 25 *kaleng* more. Since the creditor's son had repawned the remaining half for 200 *kaleng* of rice, he stood to have to redeem the balance of 175 *kaleng* himself. (The dispute was 'being taken to court,' although a year passed without any action coming to my attention.)

This sort of thing, however, is not evidence of a "factor market in land," land being simply a commodity or "real estate." We need to emphasize the lack of surveying, measuring, precise naming of neighboring fieldholders, etc., which were givens in pawns of land, and also

[4]In two instances, both involving members of different Sagala lineages, fields taken in pawn were "rented" back to the pawners before the loans were repaid. In neither case was payment to be deducted from the principal of the loans. I observed fields being worked by creditors in 1976-77; a year later, the pawner of the first planted a pepper crop for a payment of 60 liters of husked rice per year. The other began paying 70 liters of husked rice to plant coffee trees. He hoped to have the field producing a crop by the time he redeemed it. These were the only arrangements that might be construed as paying "interest" in land mortgaging. It is striking that rice, rather than cash, was the medium of "rent payments."

the degree to which pawning is limited to those in the local society. There is, as Leach said of the Kachin, "a system of pawn which approximates sale." Yet, when asked the amount of a loan they had made to acquire the use of a field, informants usually stated a figure and then added that the exact amount (in husked rice) was not significant because it was dependent on 'mutual wanting' (Indonesian, *mau sama mau*), on "complementary interests." This implies that (admittedly within limits) anyone who wants a field and has some resources can find one at the "right price." Conversely, needs of households that have disposal over fields may be met without reference to a precise standard of value of a given type, location, or area. Even though such standards probably exist, the fact that people add a caveat is significant.

An additional argument against considering the system of pawning as evidence of "a factor market in land" is that land as a rule is not mortgaged for subsistence purposes. Motives for pawning fields included paying for education, a trading or pioneer-agricultural enterprise, and medicine or other means of curing, such as certain feasts. One young man told me he would not have pawned his wet-rice field, which had been given to him when he established independence, "to buy food." "I pawned it," he said, "to be able to afford medical treatment."

Although in colloquial speech, pawning is often referred to as 'selling' and taking in pawn as 'buying,' further inquiry reveals an unspecified right of redemption upon repayment. But in newly pioneered areas on the mountain, a man can dispose of a grassland field he intends to leave the following year by a kind of sale that is referred to as 'leaving behind the hoe' (*martulak sangkul*), and the payment is said to be ' simply a sign' (*tanda*). One of the two men who opened and then "sold" a field (or the right to work such a field) spoke of the payment as the 'exchange of strength' (*tukar gogo*) and 'returning strength' (*paulak gogo*). Again, however, it is not the land being sold.[5]

Given the various means of access to land, it is not surprising that genealogical relationships do not entirely account for differences of

[5]For a parallel, see Gudeman (1978:26).

land holdings. As is seen in Table 12.4, developmental processes play a role as well. Sizes of all kinds of holdings tend to increase with age of household heads, up to age 55-60.

But as with ownership of livestock, available labor turns out to be a better index of households' landholdings than age of household heads. Despite inconsistencies, there is an even clearer tendency for households with more available labor to work greater areas of dry and irrigable land than there is for those of increasing age (see Table 12.5).

TABLE 12.4

Number of Households per Age Group Holding Valley Sawah, Irrigable Village and Dry Fields and Areas per Household (1977-78)

(r. = *rante*; 1 *rante* = 0.04 hectare)

Category	Age range of household heads (*N = number of households*)							
	19-24 (N=3)	25-30 (N=16)	31-36 (N=15)	37-42 (N=20)	43-48 (N=11)	49-54 (N=15)	55-60 (N=12)	61+ (N=19)
Number of holders	-	2	7	8	5	10	5	9
No. of *sawah* held	-	5	16	13	10	30	14	17
Sawah, irrigable fields in the Valley[a] (avg. area per household)	0	0.7r.	2.4r.	1.2r.	1.4r.	2.5r.	2.1r.	1.0r.
Number of holders	-	8	9	14	6	14	7	14
No. irrigable fields held	-	16	13	24	9	30	13	22
Irrigable fields in the village (avg. area per household)	0	1.9r.	1.7r.	2.1r.	2.0r.	4.8r.	2.4r.	2.1r.
Number of holders	3	16	15	20	11	15	12	19
No. of dry fields held	5	60	52	86	41	60	44	64
Dry fields in the village (avg. area per household)	12.8r.	21.9r.	21.8r.	30.6r.	23.7r.	31.5r.	26.2r.	21.5r.

[a]Areas are probably underreported for *sawah*. Note that the figures for the 31-36 group are skewed because two salaried men in that group have relatively large holdings.

TABLE 12.5
Correlation of Landholding and Labor Availability

	Available household labor quotients (*N = Number of households*)						
	"9—17" (N=13)	"—19—" (N=28)	"20—26" (N=14)	"27—30" (N=12)	"31—33" (N=12)	"34—38" (N=12)	"39—48" (N=15)
Number of holders	7	7	5	10	7	6	7
No. of *sawah* held	7	5	12	21	15	5	20
Sawah, irrigable fields in the Valley (avg. area per household)	0.6r.	1.1r.	1.3r.	1.5r.	2.2r.	2.4r.	2.1r.
Number of holders	6	14	12	11	10	7	12
No. irrigable fields held	9	24	18	20	17	16	23
Irrigable fields in the village (avg. area per household)	1.2r.	1.5r.	2.6r.	2.6r.	2.9r.	2.5r.	3.6r.
Number of holders	12	28	14	18	12	12	15
No. of dry fields held	28	89	61	70	51	50	63
Dry fields in the village (avg. area per household)	9.7r.	20.1r.	24.2r.	27.9r.	35.8r.	31.6r.	29.3r.

Exceptions are partly a reflection of differentials in access to desirable land on the basis of genealogical precedence.

Young men who are not oldest sons have the alternative of pioneering their own fields or leaving the village in search of land or employment. Most spend a part of their young adulthood working 'on the *ranto*,' for if their fathers are in good health and have younger children to rear, the stem family pre-empts most of the best land holdings. Judging from patterns of landholding by age and labor availability, especially of irrigable fields, and judging from life histories, men commonly leave the village, in effect, to await their fathers' "retirements" before returning to farm.

Ritual Prestation of Land

As we have seen, land is used in making a variety of gifts (to a daughter on the death of a parent, to a couple marrying intralocally, or to a son who is establishing independence).[6] Land is also sometimes given as bridewealth—at least in formal terms. The gift of land from wife-receivers to wife-givers as bridewealth seems to contravene the blessing function associated with such gifts of land, since a field is referred to as a 'shawl' field (*juma parulos*) when presented by wife-givers to a daughter and son-in-law. Vergouwen maintains that

> if land is included in the marriage payment, it is always as a pledge, *sindor* for a money debt, *sindor ni hepeng*. . . . It can be redeemed. . . . [Blessing shawls] themselves never form part of the marriage payment because these cloths come from the [wife-givers]. (1964:197)

In other words, it would be unthinkable for a wife-receiver to bestow a woven shawl on a wife-giver. Yet, while land is not always put forward in the litany of bridewealth demands—"Give us cows, horses, buffaloes, gold, money"—the notion of fields as bridewealth is not considered anomalous. However, I differ with Vergouwen's claim that land in bridewealth is explicitly associated with an outstanding debt. To say that land may be included in bridewealth payments only "as a pledge for a money debt" is to admit that it may generally be included, since postponement of full payment—outstanding debt—is the rule rather than the exception. (This, incidentally, corresponds to the usual lack of balanced exchange of the sort that Sahlins rightly maintains is "unstable" (1972:223) but mistakenly considers prevalent in hinterland Southeast Asia.)

The demand for a field in the bridewealth session for one marriage was prominent and its resolution revealing. The major themes of this chapter are drawn together in, and further clarified by, this episode: on one hand, the role of marriage as a means of effecting access to land is highlighted, and on the other hand, the specific character of land as a

[6]On gifts of land, see Ypes (1932:208-209) and Vergouwen (1964:61, 331).

good in "Batak economy" takes on definition. It becomes clear that rice terraces are "valuables" in a "prestige sphere of exchange," a theme I will develop more fully in the next chapter.

A prominent Sagala man's second daughter eloped with the second of four sons of a Sinaga family originally established in its own territory above the crater rim. The family of the groom had resided for generations in Limbong Valley as wife-receivers of a Limbong subclan and had a house in Limbong more substantial than any in Huta Ginjang. Negotiations were carried out over a period of several weeks following the elopement, and finally the family of the groom came to 'pay *adat*.' When both sides had eaten the prepared meat and rice, they sat down opposite each other.

> Sagala speaker for the bride's parents: A moment ago we asked for a cow, a buffalo, with a horse, in addition to this money. And I think you said, 'We have no cows.' But as for a field (*juma*), well, husbands-of-our-women, you must make one over.
>
> Sinaga speaker for the groom's parents: On the high plateau, forest land, [with] trees on it, we have that.
>
> Sagala: That's not what I am looking for.
>
> Sinaga: What then? That's where our land is.
>
> Sagala: Land in Limbong, land in Limbong!
>
> Sinaga: There is no land of ours in Limbong. There are bought fields.
>
> Sagala: But in my opinion you must make over one opened by that husband-of-our women there [i.e., an ascendant of the groom].
>
> Wife-giver of the family of the groom: Excuse me. . . . As for the field you request, the descent of my son-in-law here is from Parbuluan [on the high plateau]. As for a field, there is one, but in Parbuluan. As for that field, don't worry, there is that.

No objection is raised concerning the propriety of the request per se; it is accepted as a valid one, with an offer of land, however undesirable. Aware of the resources of the family of the groom, however, the family of the bride refuses:

> Sagala: Make it proper. We know precisely . . . the place of our daughter's husband; he is a landholder in Parbuluan, he has his rights (*adong hakna*) there, but he has rights in Limbong. Show us that.

Some of those on the bride's parents' side at a 'wide-mat' bridewealth session.

Sinaga: We have no right to show that, we have no rights there.

Wife-giver of the groom's father: Oh, sirs, as for this daughter's husband, he is not of the land in Limbong. We 'rule over' this person (*na hinomit hami halak on*) in Limbong.

The groom's family insists over and over that it has no right to land in Limbong. (As one informant put it, "They have fields but cannot give them to others; one must have a hamlet to be able to give land.") But the bride's side is not deterred. One of her father's clansmen calls out, "A field taken in pawn will do." This is followed by further interchanges, and then the speaker for the bride's father reiterates the seriousness of the request:

Sagala: Think, husbands-of-our-women, because the words of your in-law [i.e., the bride's father] before, were, 'You must get them to agree to one field, in addition to that cash' . . . 'Be it taken in pledge, or however, so long as it is what is called a field (*asal ma na margoar juma*) that is in Limbong.' . . . Do not imagine that I'm making this up alone.

Sinaga: God [may strike us] if we lie. As for my fields in Parbuluan, there are some, I can show them any day.

At this point, the first admission is made by one of the groom's uncles that they may possess fields in Limbong. He invokes the livelihood of his brother, the groom's father:

> Sinaga-2: To add to the words of this father . . . even if there is a field of the father-in-law of your daughter here, will not your wife-receivers live anymore . . . to care for your son-in-law while waiting for him to establish independence? Would you be at ease [if] that [were to happen]? Supposing he gave it over. . . . Will only you eat? Won't these grandchildren of yours eat? That is in addition to [the fact] there are no [fields] . . . none!

The reply contains a subtle qualification in the demand—the *naming* of a field is desired:

> Sagala: As for your answer, we are not about to pick it up and bring that field of yours here. Its name, so long as you make over a field.

A clanmate of the bride's father adds, "Because our son-in-law [the groom] there is the second-born." This speaks directly to the question, "Will only you eat?" The covert reason for the demand is a precaution

Some of those on the groom's side at such a 'wide-mat' bridewealth session, with kin and neighbors of the bride standing and looking on, listening to the repartee.

The bride (rear) sits flanked by women on the groom's side during negotiations.

that the groom, the second-born of four brothers, not be dispossessed in inheritance, which favors eldest and youngest at the expense of "middle" brothers.

> Wife-giver of the groom's father: I understand your request. . . . That is why we are speaking with care here.
>
> Sagala-3: That is why you came along to order things. . . . If [the groom] were the eldest, there would be no need for us to speak in that way here.
>
> Wife-giver of the groom's father: If there is [a field in Limbong], it goes to him [the groom].
>
> Sinaga (groom's grandfather): If there is [a field], to your son-in-law, to your daughter there, God is our witness now!

In other words, they protest that it is the groom himself who is their favorite.

The whole assembly of Huta Ginjang villagers now joins in the banter, and the mother of the groom calls out, "That's right, all you fathers, do not fear. I will give secure land (*tano hot*) to your son-in-law!" And the bride's father's older brother responds with feigned amusement:

Sagala: Are you through, father's sister?

A little while ago I heard you wife-receivers' voices: 'There is a field in Limbong. But our father's sister is already aged, what would she work?' Now, what I say is this. From the very start, the words of our older brother from here said, 'When in a gathering, prestige (*iang*) is what one fetches, prestige is what is delivered' (*iang do na nialap, iang do na tinaruhon*). . . . And it is prohibited for us to demand what is called secure land (*tano hot*). But even if so, that which you took in pawn even, that is in Limbong, as long as it is what is called a field. It is not that we want to carry it up here, or that we want to work it. But since you have come here 'making prestige' (*mariang*), well, it seems to me that whatever we request, you have to deliver, even if it is merely one.

In effect, the bride's uncle downplays the covert reason for a field as a precaution to protect the bride's livelihood, and he emphasizes the overt prestige enhancement. Indeed, it is too late to withdraw the demand, as would normally have been done at such a show of recalcitrance. The bride's father's brother, however, renounces using or taking a tithe of the produce of the field demanded. Thus he concedes to the groom's family that they are not able to transfer land in Limbong. But he continues,

Sagala: We ask for a buffalo, there is none; we ask for gold, there is none; we ask for a cow, there is none. [You say] 'We are not of the land in Limbong.' We know you are not of the land there. And the secure (*hot*) [field] that you mention [on the high plateau], of a *kaleng* seed, we know it. But the soft, there (*na mura i*), we persist in requesting, but the soft too, there is none. It is as though we were constantly contesting each other. Here, father's sister, our hearts are continually seeking at random (*lulu-lulu rohanami*).

These last querulous remarks, including a play on 'secure,' 'firm,' rights to land, as opposed to 'soft' (i.e., irrigable), 'easy' and 'cheap,' rouse the village spectators to laughter. The bride's uncle calls, "All of us are laughing, husbands-of-our-women. Don't you see us laughing?" This infuriates the groom's grandfather:

Sinaga: Always a field! Always a field! God made people who are willing to be satisfied. . . . This [lot], always a field, always a field! How was I to know [it would be like this]? I, too, now, if I release [the source of] my living expenses, thanks (*molo hupalua balanjongku, mauliate*)!

When another clanmate of the father of the bride calls, "Fetch your heart, husband-of-our-women, the one you took in pawn in '73, give that one!" he responds, faster and more furiously:

Sinaga: How was that? Is this not a gathering of men? . . . 'Fetch your heart, fetch your heart!' . . . My heart has not gone anywhere, it is here. [If] you say it until tomorrow, there is none, as for fields. [The groom's] older brother's debts are many too. How is this one going to pay them? . . . Now I make reverence to wife-givers. Now, it is impossible to divide the fields because I am still living. That's it in a word.

But the derisive banter continues, a woman married to a distant clanmate of the bride's father shouting above the rest:

Prestige is what is delivered! [For] prestige, give one of them. Don't be afraid, it will remain over there, that field. . . . Oh, mother of Limbong. Do not be like the immovable you mother of Limbong, that field, bah!

"I am not immovable," came the reply (of the groom's mother?), and the following exchange between the two women quickly passed:

They already said, 'a field taken in pawn,' give it!

Always giving, even if it is not one's land!

Prestige is taken, you get prestige, we get prestige. We are not going to drag it up here, that [field].

Suddenly, the groom's father's wife-giver, who had been conferring with those around him, put an end to the matter:

Wife-giver of the groom's father: Well, here it is. There is one field in Limbong, 'The Hoeing Road' [is the location], but its name is not here. Ask me for that. . . . But it is taken in pawn, sirs. One terrace, a broad terrace.

Immediately, a distant clanmate of the bride's father queries:

Sagala-4: How much is its seed, daughter's husband?

Wife-giver of the groom's father: Its seed is sixteen liters.

The speaker for the father of the bride replies:

> Sagala: That is the life of our daughter (*Ngolu ni borunami do i*).

He concludes with appropriate thanks for the compliance shown.

The demand for transfer of a subsistence resource is at first refused from a "politico-jural" point of view: "We 'rule over' this person in Limbong" (*na hinomit hami . . .*), says their wife-giver. Then it is rejected because of subsistence needs ("Will only you be the ones to eat?") and because, as the groom's grandfather puts it, "Now, it is impossible to divide the fields because I am still living. That's it in a word." When the demand is attributed to concern for the well-being of the new couple, reassurances are quickly forthcoming, and when this is followed by a speaker for the bride's parents asserting prestige enhancement for both parties and forswearing use of the field, the impatient banter forces the groom's family to acquiesce. This is done in a statement by the wife-giver of the groom's family, who takes it upon himself over the obstinacy of the grandfather. Thus, while the gift of land is ostensibly a bridewealth payment, it also serves, as Vergouwen put it of dowry, "so the bride will be held in esteem," as well as for a resource to sustain and nurture her new household.

The fact that there was an outstanding debt of a promised cash payment of bridewealth on this occasion does not truly account for the gift of land, as Vergouwen claimed (1964:197). While the field is a bridewealth payment, it is not given to the bride's father; 'rights' to use a field held in pawn are publicly renounced in favor of the new couple. They are to use it without impediment from or payment to the bride's family, to whom title has ostensibly passed, and if such a field is redeemed, the principal would go to the new couple, enabling them to take another field in pawn as a replacement. This gift of land as bridewealth thus served to effect the guarantee of an inheritance to a second-born son. It is an example of how the many-sided relationships that comprise village society are based on and interwoven with the complex web of landholding.

Access to Land and Self-Sufficiency in Rice

Many of the quantitative findings regarding access to land appear remarkably predictable. Sagala clan households have on the whole inherited a more favorable position than have their affines, but the Sagalas' holdings could be attributed in part to the effects of age and available labor rather than clan membership per se. To the extent that for all Sagalas, as opposed to all others, there still appears to be greater-than-average access to resources—given the small size of the sample, statistical "proofs" are not called for—certain differences of allocation among village households may be said to be culturally determined, resulting from the body of values that include the principles of clan organization and ritual perquisites of activities involving the earth.

It appears that differences stem originally from degrees of access to irrigable land. This is borne out by data on "self-sufficiency in rice" (by clan, age group, and labor availability) and on "strategies" of rice growing (Appendix D). The percentages of each clan grouping—Sagalas, their wife-givers, and their wife-receivers—at given levels of self-sufficiency in rice are very similar. Likewise, the scattered occurrences of self-sufficiency in the age groups and according to labor available indicate that neither criterion is a determinant of the level of surplus in rice production. This is not unexpected, since so many households apply much effort to crops whose prices have not been affected by government price controls, unlike the case of rice since Dutch times (Timmer 1975, *passim*). While some do without and a few men work for wages for as many as 60 days a year, most make up their rice deficit by purchase from the proceeds of other crops.

The data on the rice-growing strategies pursued and their relative success (App. D) also show a fairly even spread by age and available labor, but this is not so by clan. Half as many Sagala households grow only dry rice as do households headed by men of other clans. This is a clear reflection of their greater access to irrigable land. The same applies to the fact that 17 percent of Sagalas, but only 12.4 percent of others, grow a substantial surplus of rice. Yet, since the differences among clan groupings in terms of production are relatively small and the distribution of well-off, average, and poor households is not restricted to any clan or kin categories, it may be argued that Samosir Batak village society is highly differentiated but also highly integrated. People live in close proximity, maintain separate productive activities, grow apart in their capacities, holdings, and endeavors but continue the social cycle without extreme stratification.

PART V

MODELING SAMOSIR BATAK ECONOMY

The Toba Batak of Samosir had a rather complicated economy even before they were colonized by the Dutch. In their markets, rice was the general medium of exchange, but coins minted by distant states, though not serving as a general means of payment, were used to purchase certain valuables, to pay bridewealth, and for other ceremonial prestations. People made formal loans of either rice or cash. They made some loans at interest and others interest-free. They pawned rice terraces. They participated in joint ownership of livestock. (Many of these, as has been shown, are still common practices.) Although they were not primarily producers for the market, they had externally oriented markets and exported agricultural and forest products, apparently including rice and livestock and some manufactures. A small proportion of the population lived in debt-bondage to local "big men," or, as they put it, 'rich ones,' na mora.

Throughout my description of Batak society and culture in the Mount Pusuk Buhit area of Samosir, I have referred back to the issues of the extent and significance of monetization and of class and hierarchy that were raised in the Introduction. While money, in conjunction with other changes, certainly makes mobility easier and opens different options for livelihood than were available before modern times, it is my view—given the resilience of Batak society and of its cultural constructs of the world, which I have tried to establish—that the uses and effects of money have been more limited than might be indicated by the importance of cash for market transactions, travel, schooling, emigration, and even ritual. The question is, How may the cultural persistence be explained? or, How can it be best understood?

The explanation I propose is one that returns us to our point of departure: Viewing the sociocultural whole of Samosir Batak livelihood in terms of a "spheres of exchange" model requires—and at the same time helps make possible—an adequate account of the role of rice in the economy. Among other things, this will allow an answer to the question of why market women would not accept cash for goods in Pangururan in 1913. More importantly, it will provide a coherent framework for synthesizing the data of the three interpretive frameworks with which we began: the role of rice in Batak economy; the political economy of feasting; and the cultural ecology of both wet- and dry-rice growing. In the ensuing discussion, their joint roles in Batak livelihood will be shown to rest on their parts in a cultural system with wider, Monsoon Asian ramifications.

Chapter 13

Reciprocity and Spheres of Exchange in Batak Economy

In this chapter, I will apply and consider the merits of an economic anthropological model—spheres of exchange—which provides a way of coming to grips with the aspects of traditional hierarchy and inequality that still exist—that are in some ways integral to Batak culture—and of relating Samosir Batak beliefs and values to the material and social realities of their livelihood. In addition, it provides a means for appreciating the strong and persistent social value placed on rice in Batak and perhaps other Southeast Asian societies.

A theory or model of an economy characterized by distinct spheres of exchange—in which prestige goods comprise one level in a hierarchy of goods—was first spelled out by Raymond Firth in 1939. Writing of the Tikopia, he proposed that

> [a]t the lowest level . . . objects such as arm-rings . . . are paid for by food. . . . On the next level is the bark-cloth [and] sinnet [rope] series. . . . The third . . . is that including bonito-hooks, turmeric cylinders and canoes. . . .
>
> Apart from the three spheres of exchange mentioned a fourth may be recognized in cases where *goods of unique quality* are handed over. . . . Women and land are given in satisfaction of unique obligations. (Firth 1965:340-344, emphasis added)

Firth maintained that an attempt to analyze such a system in what might be called "formal" terms is ill-considered:

> Because the goods or services in these different spheres of exchange cannot be expressed fluidly in terms of each other, the cost of production cannot be measured exactly against exchange value. Theoretically it would seem that one should be able ultimately, by considering the various exchange transactions into which a canoe enters, to relate the value of a canoe to its cost of production in terms of that of the other items . . . and to find some common measure in the labor involved. In practice this is never done by the Tikopia. . . .
>
> [A]n attempt at constructing theoretical equations in terms of comparative costs of these items would distort the native economic ideas. (Firth 1965:341-343)

I will adopt roughly the same distinctions and refer to a Samosirese subsistence-goods sphere, a prestige-goods sphere, and a sphere of goods "of unique quality" (cf. Bohannan 1955 and Salisbury 1962).

If the process of Batak feasting is viewed in the most general terms, it can be considered a series of formalized acts of prestation and presumed or concrete counter-prestation, between humans and ancestral spirits and between people in various relationships to each other's households. I encountered the term for prestige (*iang*) only in the context of feasting and particularly with respect to ritual prestations. In the bridewealth session involving the gift of a field, that involving a quarter of a cow, and the youngest daughter's inheritance on the death of her mother, explicit appeals were made to the prestige of making the gifts. What is striking about their prestige sphere, viewing the Batak data in light of a spheres of exchange model, is that resources or factors of production—land, livestock, and capital (e.g., gold and specie)—are used as prestige commodities. An analogous situation is found among such groups as the Kachin and Ifugao.[1] In the next few

[1]In discussing concepts of property and ownership, Leach notes the Kachin use of trade (*hpaga*) objects that "may form part of . . . tributary dues." He also refers to *hpaga* as "ritual wealth objects" and "items which are specified in a statement of claim" (1965:143-144, 146). These *hpaga*, including gongs, swords, silver bullion, slaves, cloth, iron pots, silk coats, and special bead necklaces, are given along with cattle. He notes that "a few of these items are sometimes dealt with in the open market but, in the ordinary way, ritual wealth objects of this kind only change hands on certain set occasions . . . (a) marriages, (b) funerals, (c) in payment of ritual services . . . (d) on the occasion of a transfer of residence (e) as judicial compensation" (Leach 1965:147). The first three instances could easily refer to Batak blessing shawls.

Of Kachin *gumsa* land tenure, we learn that the "rights of ownership that pertain to a chief

pages I will discuss specie, livestock, shawls, and land from this perspective.

Specie, Livestock, and Blessing Shawls

In the early years of Dutch administration of the Samosir area, market women would not accept specie in payment of subsistence goods (Middendorp 1913:16). It appears that specie was a commodity handled only by men—it was men who bought the livestock for which Middendorp listed guilder prices at market. Both coins and livestock were prestige commodities used, for instance, as bridewealth.

Livestock is used as a prestige commodity, both for sacrificial offerings to spirits and, cut up in named portions, divided among guests according to relationship to the principals. But, again, the fact that the Samosirese quoted livestock prices in specie in the markets of Middendorp's time (1911-1913) and the substantial export that continued throughout Dutch rule suggests that there was a traditional export of livestock from this savannah region to the heavily forested surrounding areas.

Batak blessing shawls (*ulos*) are also a traditional prestige good that Middendorp found to have market prices quoted in guilders (i.e., silver specie). As is the case with livestock, their presumably higgle-haggle marketability, the fact that he could get prices quoted in guilders, is not anomalous, since the specie for which shawls were exchanged was also a prestige good, perhaps one of the rarest. It may be that then, as now, almost any adult could assess the exchange value of any shawl in cash—granted, of course, that bargainers often disagree

---

. . . . rest with the members of a particular lineage. . . . [T]ransfer must be carried through in ritual fashion with an appropriate exchange of *hpaga*" (Leach 1965:155).

Among the Ifugao, as Hoebel summarizes Barton, "Property is of two kinds: that which requires and that which does not require an *ibuy* ceremony to effect alienation. . . . *Ibuy* property is of three orders: 1) rice fields; 2) heirlooms, consisting of gold neck ornaments, strings of glass, agate, and bloodstone beads, rice wine jars, gongs . . . ; 3) forest lands" (Hoebel 1968:105; see also Barton 1919:46-50).

as to value—for shawls were also exported to "all surrounding regions."

The shawls were not only prestige goods but also, to a degree, utilitarian items in a society where hand weaving made cloth too rare for daily use. That is, such heirlooms were stored away, as they are now, and worn for special occasions. Some of lower grade were used daily to carry children on the back. Now trousers and dresses prevail where bark cloth was once the norm, yet shawls remain utilitarian items, as well as prestige commodities and gifts that can be sold and resold within a fairly widespread area for a fairly fixed price, in cash (adjusted to the going price of rice). Every market has stalls, often row upon row, draped in a fortune's worth of shawls. This does not appear to be drastically different from precolonial markets, except that shawls would then have been stored in homes.

Since these traditional valuables required time and materials, as well as skill and patience, women who wove them could only do so in a situation of relatively predictable "income," protected, in the first instance, from the uncertainties of want. Their production signals a relatively successful trade and a defined subsistence base. On the other hand, deficiencies of the agricultural system, hampered by an uncertain water supply in the growing of the preferred crop (rice), may have helped give rise to the prominence of weaving in Samosir Batak livelihood.

But even before the market for shawls arose, they were goods made to be alienated from their direct producers. They were cloths made by women, to be given, by their fathers or their husbands (and sometimes by themselves), to wife-receivers, to daughters and daughters' husbands, daughters' sons, husband's sisters and sisters' sons, husband's father's sisters' sons, etc. Since only a shawl received from wife-givers has value as a source of blessings in Batak ideology, a weaver of shawls must have looked to her mother or brothers' wives for her own public dress.

Whether most Samosir women wove full-time and did no agricultural work, as some Dutch observers claimed, or whether those observations were of exceptional areas or based on off-season activities, there was undeniably an export from Samosir. Those who required shawls for social ritual, whether in this area or in neighboring areas, apparently created the demand evidenced by traditional market exchange. People's pleasure in precious cloths and their liquid nature (as with the more durable jewelry) characterize their use among Batak, as do such forms of wealth among Javanese (Dewey 1962:96-97; Siegel 1986:179-184). Other sentiments and beliefs are involved in the value placed on them: the belief in the power of ritual prestation of shawls to convey blessings remains strong. This is so, even though many *ulos* bestowed by wife-givers of a feast principal are now machine-made. As those bestowing them often say in the remarks leading up to their rhymed-couplet blessings, "This shawl was made in one day," or, "The mothers no longer weave in the hamlet, due to the price of shallots. As a result, this is a shawl bargained for from the market. But although it be thin, may it be heat to your flesh!"

The character of precious cloths as prestige goods is thus a function of the modes of agricultural production that made them possible and of their sentimental value as conveyors of blessings. It is also tied to their being an export, a commercial commodity. Given the export of shawls and livestock, there was clearly a precolonial trade in prestige commodities in the markets of the area.

Jewelry may also serve as a gift or bequest, as can be seen from the discussion that followed a "soul-strengthening" ritual meal for a woman who had been badly burned. In my notes, I wrote that "her husband now believes that his pawning of her heirloom necklaces against the advice of the *dukun* (augurer) has had the predicted result, and he is full of remorse and intends to redeem them." Although the cash for which the necklaces were pawned had been for a son's schooling, an analogy may be drawn with the Tiv view of the undesirability and, in some sense, the immorality of "converting down" (Bohannan 1955). Like specie, rice, and jewelry, shawls could also have been hoarded, and they have more of an heirloom quality, particularly because they are prominent in "death dues" payments.[2]

Parcels of Land

As has been seen, parcels of land are not alienable among the Samosir Batak except in circumstances that show land set apart, a special class of resource that may be used, like shawls, as benedictory gifts. Land is not part of a factor market, at least in the homeland. It may be said to serve as insurance against hard times (in that it may be pawned), but that is not an entirely satisfactory characterization of its place in Batak culture. They consciously view land as the basis for future livelihood, of the highly valued descendants of every potential line. Fields given in public ritual, as to a daughter on the death of her mother or in bridewealth, are called 'paths of life.'

The reasons for pawning land invariably involve what Bohannan (1955) termed "conveyance"—exchange *within* (in this instance) the prestige sphere, as opposed to "conversion" *between* spheres. That is to say, land was pawned to cover expenses associated with illness (including curing feasts), education, pioneering abroad, and trading enterprises. (Given the traditional place of traders in this "peripheral market" society as acquirers of highly valued metals, weapons, salt, and other items such as Chinese pottery and gongs, the pawning of land to start a trading venture appears congruent with its culturally defined values, particularly because many imports served as prestige commodities in effecting marriages.) Granting their metaphor, all these

[2]To forestall any claim that this makes the hinterland Batak "distinctive" with respect to a "sociology of primitive exchange," I should note that the Trobriand *kula*, after all, involves exchange of prestige goods. Regarding Batak *ulos* (shawls), there is, on the one hand, as noted above, a comparison with Javanese batik cloths to be made. Both batik and gold jewelry serve as "a very liquid form of savings" among Javanese peasants (Dewey 1962:97). On the other hand, the question of "inalienability" (i.e., non-transferability), see also Weiner (1985), who describes traditional uses of Maori cloaks and nephrite congruent with a "spheres of exchange" model. Like Batak shawls, which are still used in disinterments, Maori cloaks were used to wrap bones of the deceased, and both cloaks and nephrite were "payments for ceding land title," "payment to religious experts," and "[c]ompensation for crimes" (Weiner 1985:219). There are correspondences here with the Kachin and Ifugao data cited in note 1, above.

purposes represent possible paths to a continuation and increase of the prosperity of descendants inherent in the Batak notion of livelihood (*hangoluan*). In a sense, the prestige sphere, like that of "goods of unique quality," is comprised of items that call forth magical-religious power, the source of prosperity.

The lack of a true factor market in land, as was noted, is borne out by the contention that the amount given for the pledge of a field was based on the need of the pledger and the ability to comply of the pledgee (*mau sama mau*, mutual wanting). Again, as noted earlier, when I expressed surprise that an informant had pawned his *panjaean* ('establishing-independence') rice terrace, the young man said defensively that he would not have done so "to buy food," but he had been forced to do so to meet the expenses associated with curing. This brings an indigenously recognized subsistence sphere into focus, a sphere defined in opposition to one of what are literally prestige "goods" that appear to be considered of greater importance than immediate subsistence. The cultural bias against the pawning of land for subsistence purposes defines the subsistence realm of the economy by excluding it from transactions within the realm of prestige goods and services.

In a similar vein, among the Ifugao,

> [F]amily fields may be sold if necessary to buy sacrificial animals to accompany the spirit of a deceased ancestor [or] to bring about the recovery of a family member from a dangerous illness. . . . Rather than sell a field, a trustee who needs goods to set up a funeral feast, or make sacrifices, or to pay a fine . . . will if it is at all possible, obtain a loan on a piece of his land, pledging it to his creditor as security on the debt. (Hoebel 1968:106-107; see also Barton 1922:419)

Barton also noted that "all [Ifugao] real estate values are measured by [the media] of pigs and water buffalo" (1922:430), and parallels are found among the Toraja as well (Volkman 1985:72, 104-105). In each case, as among the Batak, land is a prestige commodity, but this does not put it beyond the pale of exchange.

Critique of the "Moral Economy" View of Traditional Rice Trade

As was noted in the Introduction, M. Sahlins claimed that hinterland Southeast Asian societies were "distinctive" from ancient times:

> They are . . . engaged by petty market trade . . . to more sophisticated cultural centers. From the perspective of the advanced centers, they are backwaters serving as secondary sources of rice and other goods. . . . From the hinterlands view, the critical aspect of the intercultural relation is that the subsistence staple, rice, is exported for cash, iron tools, and prestige goods, many of the last quite expensive. It is suggested . . . that the peculiar social-economic character of Southeast Asian hinterland tribes is congruent with this unusual deployment of household subsistence surpluses. (Sahlins 1965:179)

What is the "peculiar" social-economic character of hinterland tribes? What makes it different from a characteristically Melanesian one? Surely the Trobriand *kula* trade requires deployment of subsistence surpluses, and, although their valued items are not products of a civilized center, they also give prestige when used in exchange. But Sahlins argues that

> the implication of an external trade in rice is not merely an internal ban on sharing it, or a corresponding requirement of *quid pro quo* in intracommunity dealings, but departure from ordinary characteristics of primitive distribution in virtually all respects.
>
> The engagement with the market makes a key minimal demand: that internal community relations permit household accumulation of rice, else the amounts required for external exchange will never be forthcoming. . . . [I]f internal leveling is encouraged then the external trade relations are simply not sustained. (Sahlins 1965:179-180; 1972:224)

Many of Sahlins' generalizations appear to characterize the Batak, as well as the Kachin, the Ifugao, and others. It would be as applicable of traditional Batak society (at many times, in many areas) to say, as he does of the Bornean Dayak:

> Prestige apparently hinges on obtaining exotic items—Chinese pottery, brass gongs, etc.—from the outside in exchange for rice or work. Prestige does not, obviously cannot, rest on generous assistance to one's fellows in the manner of

> a tribal big-man. . . . As a result there are no strong leaders. (Sahlins 1972:226)

But aside from the fact that powerful and renowned leaders do arise from time to time among the Batak, Kachin, Ifugao, and others (and aside from the added fact that a number of scholars have claimed that their feasts and those of others less powerful are redistributive), Sahlins' view fails to confront the fact that these peoples need to produce more than enough to eat; they need enough to save a "surplus" of rice for making gifts in many contexts, as an a priori of social life (see Scott 1976:9). Thus, in a sense, there has always been "a market" for rice, even before it was used in interregional and international exchange. That is, there have always been people needing more rice, episodically, than they had, and willing to give up valuables for it.

Another significant problem with Sahlins' focus on rice is that it ignores other hinterland exports, including jungle products such as benzoin, camphor, lac, and rattan, which were probably often more prominent than rice in the overall balance of trade (see, e.g., Lehman 1963:167-168; Wolters 1967, chs. 7-8). To focus on rice export to the exclusion of other means of obtaining the products of "more sophisticated cultural centers" and, in particular, to draw "moral economy"-confirming conclusions based on a sometime characteristic seems to be a dubious enterprise. It distorts both the internal characters and the external situations of these societies.

While "sharing in favor of need" occurs among people in all societies, Sahlins gives the impression that it is much more general in Melanesia than in Southeast Asia. This may be, but it is not borne out by such observations as those of Pospisil on the Kapauku Papuans, among whom "some natives, especially children from poor homes . . . develop severe symptoms of undernourishment, while individuals from prosperous households are well fed" (Pospisil 1963b:403). Nor is it borne out by Sahlins' own observation that the Melanesian leader "[deploys] his resources carefully" and "uses wealth to place others in his debt" (1972:136; cf. Sahlins 1960:405-406).

Sahlins also fails to take account of the key difference between tubers and cereal crops, particularly rice. Let us pause and go back for a moment. Note that Sahlins' viewpoint on the socioeconomic effects of rice export is entirely in keeping with that of Polanyi. Based on the same outlook, formed by Malinowski and Mauss, regarding reciprocity as the most fundamental source and expression of human nature,[3] Sahlins goes further than Polanyi. He is not saying just that production for exchange has a certain effect socially, as Polanyi does, but that the production of a specific good—rice—for exchange—does so. This is so particularly because rice is *food*. What could be shared, says Sahlins, is instead hoarded and then traded out.[4] But this is merely one of its aspects (see Gudeman and Penn 1982). A broad-brush account of the centrality of rice in Asian societies is necessary in order to account for its strong and enduring social value. The following outline of the terms in which rice in Asia may be said to have higher "social value" than any other crop is also fundamental to the third major interpretive framework in this study: the cultural ecology of its cultivation by unusual, dry-field methods as well as in flooded terraces.

It is something of a cliché to regard rice in Asia as having a special significance, since it is the preferred staple in much of the area that includes China, Japan, India, and Southeast Asia. It is time to enunciate the aspects that have contributed to this widespread taste preference.

In the first place, rice stores very well, especially when kept in the husk. By contrast, corn gets worms in tropical areas, and most tubers rot in a short time after they are dug. Storability makes rice a potential medium of exchange, since it has intrinsic value as food, but whereas rice could serve indefinitely as a store of value,[5] relative to rice, even

[3]See Meeker, Barlow, and Lipset (1986); and Mitchell (1988), on the relevance of gambling.

[4]In a sense, Sahlins is simply echoing Lévi-Strauss' observations, based on the Bemba example (Richards 1939:199-200), preparatory to his theory of "exchange of women," viz., that in view of the alternation of seasons of plenty with those of great want, "it is not unusual that primitive thought should be incapable of regarding food 'as something which could be procured, owned, and consumed by one individual alone. . . .' " (Lévi-Strauss 1969:33).

[5]Akira Oki (1977:43, 1984:100-101) reports records of Dutch observations in South Sumatra in the 1910s of thousands of tons of inherited stocks of heirloom rice, some of which were 100 years of age. The Dutch requisitioned it to feed corvée labor engaged in road building. (I am grateful to Dr. Tsuyoshi Kato for bringing these sources to my attention.)

yams keep only temporarily—six months (Weiner 1976:138). This contrast has broad cultural ecological ramifications.

To ensure its reproduction, an agricultural community must be able to provide its food in the off-season and particularly during years of pestilence or drought. As Meillassoux notes (1981:26), for societies that grow mainly tubers, "[i]t is not possible to accumulate reserves for several years." Yet,

> the ability to keep enough in reserve to cover a period roughly equal to the greatest length of probable catastrophe indicates the minimum productivity that agriculture must reach [to guarantee repetition of the cycle]. In this respect, it is clear that cereals, storable for a period much longer than the agricultural cycle, lend themselves to the development of the domestic community far more than do root crops. (Meillassoux 1981:34)

This contrast of the characteristics of basic staples is ultimately a contrast of the ecological "holdings" of Southeast Asian as opposed to Melanesian peoples. The inherent differences between rice and tubers do have implications, but not those that Sahlins claims. The qualities of rice as a compact and storable food, a natural store of exchange value, predisposed it to being traded in the marketplace.

We can get a better purchase on the role of rice in shaping the socioeconomic character of Batak society by considering the fact that, although rice is the only starch fit to serve in any formal gathering, it is not the only subsistence staple. Marsden reported that by 1772 corn was grown by Batak of the interior as a frequent substitute for rice (1811:371). Indeed, according to the observer whom he cites, "The ordinary food of the lower class of people is maiz [sic] and sweet potatoes; the *rajas* and great men alone indulging themselves with rice. Some mix it together" (1811:380)—perhaps a majority, in fact, did so. And Burton and Ward (1827) reported substantial cultivation of tubers in 1824. Thus, even households whose rice production was greater than their staple needs could rely on other starches for subsistence and save their rice for ritual (in which case it would be consumed locally), to dispose of in trade, or to loan at interest.

Because rice stores so well, it serves as insurance, which gives it special value. Those who grow more rice than need and prudence require can easily dispose of the surplus. Both storage quality and attractiveness in trade are also partly the result of its compactness. That, in turn, makes it easily measurable in any given volume measure.

The storability of rice in the husk compared with that of tubers or corn provides a potential guarantee of societal survival in the event of widespread natural disasters in any given year. Cultivation of wet rice flourished in Asia in part because it provided such guarantees. But, looked at in broad, area-wide perspective, this was probably accomplished not only through on-site storage but also through trade, at first intraregional and, later, interregional and international. At some point, trade and perhaps tribute became the main means by which lowland civilizations based on rice cultivation came to guarantee their survival—by drawing on hinterland surpluses—in case of widespread flooding or drought.

For those hinterland people who do not grow enough rice, tubers become a dietary staple unless they are willing to pawn some valuable for rice. As Freeman writes of the Iban, "If there is only a small deficit, a family may elect to part with one or more of its gongs . . . in exchange for *padi*." For the Batak, this might read: ". . . elect to part with one of its *ulos* shawls." The point remains that

> [i]n good years, when a surplus of *padi* [unhusked rice] has been gained, it is exchanged for [valuables]. . . . Each season, some families succeed in producing a surplus, while others find themselves with a deficit; and so, year by year . . . scores of different families [in an area] exchange [valuables] for *padi* or *padi* for [valuables]. (Freeman 1970:267)

Does this mean the Iban (or the Batak, or the Kachin—some of whose prestige valuables, according to Leach, "are sometimes dealt with in the open market" [1965:147]) do less "sharing in favor of need," as opposed to hoarding or trading for profit, than people in Melanesian big-man societies, such as the Melpa (Strathern 1977)? Before we concede the possibility, we must note that even in the Southeast Asian hinterlands, there is a *degree* of sharing "in favor of need." It is done through a variety of means. For instance, Freeman notes the "[ancient] custom" *(adat lama)* of selling rice to members of the longhouse and other Iban for one-fifth its market value (1970:272). He also mentions that "occasionally grain is given to close relatives, but always on the general understanding that it will be repaid when conditions permit" (Freeman 1970:272). Similarly, among the Ifugao, "no interest is charged" on some rice debts (Barton 1922:425). And among the Batak, I confirmed Vergouwen's report (1964:295, 332-333) that the terms for interest-bearing and non-interest-bearing loans apply equally to rice and cash.

In spite of what may be considered a moral imperative against "converting down" (against exchanging prestige goods for subsistence staples), all kinds of "conversions" undoubtedly took place in precolonial Batak and other hinterland societies, as they do in modern ones. The fact that, in addition, there are loans of rice at no interest or sales for a fraction of the going rate suggests that the Bataks' trading of grain is not an adequate basis for judging the amount of uncalculated sharing that they practice. Admittedly, they share selectively, as would people anywhere, but it cannot be assumed that, because in some societies subsistence staples are only bartered for other subsistence staples (Sahlins 1972:217-218), this is necessarily the case for all such staples in all societies having multicentric economies. Some foods have more intrinsic value than others because they keep better, and rice keeps better than any.

Moreover, Sahlins does not adequately consider the fact that feasting and ceremonial prestation are still common activities of Batak and other Southeast Asian peoples, as they are in the big-man societies of Melanesia. Although noting that "[p]restige apparently hinges on obtaining exotic items (Chinese pottery, brass gongs, etc.) in exchange for rice or work" (1972:226), Sahlins slights the use of such items in what Bataks call 'paying *adat* [custom]' in feasts and other rituals, and he makes bare mention of their use in bridewealth. Thus he evades the major implications of considering such economies to be multicentric: (a) the coexistence and operation of the various spheres of exchange, and (b) the fact that in all societies with ranked spheres, some items obtained through outside trade serve as prestige gifts or counter-gifts.

Spheres of exchange do not simply exist at a moment of non-exchange or inconvertibility (cf. Sahlins 1972:277). Rather, such spheres coexist because conversion is possible between them, and therein lies the continued importance of hinterland rice. The demand, though sporadic, must have been intense, with all kinds of valuables offered for the grain at certain periods of the past.

The Place of Women, the Role of Rice, and the Maintenance of Multicentric Values

One of my village neighbors commented on the tape recording of the bridewealth session involving the field: "There had to be either a cow or a field named at that gathering, so it would be esteemed. That is what is called prestige (*iang*), fame (*barita*)." This brings us to the place of women in the spheres of exchange. As among the Tiv, Tikopia, Santa Cruz Islanders (Davenport 1961:66), Lele (Douglas 1958:120-121), and others, women constitute a category of "goods" for the Batak but one more highly valued than all others—one of "unique quality." The blessings of their reproductive and nurturing powers are acquired in return for bridewealth demands for prestige goods—"gold, cows, horses, fields"—that are today often satisfied with cash. The view being proposed here is that in spite of the prominence of cash in bridewealth, women continue to comprise a sphere apart and multicentric values are maintained. The role of rice, while somewhat ambivalent in the very nature of the case, is of great symbolic importance in the process of bridewealth marriage, which might be described as being characterized by persistence amid change.

At present, land is most often pawned for a volume of rice (or its cash equivalent), though rarely is the rice to be used for subsistence. In the traditional economy, "conversion" occurred in exchanges of prestige goods given for those of "unique quality," and in emergencies, conversion of prestige goods for subsistence items must also have taken place. Indeed, such "conversion" was an implicit but open possibility in the management of every household. The possibility of exchange of a valuable for rice, a subsistence good, is attributable to rice's potential ritual uses on the one hand and its value as a staple on the other. In many instances already noted, cooked and uncooked rice is symbolically used to transfer blessings and as a prestation—that is, in making an obligatory ritual payment. What E. Wolf (1960) calls the "costs of social representation" (feast contributions, condolence offerings, returns for minor bridewealth payments, and other such customary "dues") are often paid with rice.

The role of rice can best be viewed as that of a mediator, a common denominator, a medium of exchange. That rice should have gained the position of mediator of distinct, differentially valued spheres is probably traceable to its storability and food value and its consequent value in trade. (In a sense, these are, in turn, dependent on the complementary means of growing the grain.) Blacksmiths, traders, canoe carvers, drummers, and the like have always needed rice to supplement their households' agricultural endeavors. It was probably traditionally in demand as compensation for such special services, and it continues to be for some of them. Again, it may be said to have acquired its strong and persistent "social value" by virtue of a threefold attraction: (a) the taste preference that everyone in this part of Oceania professes—i.e., it is the favorite staple, far more so, even, than bread in the West; (b) its compactness, which makes it storable, transportable, as well as easily measurable; (c) its attractiveness as an export in a world of seaborne powers like Śrivijaya, of the Palembang region of south Sumatra, which forcibly exacted the "business" of shipping using the Straits of Malacca in early historical times, practicing what van Leur termed "compulsory stapling . . . enforced upon the international trade" (1955:105).

As was noted earlier, rice continues to fulfill what some theorists have abstracted as the four main "functions" of money (Melitz 1974 *passim*): a store of value, a means of payment, a unit of account, and a medium of exchange. For the Ifugao, in 1922, R. F. Barton argued that "[r]ice was and still is, to an extent, money."

> While somewhat cumbersome, it still has more of the qualities of a perfect medium of exchange than one, at the first glance, would be ready to admit. Rice

> keeps indefinitely. . . . It has a regular yearly fluctuation in value, but this can be depended on as . . . a regular occurrence. (1922:428)

> Rice was [the Ifugao's] one universal medium of exchange. . . . and he could even today get along with it almost as well as with money so far as his domestic trade is concerned. (1922:430)

But, as pointed out earlier, while rice may have some of the functions of money, that does not make it—a staple food—money. The customary place of rice in Batak economy, nevertheless, obscures the existence of spheres of exchange as traditionally constituted, and the recent adoption of cash as "general-purpose money" compounds the problem of ethnographic and ethnohistorical winnowing attempted here. In part, the difficulty of distinguishing such spheres increases because, once the possibility is broached, the strange, multiple role of rice comes into focus.

While it is necessary to conceive its role as a mediator, rice also functioned as money in the market; it served as a medium of exchange—i.e., as a common denominator. Note that it was so used in a rice-deficit area, Samosir, only parts of which produced surpluses. Still, the fact is that food served as a (general-purpose) medium of exchange, in a market where cash—coins, not bills—served as a (special-purpose) medium of prestige-good exchange. To accept the simultaneously subsistence and prestige nature of rice in the Batak economy and to admit the possible traditional system to have been of differentially valued and otherwise mutually incommensurate spheres of exchange, we must confront some widely heralded ideas on the influence of money on such a system. In describing a similar situation among the Tiv, P. Bohannan (1955, 1967) claimed that it was the British forcing them to abandon the use of brass rods for bridewealth in favor of coinage ("general-purpose money") that destroyed the distinctions between the spheres, "making everything exchangeable for everything else."[6] Among the Batak, general-purpose money has likewise come to

[6]But probably of greater effect was that the British *outlawed the favored form of marriage* (Bohannan 1967:127), by patrilateral exchange. Marriage by bridewealth payment was decreed to

be used as a means of evaluating and acquiring many goods and services. If it be granted that trade in traditional commodities, including rice—which also served in conversion among traditional spheres of exchange—did not give rise to what P. Bohannan termed a "unicentric" economy before the adoption of cash, the question of whether general acceptance of Indonesian currency has occasioned this or other fundamental changes must be addressed.

Although the Batak use cash for most transactions in ritual or mundane spheres of exchange, there is no clear reason to believe that people whose cultural codes and values appear to be largely intact and whose lives are enmeshed in many kinds of economic interchanges will cease to distinguish between the traditional spheres of their social economy—subsistence goods, prestige goods, and women—or cease to recognize the differences among the spheres. As I suggested, by analogy with the Tiv and the Tikopia, it can be argued that women remain the basis of a separate sphere of exchange, in which widely ramifying kinship groups are brought into new alignment by a series of prestations and counter-prestations. This appears to be the case for patrilineal, largely patrilocal Southeast Asian hinterland societies, like the Lamet, Batak, and Kachin, which idealize men's marrying matrilateral cross-cousins. The continued use of livestock and parcels of land as bridewealth in Samosir and the use of shawls as gifts to wife-receivers indicates that the Batak still view the transactions with "multicentric values"—as, indeed, Bohannan admits that the Tiv still view "the institutionalization of [their] economy" (1967:134). To be sure, were it not for language and ritual, those distinctions would perhaps evaporate. Yet, given the blessing transference carried out in the making of such gifts, there is continued call for their use. Ritual continues to instill the scheme of values and, in a sense, to give traditional spheres of exchange palpable reality, and spheres of exchange in turn continue to have an important effect on the social organization of Batak livelihood.

As I have said, a common feature of some societies being considered

---

be the only legal form. None of the shocks—many of them temporary—to which the Batak were subjected would seem to have been quite so severe.

appears to be the integration of products of outside trading circuits with the internal system of marriage. Bridewealth marriage, transferring rights in the procreative and child-nurturing capacities of a woman, is not a sale. But, being what Firth termed of "unique quality," women may serve as the mainspring for the movement of goods and services that comprise much of the prestige sphere of exchange in Batak and similar societies.[7] The society perpetuates itself by the practice of its rituals of passage and of prosperity/power, the parameters of which are established by marriages. As Singarimbun (1975) wrote of the Karo Batak, women are "bridges" between lineages, and the same holds for bilateral peoples, between "houses" (Volkman 1985). Where this occurs, "the principal reciprocal relation between [hill tribe] households" is not "calculated labor exchange," which results from rice accumulation for export (Sahlins 1972:225). Rather, marriage is the principal reciprocal relationship between households. In fact, it often gives rise to *uncalculated* exchange of labor service. Other reciprocal relations include labor exchange and uncalculated help. Indeed, Batak reciprocity in labor arises in one of four ways: through marital relations, voluntary association, contract (e.g., in exchange for plowing), and, formerly, through debt.

This is not to say that some Batak do not feel some discomfort about the new prominence of money in bridewealth. One may even hear it said that "these days, women are just sold." But one also hears (of young men with academic titles) that "these days, it is more a matter of buying a son-in-law, not of selling daughters anymore." Almost without exception, both viewpoints are exaggerations. 'Buy' and 'sell' are applied to pawns of land as well, though it is acknowledged that such transactions are not permanent transfers.

Valuables change hands, and women move in weddings: they shift from the "jural control" of fathers, brothers, etc., to that of husbands and husbands' lineages (Sherman 1987:877). But statements about women being "sold" do not necessarily indicate that they become

[7]Prestige "imports" may also be used, if not as counters in the "circulation of women," then, as in the case of the Iban *bilek*, as household-establishing wealth. A sacred strain of rice from the parent *padi pun* also forms part of such wealth for the Iban (Freeman 1958).

"livestock" when money enters a bridewealth system of marriage, as Meillassoux claims (1981:74). Perhaps the most telling point against interpreting bridewealth marriage in terms of women as chattel is that the ideology takes no account of the power of women to choose their own mates. The notion of women as chattel takes too literally the named 'payments' of bridewealth and ignores the substantial meal that must first be presented, parts of which must be apportioned among the recipients, as well as the return, packaged food, with which the groom's party is sent off. It also ignores the fact that the weddings of the rich, although they involve far larger expenditures and exchanges of wealth than those of the poor, accomplish the marriage of only one couple. Most important, the notion of women as chattel ignores the place of women—their roles in interlineage relations, the unique value conferred on them, and, thus, what Weiner (1976) calls women's "power." This analysis corresponds both to the Batak point of view and the objective roles of women in Batak society. These were seen repeatedly in the description of Batak life. Women are indispensable partners in livelihood-seeking, be it village production, out-migration, pioneering, or ritual.

Models of Non-Asian Feasting Economies in the Southeast Asian Highlands

We now turn to the political economy of feasting. Sahlins' view of the rice trade precludes his endorsing the "redistribution" theory of hill-tribe feasting. He avoids the mistake of considering hill-tribe feasting to be a means of leveling wealth differences, "a continual narrowing of the margin between the haves and have-nots," as Stevenson wrote of the Chin (1943:164). Leach makes similar statements: "Since rich people make larger sacrifices than poor people, sacrifices have the effect of equalizing consumer distribution. . . . Meat will always be shared around the whole village" (1965:172-173; 1966a:93).

Though it is true to some extent that consumption of meat is equalized through feasting, Stevenson's own account—the most detailed of any Southeast Asian feasting system—stands in contradiction to such a view of the institution. In his tabulated "Statement of Kinship Obligations at Feasts of Merit" (1943:143f.), there is a clear balance shown between the amounts of beer or meat contributed and the amounts received in return by nonpatrilineal kin. He writes:

> Only the help of bondfriends and relatives makes the holding of the feasts possible, but an account of what they give is valueless unless compared with what they get, and what they get is in turn governed by the vested interests of the *hausa pawl* (. . . members of the Feaster's Club [analogous to the Batak *bius*]) progress among whom is one important raison d'etre of the whole series. (Stevenson 1943:137)

Instead of an 'evening out' effect on consumption and economic inequalities, we learn that

> As a consequence of gaining the top ranks of [feasters] a man opens for himself through elevation to the village Council avenues to a further wide range of economic advantages including participation in entertainment of village guests and communal sacrifice, both of which yield a fairly constant supply of beer and meat. (Stevenson 1943:140).

> [T]he individual householder . . . can not by any manner or means hold these feasts on his own resources. (Stevenson 1943:147)

Furthermore,

> In the main the elders and priests get the lion's share of the flesh and the best of the beer. As a rule only men attend and therefore the consumer benefit is confined to a relatively small circle. (Stevenson 1943:161)

It is hard to see how this last observation could have given rise to a notion of redistribution or leveling. Unlike most of the others, it does not hold for the Batak, among whom women attend and are fed at feasts. For both, however, there is a cyclic distribution of meat and grain—not a redistribution of wealth, but a system in which participants appear to draw their due in proportion to what they have contributed over the long term.

This viewpoint renders the Chin data congruent with the Batak ideal that the giver of a large feast should take in more (in rice, blessing shawls, cash, and other contributions) than the outlay for food, orchestra, and other needs. While the achievement of this ideal is rare, I was present at one final reckoning for a very large feast in which what was received, evaluated in rupees, surpassed the expenditure of the principals. This corresponds to Vergouwen's observation that "a scribe notes the names of the guests and their gifts which, in total, sometimes exceed the outlay for the occasion" (Vergouwen 1964:305). It is true, as can be documented in any society, that "stinginess is not commendable; liberality is praiseworthy." Nevertheless, as Vergouwen also put it: liberal hospitality on the part of a "chief" is "no demonstration of benevolence toward the poor . . . but a public demonstration of one's wealth, a fulfilment of the obligations" (Vergouwen 1964:132).

I also recorded a discussion on the difficulty of limiting the number of guests, given limited resources, which indicated that the discussants saw nothing wrong with profiting from a feast—that, indeed, they thought it quite proper, though unfortunately rare. The first speaker was a man of about seventy (who may have been referring to the Dutch ban on large feasts—of which I was then not aware):

> Ompu D.: It used to be, they would take a chicken, and make soup, and everyone would dance. These days, if there is not a lot of meat, you can't have a *gondang* (feast with an orchestra).
>
> A.R.: Just listen a minute. It's according to the times. In the past two chickens were enough. One goat. Right? So they would invite one person per household. Now, though, even for a water-heading feast it is a cow. More than 60 kilos [of meat].
>
> O.D.: Let me tell you, you know about gain. Nowadays, if you have a *gondang*, let me tell you, if you say you want to make a profit, don't do it. Any way you do it you have to lose a lot.
>
> A.M.: On purpose, you mean.
>
> O.D.: On purpose! Loss! That's the only way. If you are going to borrow money on interest, you want to have a *gondang*, don't do it, don't!
>
> A.M.: You'll be ruined, ruined.
>
> A.S.: Just look at our brother-in-law here. There was no lack of people at his feast.

This conversation indicates that people do think of feasts as potentially profitable—but what is so strange about that? Feast-givers explicitly ask spirits to make them more prosperous. Should the feast itself not do so and thus tend to reinforce their faith? Certainly, if it did, it would not contravene its purpose. The only reason this might shock us is if, for whatever theoretical reasons, we expect feasts to be redistributive, for how could they be if sponsors take in more than they expend?[8] In fact, this situation is not very different from Sahlins' own observation that Melanesian leaders deploy their

> skills and efforts . . . towards amassing goods, most often pigs, shell monies and vegetable foods, and distributing them in ways which build a name for cavalier generosity, if not for compassion. (Sahlins 1963:291; see also Meggitt 1971:196; 1974:189-191)

Neither in Melanesia nor in the Southeast Asian hinterlands do we find indigenous expression of the egalitarian ideal, "to each according to his needs; from each according to his abilities."

In part, as one of my informants said, "the reason for holding a feast. . . is to get prestige and fame, to make one's name big, to gain honor." Another said that "in the old days funeral festivities could take a month. They ate and ate, to give notice of their wealth, that they were rich and majestic people." Yet prestige, which accrues to the members of a Batak lineage who pool their resources to hold a feast, is only partly derived from the "fame" aroused by any conspicuous gathering. In fact, this reason for the status enhancement of a feast is downplayed in the oratorical praise heaped on feast principals by their guests. The statement repeated by almost every speaker at a large feast, "Many people are rich, but not many can unite in one purpose, not many can be of one word, one agreement," refers both to the

[8]The acceptability of a feast-giver's profiting materially from his endeavor is also found elsewhere in Southeast Asia, as Firth writes of "the North-Eastern Malay peasant institution of a ceremonial feast": "The organizer of this, normally having a marriage or other social event as the prime reason, receives payment from his guests, which is in part a mobilization of his credit with them, and in part a contraction of new credit obligations. *If he makes a profit* he can use this either for expenditure on consumers' goods for his own pleasure or for investment in some item of producers' equipment such as a fishing boat." (Firth 1964a:28, emphasis added).

cooperation of the principals and the support of "attending" wife-receivers.

How has the practice of feasting in such societies come to be considered one of the primary mechanisms of what J. Scott (1976:41) calls "social controls which act to provide for the minimal needs of the village poor"? For one thing, the distribution of meat to a great number of guests is impressive. Domestic animals have traditionally been slaughtered only for communal functions, so there is some "equalization" among rich and poor in consumption of livestock. The inductive process, from wide distribution of meat to "leveling of wealth differences," appears to have been facilitated by the fact that in Melanesian feasting systems, as Burridge put it, "the significant wealth produced, perishable foodstuffs . . . was consumed as its handling and apportionment translated work into moral qualities" (1975:94). The point here is that contributions of rice (whether husked or unhusked) at a Batak feast did not have to be consumed or redistributed so as not to be wasted, as do most of the vegetable foods used in Melanesian feasts. Rice could be stored and used for other purposes by the recipients.

However, I do not want to replace one set of misconceptions—feasting as redistribution—with another: feasting as balanced, reciprocal exchange. It often has outcomes other than the sponsors' breaking even. Giving sacrificial feasts, for example, is a well-known route to poverty for those overly lavish of their means when a family member is subject to incurable illness, thought to be caused by dissatisfied spirits. My point is that even those who thus become impoverished do not look to the feasts of others to fulfill their minimal needs. While there is accumulation and redistribution of considerable surplus product, it is difficult to consider the feasting system as the mainstay of what Scott argues are universal "subsistence guarantees" in non-market-based societies. Such guarantees do exist—old, young, and disabled are cared for by close relatives as part of the natural course of life. But the contribution of feast meals to subsistence of the needy could never have filled more than a minor portion of their needs.

The problem of "social insurance" or provision for the needy is one that Batak society appears to have developed other, more direct means of solving, including the capacity and willingness to store and lend rice. As Scott himself points out, one who is in need borrows, and, as he quite rightly adds,

> It is evident that as soon as a peasant leans on his kin or his patron . . . he gives them a reciprocal claim to his own labor and resources. . . . [T]here is a tacit consensus about reciprocity, and their assistance is as good as money in the bank against the time when the situation is reversed. (Scott 1976:28)

Instead of expelling, the society harbors and nurtures its members, but not always without cost in supplemental repayment. Among the Batak, again, one of two alternatives is brought into play, depending on the relationship between borrower and lender: the lender stipulates a return of the amount loaned (receiving "social insurance" for the use of his rice or money) or of the original amount plus interest. Apparently the choice of whether interest is required on such loans of rice is not determined solely by kinship considerations—loans with no interest were invariably between those who were at best distantly related, though they were often age-mates and companions.

What is crucial is that there were two traditional, alternative means of borrowing rice. Loans are particularly significant in relation to the feasting system, given the planning required for any feast. Let me explain. The competition for prestige in feasting may be considered an ancient and effective incentive to production, as Sahlins (1972) argued in his essays on "The Domestic Mode of Production." The importance of such competition in a rice-based system of production may be seen more clearly in the following hypothetical set of contingencies. Three households, or household heads, have been, respectively: (1) just making ends meet, (2) "investing" surplus rice in return for heirlooms, or (3) saving rice for a feast, plans for which have been set in motion, though not definitively settled. In the event, say, of widespread crop failure due to an unusually prolonged drought or of local failures resulting from any of a number of causes, the households' alternatives might turn out to be that: the first must borrow the rice needed for subsistence; the second may borrow rice or exchange a valuable for it by pawn or sale; the third may find that those whose contributions have been counted on for the feast begin asking to borrow rice, and may then have to decide whether to postpone the feast (and instead loan rice). If we assume that in any given year some households will have been harboring their rice stocks for projected ritual or trading purposes, such a hypothetical quandary is not unlikely. As this scenario suggests, differences in accumulation of rice open the possibility of relationships of dependence arising.

The storability of rice is, thus, a cultural-ecological aspect not only as it contributes to its attractiveness as an export and its consequent convertibility, which have long allowed trade and social differentiation based on display and gift of imported luxuries. Its storability also has cultural-ecological implications because differential success in growing rice opens the way to those with stocks to provision others in temporary need of subsistence aid, "to put people under obligations" (Lingat 1949). This, in turn, has further consequences. It sometimes led, for example, to debt-bondage, but the possibility of flight of those who became too deeply indebted may have tempered the demands of creditors in a position to exact service from debt-bondsmen. As Vergouwen noted (and as in several cases I encountered, such as a threat of foreclosure on a pledged house, for a loan 18 years overdue), there is a custom, the *adat parsingiron,* "that payment of debts that have accumulated or of debts that it is hardly possible to meet fully, should not be claimed to the last farthing" (Vergouwen 1964:312). (Again, this custom is not congruent with Sahlins' analysis.) The outcome of inadequate subsistence resources (particularly of land and water) was, then, not generally one of debt-bondage nor of the tacit reduction of a large proportion of inhabitants of an area to the status of tenants.[9] The outcome was, rather, the foundation of new hamlets, offshoots of mother villages, by pioneers who, as at present, were probably often dependent on family members maintaining the home base. This is borne out by the oral tradition of an outward spiral of genealogical branching and foundation of new hamlets.

[9]Keyes (1983) comments on the relative rarity of such a situation.

The social value of rice in such a system can also be seen in terms of its role in social reproduction. In his essays on the "Domestic Mode of Production" (1972), Sahlins claims that the "household system" is not organized for production of surplus above producers' subsistence requirements (presumably these are "minimum dietary requirements"—"subsistence" surely does not connote "ritual requirements"). He goes on to argue that the drive to produce above need is set in motion by individual seekers of power or wealth, on the big man model.

But the problem with this notion of "subsistence," as opposed to "surplus," production is that there are innumerable occasions on which gifts of rice are de rigueur social or ritual requirements in the daily life of Samosir's tribal peasants. The desire to accumulate surplus is undeniably motivated at times by the desire to give a feast—to improve one's chance of future success, as well as to acquire or validate prestige or to participate in social life. So what is wrong with Sahlins' assertion that "the household system" per se is not organized for production above subsistence needs? We can abstract a process called "household developmental cycle" but there is no clear-cut way to distinguish subsistence from surplus production.[10] Among the Batak one cannot recruit a cooperative labor group without rice and fish to serve. One cannot attend a wake or a village wedding or a feast of one's wife-givers without bringing rice. One can hardly begin householding without a stock of rice held by a relative to see one through a harvest. Similarly, a person who wishes to start a trading venture pawns fields for rice (which may be lent in cash, and which, if repaid, will be repaid in the current cash equivalent of the rice, not the amount of cash borrowed). Thus, perpetuating a household or a lineage *requires* "surplus" production—so it is not really surplus.

[10]As Godelier put it: "The concept of 'subsistence economy' . . . —used frequently to characterise primitive economies—should be rejected since it masks the fact that these economies do not limit themselves to the production of subsistence goods, but produce a 'surplus' destined for the functioning of the social structures (kinship, religion, etc.). It also masks the existence of many forms of exchange which accompany this functioning." (Godelier 1977:110)

Kinship and Economic Differences

Although it may be said that in Samosir "economic relations are embedded in a kinship structure" and that "the kin structure pervades the entire society," it does not necessarily follow that "minimization of the attempt to gain" and "maximization of mutual aid" need be considered "the principles of [the] entire economy" (cf. Sahlins 1960:409). Maximization of mutual aid is, indeed, a principle, an ideal expressed in certain situations and in the context of differing principles such as: (a) seeking good fortune (prosperity, high status, fertility of humans and animals, productivity of the land) through ritual activity; (b) reciprocity in a variety of forms (agnatic and both affinal varieties and extrafamilial reciprocity, arising from "credit arrangements" [Mauss 1967:35, 45, 60]); (c) the principle of substitution, whereby a ritual payment (of bridewealth, for instance) is called by the same term, no matter what, and no matter what quantity is given (Leach 1965:148f.), making it possible for a poor man to satisfy the same code as a rich man.

There is mutual aid and cooperation, to be sure, often among neighbors and for situational reasons. But there is also maximization of gain in all sorts of exchanges. Although households belong to lineages (and it is those that persist over time), in "getting a living" households expend a large proportion of effort, in fact, operating as autonomous enterprises. When cooperation occurs, it is not generalized but, rather, with selected members of the community. Personal compatibility often has as much to do with involvement in nonritual endeavors as does kinship in ritual endeavors. Kinship relations continue to be adjusted to material or political need (as, in the past, with the tacit adoption of debt-bondsmen or a marriage as part of a feud settlement).

J. Scott claims that "Well-to-do villagers avoid malicious gossip only at the price of an exaggerated generosity" (1976:41), and I did indeed hear such gossip. But if people were as sensitive to gossip as he implies, wealth differences would not arise or be maintained. For any number of reasons, however, they do arise and do persist, some for generations, some for active lifetimes. There are households that grow poor through sickness, for instance, or profligacy, or badly conceived trading ventures. Others build up a greater-than-average number of irrigable holdings, which they can give out for sharecropping while maintaining a high level of production on fields they work themselves.

While I do not consider precolonial Batak society to have been stratified, into "nobility," "commoners," and "slaves" (cf. Loeb 1935), there is a resemblance between the successful hamlet headman and the Melanesian big man, as well as the typical "patron" of "entourage" formations in central and northern Thai ethnography (Hanks 1966; Van Roy 1971). As among the Melanesians and the Thai, a characteristic of Batak who rise to prominence is the tendency to form alliances with those of similar prominence outside the immediate area, with whom they can engage in exchanges roughly on a par.[11] Given the ancient market network in the Batak highlands and the roles of hamlet headmen, trade may have been a central feature of this tendency.

Economic inequality among villagers is congruent with the hierarchically defined kinship relations of wife-givers and -receivers, as well as with a "spheres of exchange" model of the economy. As Firth puts it, of the latter, citing Salisbury,

> [T]he presence in non-monetary societies of discrete scales of value, each dependent upon a different standard of evaluation, is not an unfortunate accident. It is a relatively simple mechanism which helps to maintain a basic standard of life at the same time as an allocation of status and power in the society. (Firth 1967:19)[12]

Perhaps the reluctance of Scott and others to view rice loans at interest and the pawning of valuables like shawls or gongs as mechanisms providing for the needy is due to the superficial resemblance of such institutionalized transactions to capitalist factor markets.[13] There is a

[11]See Paynter and Cole (1980:89-94) on the implications of the work of Pospisil, Meggitt, and others for appreciating "the importance of regional processes," as evidenced by "extra-parish big-men connections" and "the extravillage character of labor reproduction."

[12]See also Salisbury (1962:212) and Weiner (1976:220) on the implicit power relations in exchange.

[13]But cf. Scott (1976:176).

tendency to assume that they arose in response to penetration of and "contamination" by mercantile capitalism, which supposedly undermined prior leveling processes. But they may have originated without the pressure of outside demand for products of crafts or of the soil.

From the viewpoint I am proposing, contradictory principles of local social relations appear to compete but coexist. On the one hand, there is what might be termed "limits on 'familism,'" and on the other hand, the maximization of solidarity, an ideal of unity or, as Toba Batak put it, 'to be of one word, one agreement,' *marsahata-saoloan*. Some remarks on each of these aspects of their social organization of livelihood are in order.

As was noted in Chapter 8, there is a dearth of village cooperatives, in part because usually only limited trust is generated by a village leader who attempts to convince those of his own or other descent lines to join in cooperative ventures. This might be interpreted as an example of "amoral familism" (Banfield 1958) or of the "individualistic" tendencies of Mexican peasants discussed by G. Foster (1967) or O. Lewis (1951). As Greenwood puts it, Banfield proposed that southern Italian peasants were

> backward because the people had a "culture of amoral familism." The term refers to an attitude of total suspicion toward those outside the family and a consequent inability to cooperate in the collective interest. (Greenwood 1980:10)

As Greenwood points out, however,

> There are many studies now contradicting this . . . [whose] authors emphasize [that] the extremely unequal distribution of property and power [is] a legacy from an extremely long colonial past [and] an economic system that forces the poor to compete harshly for tiny opportunities. (loc. cit.)

No such millennia-long colonial past can be posited for the Batak, nor can it be said that they have an attitude of total suspicion "toward those outside the family."

Batak 'familism' is neither homogeneous—attitudes to kinfolk depend both on the kind of family (agnatic or affinal) and on personal relations and circumstance—nor is it the only traditional principle of social and economic behavior, as is clear from the existence of long-distance trade, as well as from the institutionalized or formal means of access to land, livestock, labor, and capital.

As for traditional trade, although I have rejected Sahlins' inferences from the evidence of hinterland rice export, I agree with his premise that "the engagement with the market makes the key minimal demand: that internal community relations permit household accumulation of rice" (1972:224). Without such accumulation, a household can neither develop nor thrive—let alone engage in trade. Traders have to eat, and rice may provide their sustenance and sometimes their capital. This becomes an analytical problem only when one takes the perspective that "where economic relations are embedded in a kinship structure," "maximization . . . of cooperation" ought to be the primary motif of local social organization (Sahlins 1960:398-409). Granted that trade demands accumulation; but the fact that households accumulate rice in every sort of society throughout Southeast Asia is primarily a reflection of the minimal demands of subsistence and "surplus" needs (i.e., for ritual and mobilizing labor). Presumably, it is only secondarily a response to demands of trade. Since accumulated rice is subject to a variety of dispositions at the behest of its storers, its storability predisposes to, or constitutes, a potential limit on "familism." (This is what I meant when I said there has always been a market for rice, even before it was exported.)

Second, means of access to rice-growing land—by sharecropping arrangements, gift to affines, taking in pawn, loan, and others—constitute another set of potential limits on "familism," that is, of "devices" for restricting access on the part of (some) close relatives by a variety of temporary arrangements that may or may not be with relatives. Even if such arrangements were traditionally made only with relatives, they provided formal means of being generous to some at the expense of others. The arrangements are, indeed, made using kinship terms, if among those who know of no ancestral ties below the clan level. As one Sagala man put it when asked what kinfolk had sharecropped the fields pledged to him, "The poor search for kinship relations (Indonesian, *kekeluargaan*). Owing to this *marga* (clan), it is possible, even though there has never been a family relation" (*Ala ni marga on, boi do, tung pe ndang hea marpamili*). He was the relatively well-to-do teacher, whose younger sister received a field at their mother's funeral, and he had a number of less-well-off lineage mates with no irrigable holdings. The latter were, in effect, denied access to his fields by his acceding to the requests of men who called him brother-in-law (although they belonged to lineages that had no affinal relations with members of his). By the same token, he had either disposed of stores of rice or capital without "redistributing" them to his kin, in taking the fields in pawn in the first place, or he may have gotten fields from those kin in return for loans.

Such limits on the access of close kin to factors of production remain integral to the social organization of Batak livelihood. Yet, in spite of such divisiveness, a variety of forms of social solidarity arise among those within the homeland, as well as among those who have emigrated. Again, the degree of unity or social solidarity in Batak society lies in the eye of the beholder. G. Foster claims "the image of the limited good" in peasant society is a "total cognitive view," what Honigmann termed

> the implicit belief that good of all kinds is limited. There is only so much respect, influence, power, and love in the world. If another has some, then somebody is certainly deprived of that measure. (Foster 1967: 305, n. 6)

An analyst intent on demonstrating an unexpressed, indigenous "image of the limited good" and consequent lack of cooperation in Batak society could easily do so. But there are numerous situations in which strong ties are expressed and enacted.

As we have seen, lineage unity is most overtly manifested in the lineup of principals arrayed on one side of the courtyard during the *gondang* dances, meeting each of the guests who dance past with appropriate embraces. Even when one household or a group of first cousins acts as principal sponsors, other members of the minimal lineage to which they belong dance in a row at their side. (The order of the lineup may be a cause of drawn-out debate, but eventually a line forms.) The formal meeting of household heads of any localized lineage to agree on the joint contributions and strategy of marriage for any sons or daughters is similarly striking, even though it may occur in response to a *fait accompli*. Again, it is particularly at large-scale feasts that the ideal of solidarity, "to be of one word, of one agreement," is lauded by guests and invoked as a source of strength and well-being. It is generally declaimed in formal oratory, but, not infrequently, it is a message of a spirit possessing the wife of one of the principals. In an indoor ceremony at the end of a three-day feast of ancestral spirit power, two women successively became possessed and, in answer to the advice-seeking principals, the first cried out:

> Do not oppose [your] hearts [to one another] (*Unang maralo roha*), that is what I have to say. Agree with each other. Do not bicker with each other. Make pe-e-ace.

Then, after several more dances, the second one gave forth with a wail:

> Do not try to show the greatness of your knowledge, in encounters with your older and younger brothers! Do not look [at each other's fields] with jealous eyes, from now, for as long as you may live!

An often-quoted *umpasa* (rhymed blessing couplet) referring to the loom used to weave blessing shawls expresses similar values:

> The spindle, the loom-bar, the foot-rest, the back-strap;
> Those who are willing to agree with each other are really blessed.
>
> *(Anian do pagabe, tundalan sitadoan;*
> *Na nian do halak gabe, na olo marsipaolo-oloan.)*

Although people's actions may often conflict with such ideals, the fact that they continue to invoke them is relevant to their continued success in maintaining an ongoing community. Focusing on the mediating role of women, as the metaphorical image evoked by the saying tends to, also brings into relief the contradiction noted earlier—of limits on familism versus an ideal of solidarity. In order to reproduce, a sedentary, patrilineal, agricultural community must acquire wives from, and ultimately provide daughters in exchange with, others. The solidarity of the group for which marriage is the primary shared concern, the localized minimal lineage, remains an important factor in validating marriages and thus in assuring the continuity of each member's line. Hence the contradiction: a patrilocal solidarity inherently aims to simultaneously extend beyond the local. And, in turn, formal means of access to productive resources serve to impose limits on, rather than to induce, familism.

Chapter 14

Change and Persistence in the Worldview of Samosir Villagers

In closing, I return to some issues noted in the Introduction, such as Meillassoux's claims that the domestic mode of production is "both maintained and destroyed" through contact with the capitalist mode.

There is little doubt that even the ethnic consciousness, so proudly vaunted by contemporary Batak, is a modern phenomenon, and it may be, as Fried (1975) suggests of "tribal" peoples generally, that their ethnic identity was initially made manifest to them by the scorn of more cosmopolitan neighboring peoples and their colonizers.

Yet to take the viewpoint that political, economic, and religious changes have "undermined traditional Batak social institutions" would imply that much Batak social ritual is a sham. It is certainly arguable that in traditional Batak society, households able to produce an initial stake and to mobilize their lineage mates and affines to contribute sufficient stores and labor for staging sacrificial feasts, great weddings, and ten-night-long funeral dances would have held high social status. They might, in part, thereby have gained followings ready to heed their calls for armed forays, trading expeditions, acquiring the materials for a great house, or moving a hamlet and building new walls. One may surmise that the head of such a household, with the untold support of one or more wives, must have been gifted. To a degree, the structural position accorded the potential Batak "big man" by accident of birth (locale, birth order, and lineage of both parents) was and remains important in determining eventual success. But why is feasting yet so prevalent both among rural folk and their emigrant urban and peasant kin?

While traditional feasting was perhaps the primary means by which a man achieved a status analogous to that of a Melanesian big man, high status is now conferred by government appointments in education, administration, and other fields, which effectively remove the successful actor from the local arena. Local residents who stage feasts, in fact, attain greater social standing by 'showing their wealth' in this traditional manner, but the participation of those who have emigrated and their children requires some explanation. One assumes that even those who make substantial contributions do not reap prestige among their immediate neighbors in Jakarta, Ujung Pandang, or wherever. Even if they are Batak, those neighbors are not invited. Nor can emigrants be viewed as motivated by the desire to attain authority and economic advantage in manipulating debts of livestock or other goods, which comparison with Melanesia suggests may have occurred traditionally.[1] Another explanation is called for. Volkman (1985: 135-136) claims that what is involved in the analogous Toraja "feasts of honor" is feasting to validate or lay claim to status, by bilateral extended households, to which emigrants belong and often return. But while status is of course universally valued, we can come to a better understanding of such participation and sponsorship by emigrants through consideration of Batak ideas of power in their Indonesian context. (The Toraja data are perhaps amenable to a similar interpretation.)

Castles (1975:75) points out that the Batak idea of "power" is analogous to that which Anderson (1972) argues is prevalent in Javanese culture. For Javanese, according to Anderson,

> Power is that intangible, mysterious, and divine energy which animates the universe. . . .
>
> The total amount of power within [the cosmos] remains fixed . . . even though the distribution of power in the universe may vary. For political theory,

[1]See Burridge (1975:90); Meggitt (1971:195f).

> this has the important corollary that concentration of power in one place or in one person requires a proportional diminution elsewhere.
>
> . . . In a real sense, there were no political frontiers at all, the Power of one ruler gradually fading into the distance and merging imperceptibly with the ascending Power of a neighboring sovereign. (Anderson 1972:7-8, 28)

Allowing that the Batak worldview is in many ways analogous to that of the Javanese permits a better understanding of traditional social interaction between households, villages, and territories, as well as providing insight into the motives of contemporary feast-givers. The attempt to harness "power" may have been as much a characteristic of traditional feasting as was reinforcing agnatic solidarity and affinal alliances. In the past, such rituals were important in defining and defending territorial and other spheres of influence of Batak settlements, of varying extent and definition (and at varying complementary levels of social organization).[2] In addition, the pursuit of long-term series of feasts by households, lineages, and even whole territories may be interpreted as the primary means of competing for the finite quantum of "power" in their world, and this, I believe, is still true. It helps explain why feasting continues to be a crucial part of the lives of contemporary Bataks. It is true that participants are maintaining the most important relations that define their identities (Volkman 1985:159, 162), but by sponsoring and contributing to feasts, they also seek to maintain and improve their fecundity and well-being, and to ensure continued access to the known sources of *sahala*, 'soul force'—i.e., "power"—"that intangible, mysterious, and divine energy."

After the lifting of the decades-long Dutch ban, it was to be expected that feasting would become attenuated and that *bius* priests would lose some of their former influence. This raised the question of a possible "loss of faith." But, to reiterate what was said in Chapter 4, although there was undoubtedly a loss of confidence, it probably arose from the fear that human inaction (of appropriate sacrifice, prayer, etc.) had irrevocably broken the reciprocal cycle of human-divine interaction. This point of view may now be reinforced. In effect, since no one was

[2]See Meggitt (1971:198, n. 12); (1974:171, 198-199).

feasting, no area or clan or lineage could "gain the upper hand" in the quest for "power," but as soon as the ban was lifted and the priest-magicians in one area set the time for a *bius* feast, their neighbors had every incentive to resume feasting themselves. This appears to be exactly what happened. Although the initial revival only lasted six years (before the Dutch gave way to the Japanese), the system is again in full bloom. The same kind of competition apparently underlies the proliferation of concrete tombs and perhaps even that of churches, particularly in new areas of Batak settlement in the lowlands, where mosques are plentiful. In considering the supposedly reduced scale of contemporary feasting, we need not take the view that such reduction indicates "cultural disintegration." Rather, the Batak were able to adjust the number and duration of feasts to conform to modern conditions. Church ritual today, even with fire-and-brimstone preaching and melodious hymns, does not approach the emotional intensity of feasting.

Anderson's analysis of the Javanese idea of "power" also has relevance in relation to Foster's hypothesis of a universal peasant "image of the limited good." As I noted, Foster takes the position that all peasant action is guided by a "total cognitive view" that "good of all kinds is limited." He claims there are only two possible outcomes, "maximum cooperation" or "extreme individualism," and he adds, "Peasant societies seem always to choose the second alternative" (1967:310). This indiscriminate "image of limited good of all kinds" notion fails to allow for the equally strong evidence that hinterland Southeast Asian villagers like the Samosir Batak overcome individual interests in dealing with a range of problems, including social reproduction, common defense, distribution of meat, and, most importantly, the supplication of divine sources of "power." On the other hand, although the ideology supports group solidarity, that does not mean that the ideology supports an altruistic notion of "turn the other cheek" or of a common "brotherhood of man."

In its quest for "prosperity" (*panggabean*—not merely subsistence and reproduction, but also access to a continuing source of fertility), the most feasible way open to the typical Batak household to draw to itself the greatest source of blessing (i.e., of "power") is by appeals to the highest localized ancestral spirits, the *sombaon*. Appropriate sacrifices *must* be undertaken with a large group of agnates and their affines, since the spirit gives proof of having disposal over great "power" by the number of its descendants. And, in practical terms, no household, however well off, can invoke the blessings of such an ancestor without the participation of lineage mates, wife-giving kinfolk, or wife-receiving attendants. What Sahlins called the "social-economic character" of such a society is neither exclusively "maximum cooperation" nor "extreme individualism."

The social economy was traditionally based on a multicentric economy, and it remains so. A system of spheres of exchange operates, and rice continues to serve as mediator between the spheres. Cash entered the system as a prestige good but later also became a mediator among the spheres. This suggests that the aspect of social organization that we designate as the economic system has not changed fundamentally in rural settings or in many urban settings. Indeed, it is arguable that it is being maintained, not only through the traditional productive activities of agriculture and local trade and the reproductive activities of marriage and ritual, which were, in the main, internal to the society, but also through participation in the cash nexus of bureaucratic employment and professional specialization of other kinds on the part of out-migrants. Many of the latter maintain their ties to their village of origin, and some contribute large amounts of cash, in lieu of other prestige goods, to traditional feasts. Cash can be used for anything, from a buffalo or an irrigated terrace to a wife, as well as for subsistence staples. Its use as bridewealth breaks down neither the culturally defined economy nor the distinctions between the spheres of exchange, any more than the use of rice broke them down when *it* was the sole commodity that functioned as mediator—in part, due to its use in obtaining the valuables needed in bridewealth.

Though the advantages of cash, in terms of portability and ease of measurement, are undeniable (as, disadvantageously, the ease of robbery), the Batak, like other Indonesians, have become aware of a tendency for inflation and currency devaluations, which makes hoarding cash a high risk. Cash is also difficult to acquire in significant amounts except by those who are highly educated and well positioned, or otherwise especially gifted. This contrasts with the relative ease of access to (generally small surpluses of) rice. Rice's bulk admittedly puts a limit on its marginal utility to the producer or to the potential hoarder, landlord, etc. (as H. K. Schneider [1968:435] suggests of wealth in grain versus that in livestock). But just as other commodities have always been convertible to rice, rice could always have been exchanged for more durable and portable prestige goods—"converted up"—and this is still so.

For reasons already enumerated—reasons whose grasp requires an understanding of the agricultural and cultural systems—rice serves as the pivotal standard of value. Perhaps as much as anything else, this gives it "strong and enduring social value." It can therefore be argued that for the Batak, a multicentric economy operates as a cognitive system structuring values and that, although cash may have partly taken over the mediating role of rice, the economy continues to operate in terms of spheres of exchange, because those spheres rest on agricultural and ritual components of Samosir livelihood. They involve land, livestock, and other goods as prestige valuables, and women as goods of unique value. Thus, in spite of many overt changes, a largely constant set of beliefs and values has been maintained and continues to shape the principles of social organization. Such a generalization may apply more broadly to other hinterland Southeast Asians.

Recently, several works have appeared which make major contributions to the analysis of the ways that changes in political-economic contexts affect traditional institutions.[3] R. S. Oboler (1985) describes the British deeding of land to Nandi men and the commoditization of milk and cattle and their effects on the position of women; and Sahlins (1985) describes the collision of Western concepts with those of Hawaiians, Maoris, and others. In terms that could well apply to Sahlins'

[3]R. Firth has put forward one of the most balanced views concerning sociocultural change in such situations in a number of statements (1929:447 and cf. 470-471, 476; 1964b:48, 187, and cf. 188; 1966:89 and cf. 113-115, 117; 1971 *passim*; 1972:469). See also Belshaw (1954, 1965) and the essays in Force and Bishop, eds. (1981).

subjects, Moore claims that "[i]n the economy of social relations and cultural ideas, there is sometimes a special convenience in using existing forms for new purposes" (1986:226). "It would be a serious error," writes Moore, "to mistake the present traditional forms [of the Chagga] for replicas of the earlier ones they strongly resemble" (ibid.:227). This is undeniable. But, as she puts it, "participation in a cash economy did not change everything" (ibid.:232); and, with eloquent ambivalence, "the taking on of utterly new ways of doing things has not precluded an invigoration of selected traditional cultural forms. The two transform each other" (ibid.:243).[4]

While traveling from the village to the city where I had to renew my research permit, on one occasion, I was talking to a fellow passenger, and as we passed a military base the man remarked that rice was part of the soldiers' wages. In fact, I learned further, rice was part of the wages of all civil servants in Indonesian government departments, including the Department of Agriculture. (I have since verified these facts with civil servants.) At the time, I was somewhat taken aback, but could not understand what was significant about the means of payment. An Indonesian military base in northern Sumatra, seen from the road, looks like a group of bungalow compounds, with whole families evident, laundry of every description drying on lines, and chickens scratching the ground. Hence, the fact that rice was part of the soldiers' wage did not strike me as particularly significant. It puzzled me but I had not even an inkling of its significance. But in light of my analysis of economy, culture, and society in a Samosir Batak village, much of its significance is now accessible.

For one thing, given endemic inflation, it is understandable that the Batak have not abandoned traditional valuables, including rice, the more so when we consider that in their model of the economy, such valuables, used ritually, have positive effects on social reproduction. It may well be that spheres of exchange no longer play the dominant

[4]Cf. also Moore (1986:130, 215, 306-307, 317-319); and see her descriptions, *passim*, of oaths, sorcery, and cursing. The African socialism of the Tanzanian polity has made no difference in the righting of local-level injustices or unequal distribution of patrilineage lands.

economic role in channeling the distribution of the products of either labor or trade. This does not mean, however, that the distinctions between them have broken down or that the goods that comprise them or that serve as mediators between them (e.g., rice) have been entirely replaced by money. To the contrary—although as Crump (1981) suggests, the system of redistribution (hierarchical in terms of opportunity) that formerly prevailed has come to be dominated by a "corporation in the form of the state"—the pre-eminent position of rice in rural Batak economy has been maintained. Moreover, the state in Indonesia, Thailand, the Philippines, and other countries of the region (as well as the adjoining South Asian continent) not only maintains a monopoly on issuing scriptural money, but has also entered the rice economy with a vengeance. Price controls and tariffs, based on attempts to control supply, defuse local shortages, increase production, and the like, bespeak what I view as deeper underlying realities of the social value of rice.

Anil Sadgopal asks, "Why are the storehouses full while people who produced the grain go hungry?" (1981:34). The answer, although painfully ironic, is nevertheless eye-opening. The godowns must be full because a widespread harvest failure might curtail future supply. That appears to be a given in Oriental civilizations; it is part of their historical consciousness. Since lowland and many highland social organizations in these regions are hierarchical, people who have the means naturally tend to maintain stores of grain, first for their own needs and secondarily for their less-well-off neighbors' sustenance. In the event of widespread shortages, presumably, those who would normally sell an occasional bag of grain will at least survive. If shortages continue, it is possible that supplies in one area will be sold to less-well-endowed areas. In effect, grain is one of the most speculatable commodities produced by humans. By its nature it induces risky investment since its value at any given time depends on a host of unpredictables—weather, world production and demand, information on shortages—all of which render it of great value if stored through periods of oversupply.

This suggests that there are logical and compelling reasons why governments such as Indonesia's maintain a keen involvement in rice provisioning, following the colonial tradition of ensuring urban supply at affordable prices, and thereby depriving farmers of full market value for their surplus. In fact, on a number of occasions in Indonesia, prices spiraled out of control, owing to the low planting rate of many Javanese peasants (who had been forced the previous season to sell their rice to government troops below market value) (see Timmer 1975; Mears 1981).

To view money as somehow different from rice is not incorrect: money's value lies in confidence in the issuing state and in the potential liquidity of the money itself. But this is not a sufficient basis for an economy, as the centrality of rice policy in many Asian countries makes clear. In terms of subsistence provisions, the future is ever present in the minds of human consumers. Thus, the use of rice as a symbolic and actual store of transferable value and its mediating role in Batak spheres of exchange bring into relief the more widespread, general qualities and underlying values of rice—as a widely producible and indefinitely storable resource.[5]

There remains a tendency to consider social and cultural change in response to Western penetration in terms of "disintegration" (Meillassoux 1981; Fried 1975) rather than of selective, syncretistic adoption of the new. The appeal of the former viewpoint may be due to the complementary axiom of "culture" as a seamless whole, without internal contradictions, and as something wherein change in one part changes all the others. Though such axioms may seem useful for teaching introductory anthropology courses, they are belied by many studies of cognitive dissonance and social discontinuities. On the other hand, in spite of quite real discontinuities, it must be recognized that any group we gloss as a persisting "society" or "culture" has a set of values that are held with greater tenacity than sets of secondary beliefs.

[5]Recent years, with the exception of 1987, have been blessed with large surpluses, in Indonesia, creating storage problems, including soaring storage costs (having to do with such problems as insect and rodent pests, roof leaks, pilferage, etc.—which are far easier to manage on a household than a warehouse scale).

For the Samosir Batak, these are based on what Gudeman (1986) calls "metaphors of livelihood," involving both long-term relationships between lineages through marriages and the use of parcels of terraced land, shawls, large and small livestock, rice, and cash as prestige goods.

On the whole, this viewpoint avoids two inappropriate clichés about non-Western peoples: first, the notion that their societies are in the process of disintegration—that contact with Western culture dissolves their cultures—which implies the assumption that nothing is integral except Western societies; and second, the notion that all societies must pass through the same stages of development, and can all be located along a single developmental trajectory—what Hill (1986) refers to as an "historicist fallacy"—which carries the corollary that the assimilation of Western values is a matter of course.

Appendixes

Appendix A

Methods of Data Gathering

> Informants were not randomly selected. . . . [S]uch a procedure would have impaired the quality of the information collected and would have meant, also, that willing informants, who happened not to be included in the sample, would have been ignored. (Hill 1963:197)

For the first year and a half of the two years that my then wife, Hedy, and I spent in Huta Ginjang, Sagala, the bulk of my time was devoted to observing and recording the farming enterprise of some 112 subsistence households who lived in approximately 100 residences.

I attempted to gather socioeconomic data about all the households in the village, but it was impractical to question families each evening on what each member had done during the day. On many days villagers worked from early morning to sunset, and it would have required numerous assistants to catch them in the off moments of preparing for the evening meal. It would also have risked disturbing people while they were eating, which is not only bad etiquette but thought to be detrimental to the diners. I opted for the more time-consuming method of walking as wide a daily circuit of the village fields as possible to record the agriculture. The project gave me something to talk to people about on the great majority of days when nearly everyone in the village was busy working, and it gave villagers a means of understanding my presence and of explaining it to people living in the surrounding area. In spite of attempts to explain my research aims, they decided that the reason I kept clambering about their fields asking about their efforts was that I was an "agricultural scientist" (*Ingenieur pertanian*), and the teachers spread the word that Western education requires seeking *praktek* ("experience") to complement "*teóri.*" Only as they watched me attend, participate in, record, and, much later, transcribe many rituals I was invited to, did they become convinced that the research was not limited to agriculture.

I spent much of the first six months mapping fields and recording crops being grown. Because we moved to the village in July, the middle of the dry season of 1976, rice had already been harvested, and the main crops being grown in the village were irrigable bulbs (shallots and garlic), cassava, and corn. Dry fields for planting rice at the outset of the rains were opened during those months, and with the onset of the rainy season, rice, additional bulbs, sweet potatoes, and coffee seedlings were planted in a seemingly unending series of newly readied fields.

After I had learned the fields in cultivation and had gotten acquainted with most farmers without an intermediary (which took six months), I realized that the task of keeping up was hopeless—because of the physical difficulties of the situation and because of my wishes to talk for as long as possible to those whose fields I passed and occasionally to work alongside them for part of a day—and I hired three village youths successively as assistants. This enabled me to keep abreast of almost all dry and irrigable fields and who was opening fields for later cultivation. I usually planned our itineraries for complementary areas. Data on the kinds of work done, by whom, kind of labor (cooperative, wage, etc.), and inputs such as seed and fertilizer were gathered daily and later recorded by Hedy in household files, chronologically, by field. Yields often proved difficult to verify, since many crops ripen and are harvested in stages, but persistent questioning usually achieved what direct observation could not (see App. B, on means of measurement and margins of error). Even in cases where record keeping gave only a sketchy account of labor, it ensured a complete overview of the farming strategies undertaken by each household. I felt that the only way to avoid unconsciously selecting some segments of the population was to pursue this course. Biases were, in any case, built into the endeavor. One tends to gather more information about households with accessible fields or whose members have sunny dispositions than about those whose fields are hard to get to or whose members are reticent or uncooperative. I also found that I was getting more data about villagers related to the founder's lineage (V) when we lived in the lowest hamlet, Lumban Godang (see Figure 3.3 and Map 3.1), and partly for that reason moved to Lumban Buntu, the uppermost Sagala hamlet (Figure 3.4) for the last six months of our stay.

As the research progressed and the range and variety of farming strategies became clearer, a relative dearth of data for many households forced me to conclude that using a survey questionnaire would be necessary. By this time, with Hedy's help, I had earned the sometimes grudging trust of all but the most reticent villagers. We developed comprehensive data sheets on each household, and I used them as the basis for a questionnaire to round out sociological and agricultural information on as many households as possible. The data sheets were prepared during the 15th through 17th months of research, and I administered the survey in the 18th month. Fortunately, most villagers had come to accept my ceaseless questions on their farming activities and knew that I would double- and triple-check their assertions and question discrepancies. (I must admit that by and large there were few discrepancies.) Although many people proved too impatient to be asked everything I wanted to know (e.g., means or costs of acquiring building materials for houses), only one part-time resident was overtly mendacious. All the rest contributed to this study beyond the demands of courtesy, putting me heavily in debt to them. It is my hope that this book will partly recompense them.

Appendix B

Means of Measurement and Their Margins of Error

> Which of us is free from the semi-mystical belief that if you add up enough figures the errors are apt to cancel each other, the total having a significance altogether different in kind from the component figures? (Hill 1963:8)

Before the coming of Europeans, the Batak of Toba-speaking areas had a variety of volume measures, such as the *solup*, which were made of sections of bamboo. I was given the following conversion factors: 1 *solup* = 4 *bale* = 1 *tangkar*. The Dutch ordered the *solup* to be replaced by open "cans" (made of heavy-gauge metal), referred to as *tumba* or *liter* (though a *tumba* holds two standard liters). 1 *tumba* = 6 *tangkar* (condensed-milk tins), so a *tangkar* is 1/3 liter.

To measure by counting out level containers of a given volume is *marsuhat*. Contemporary market transactions employ *tangkar* and *tumba*, mostly the latter, as grain measures. Seed bulbs are weighed rather than assessed by volume in the market.

It was said that rice sacks called *tuhuk* (and before that, baskets called *ampang*) held 3 contemporary *kaleng* (1 *kaleng* = 10 *tumba*, or 20 liters)—i.e., 60 liters. They have been replaced by gunny sacks (*goni*) having one, two, or three stripes, respectively holding 5, 6, or 7 *kaleng*.

To my knowledge, indigenous measures of weight did not exist, except perhaps for gold (and opium?), of which I heard no mention. A very common implement, still in use, is the equal-arm balance, called *hatian*, which resembles our Scales of Justice. These are used for dividing a given mass into equal portions (*margugungan*), as is done with the meat of an animal jointly purchased by a group of villagers to provide meat for Gregorian-calendar holidays (such as New Year's Day). A Batak saying, declaring the imperative of unbiased administration of justice in disputes, refers to the equal-arm balance:

> The scales of integrity, the furrow that cleaves the rope,
> Neither wobbling upward nor dipping downward.

Hatian habonaran, parningala sibola tali,
Tu ginjang so olo munggil, tu toru so olo telleng.

The only possibly indigenous measure of length I encountered was *sangkolak*, an arm's breadth (though it is not reported in Warneck [1977]), of which 10 by 10 is said by some to be a *rante*. More precisely, in areas where land can be bought outright, a *rante* measures 20 meters on a side (400 square meters). Since 25 of these equal 1 hectare, 10,000 meters square, *rante* may well be an introduced measure of area. Typically, villagers speak of (our) "field area" in terms of the volume of rice or bulb seed needed for planting rather than in *rante*.

Long distances are usually referred to in terms of the time required to cover them on foot or by analogy to known walking distances. Sometimes the distance between two places may be referred to by the number of *batu*, 'stones' (set up at 1-kilometer intervals in building sections of roads under Dutch direction).

Partly because measurements of distance or of area in geometric terms are alien to the Batak, most of those I asked expressed misgivings about letting me measure their fields with a tape measure.[1] However, they had no objection to my walking through or around fields. By being present when plots were planted, noting the amount of seed of rice or roughly equal-sized bulbs, and then pacing the plots in broad, flat terraces and measuring my paces separately, I derived a standard figure of "area" according to given volumes of different kinds of seed. While the procedures could not provide truly precise measurement of area (and therefore all yields per area and areas under cultivation reported in this study are subject to some degree of error), the deviation was constant throughout the survey. I double- and triple-checked amounts of seed, and my paces, likewise, were deliberate and had, in the long run, a constant degree of idiosyncrasy. When crops other than rice or bulbs were being planted, most adults could give equivalents in the amount of rice seed necessary to plant the same field. Furthermore, since many fields were actually sets of terraces of uneven widths, peppered with rock outcroppings of different dimensions, the seed-to-area figures that were worked out on wide, flat fields made it possible to gauge the workable areas involved, whatever the terrain.

A variety of means (other than relatively infrequent direct observation) were employed to check the accuracy of reported yields. I asked both husbands and wives the same question whenever possible and pursued discrepancies. I noted horseloads of sacks of various crops, as well as basketloads, and these figures provided a check of sorts in later interviews. I complained to reticent or mendacious informants that they could not expect me to try to answer their own incessant

[1]Freeman (1970:156-157) has remarked on the difficulties encountered in attempting to measure parcels of land among the Iban.

questions on improving yields if I could not get a clear picture of their endeavors, methods, and results.

The villagers gradually grew accustomed to my prying questions. Perhaps they came to believe my insistence that I would not give out accounts of individuals' assets or income but would use the data only to arrive at statistical averages. Somewhat to my surprise, when I repeated the questions on the harvested yields of major crops like rice after a lapse of six months or even after a year, their recollection nearly always tallied with initial reports. (But since they measured their yields and calculated projected shortages many months in advance, this was nothing to be surprised at.)

For manure use, as for crop yields and labor, the totals given in the text are based on a large amount of direct and indirect observation, and only in rare cases on verbal assertions alone. They are, in all probability, understated rather than overstated. If an informant could not recall quantities with some certainty, the data were not used in arriving at totals.

Appendix C

Regulations Promulgated at a Church-Sanctioned Feast

The following is a translation of a promissory note (*Surat Perjanjian*—a title also used for land-pawn contracts), which is read in the inaugurating salutations propounded by a church minister at the start of most large feasts in Sagala. It was recorded at a bone disinterment feast in 1977, in Panjaitan, at the northern edge of the valley.

I, who have signed below, that is, the principal of this feast of the *gondang*, make everything in this endeavor subject to the rules of the Protestant Christian Church of Indonesia (GKPI). And these rules are as written below.

1. We shall not carry out a spirit-worshipping endeavor, such as purification [with water from the source of a spring], burning incense, putting up *Dracaena*, lemon leaves, or *Gandarusa* above the door, nor anywhere else.
2. Making oblations [and] offerings to the spirits of ancestors will not occur, since there is no meeting [lit., agreement] of the dead and the living.
3. Bringing about possession so the spirits of the dead come will not occur. If someone is nevertheless possessed, then the orchestra will be stopped and they will be reminded, so that they do not continually get possessed. [If they are asked one last time] they will be taken to a more solitary place [forced to leave].
4. They cannot rejoin the feast at any time of its duration.
5. Only after they have been removed can the feast be continued [lit., can the orchestra resume].
6. If it is not done like that, the feast will be paid no more attention by the workers of the church at its conclusion. And we the principals, we will be put out, punished by the church, if we willfully engage in spirit worshipping.

Thus we undertake this letter of promise, this oath-taking, with a pure mind, in front of God as well as in front of the clergy of the church of the principals.

Appendix D

Rice-Growing Statistics

The following three tables expand on the data presented in Table 6.3, that is, percentages of households with surplus, sufficiency, and deficit of rice produced. The "greater than," "(approximately) equal," and "less than" signs in these tables refer to surplus, sufficiency, and deficit, respectively (>, large surplus; ≥, small surplus; ≈, sufficient rice; ≤, small deficit; <, large deficit). The "strategies," which are referred to on the left in the tables, below, are the following:

A. Grows no rice (excluded)
B. Grows dry rice only
C. Grows dry and wet rice
D. Grows dry rice and sharecrops someone's wet rice
E. Grows dry rice and gives out wet rice for sharecropping
F. No dry rice but wet rice given out for sharecropping
G. Grows wet rice only

As for other tables in Chapters 9-12, referring to clan, age, and available labor, the same patterns were evident in the aggregate data for all households, i.e., including widows, childless couples, traders. Aggregate data for many of those in Chapters 9-12 for which only nuclear family household data have been presented in this book may be found in my dissertation (1982).

TABLE D1

Self-Sufficiency in Rice and Strategies Pursued by Clan

(81 nuclear households; percent of column in square brackets; percent of total in parentheses)

Strategies, and relative surplus		Sagalas		Wife-receivers		Wife-givers	
Substantial	B >	4		2		0	
surplus	C >	4	14 [34%]	2	8 [29.6%]	2	2 [15%]
>	D >	0	(17.2%)	1	(9.9%)	0	(2.5%)
	E >	4		3		0	
	G >	2		0		0	
Small	B ≥	3		4		1	
surplus	C ≥	1	6 [14.6%]	0	4 [14.8%]	0	2 [15%]
≥	D ≥	1	(7.4%)	0	(4.9%)	0	(2.5%)
	E ≥	0		0		0	
	F ≥	1		0		1	
Sufficient	B ≈	0	2 [5%]	1	1 [4%]	1	1 [8%]
≈	C ≈	1	(2.5%)	0	(1.2%)	0	(1.2%)
	D ≈	1		0		0	
Small	B ≤	1		5		3	
deficit	C ≤	2	6 [14.6%]	1	6 [22%]	2	5 [39%]
≤	E ≤	2	(7.4%)	0	(7.4%)	0	(6.2%)
	F ≤	1		0		0	
	B <	6		5		3	
<	C <	3	11 [26.8%]	2	8 [29.6%]	0	3 [23%]
Large	E <	2	(13.6%)	0	(9.9%)	0	(3.7%)
deficit	F <	0		1		0	
Unknown	E	1	2 [5%]	0	0%	0	0%
	F	1	(2.5%)	0		0	
TOTAL		41		27		13	
			51%		33%		16%

TABLE D2

Self-Sufficiency in Rice by Age 1976-77

(81 Nuclear Households; percent of total in parentheses)

Number, strategies, and relative surplus	Ages 19-24	25-30	31-36	37-42	43-48	49-54	55-60	61+
B >	1	2	1	2				
C >		2		4			1	1
24 > D >		1						
E >			1	2		2	1	1
G >					1	1		
Subtotals	1(1.2%)	5(6.2%)	2(2.5%)	8(9.9%)	1(1.2%)	3(3.7%)	2(2.5%)	2(2.5%)
B ≥	3	2	1	1				1
12 ≥ C ≥		1						
D ≥		1						
F ≥						1		1
Subtotals	3(3.7%)	4(5%)	1(1.2%)	1(1.2%)		1(1.2%)		2(2.5%)
B ≈		1	1					
4 ≈ C ≈					1			
D ≈		1						
Subtotals		2(2.5%)	1(1.2%)		1(1.2%)			
B ≤	1	1	3			1	1	2
17 ≤ C ≤			2			2	1	
E ≤					1	1		
F ≤			1					
Subtotals	1(1.2%)	1(1.2%)	6(7.4%)		1(1.2%)	4(5%)	2(2.5%)	2(2.5%)
B <		1	1	3	2	1	3	3
22 < C <				2		2		1
E <				1	1			
F <						1		
Subtotals		1(1.2%)	1(1.2%)	6(7.4%)	3(3.7%)	4(5%)	3(3.7%)	4(5%)
Lacking data E							1	
2 F					1			
TOTALS	5 (6.2%)	13 (16%)	11 (13.6%)	15 (18.5%)	7 (8.6%)	12 (14.8%)	8 (9.9%)	10 (12.4%)

TABLE D3

Self-Sufficiency in Rice by Available Labor Quotients

(81 Nuclear Households; percent of total in parentheses)

Number, strategies and relative surplus	Available Labor Quotients "19"	"20-26"	"27-30"	"31-33"	"34-38"	"39-48"
B >	2	2	1			1
C >	1	2	2	1	1	1
24 > D >	1					
E >	1			2	2	2
G >		1				1
Subtotals	5 (6%)	5 (6%)	3 (4%)	3 (4%)	3 (4%)	5 (6%)
B ≥	7			1		
C ≥	1					
12 ≥ D ≥	1					
F ≥	1		1			
Subtotals	10 (12%)		1 (1%)	1 1(%)		
B ≈	2					
4 ≈ C ≈					1	
D ≈	1					
Subtotals	3 (4%)				1 (1%)	
B ≤	4	1	1	2		1
C ≤	1	1	2			1
17 ≤ E ≤			2			
F ≤	1					
Subtotals	6 (7%)	2 (3%)	5 (6%)	2 (3%)		2 (3%)
B <	1	2	3	1	3	4
C <			1	2		2
22 < E <			2			
F <					1	
Subtotals	1 (1%)	2 (3%)	6 (7%)	3 (4%)	4 (5%)	6 (7%)
Unknown						
E					1	
F				1		
TOTALS	25 31%	9 11%	15 19%	10 12%	9 11%	13 16%

Reference Matter

References Cited

Alexander, Jane, and Paul Alexander

1982 "Shared Poverty as Ideology: Agrarian Relationships in Colonial Java." *Man* N.S. 17: 597-619.

Anderson, Benedict R. O'G.

1972 "The Idea of Power in Javanese Culture." In *Culture and Politics in Indonesia,* C. Holt et al., eds., pp. 1-69. Ithaca, N.Y.: Cornell University Press.

Anonymous

1977 "Anggi di Partubu, Haha di Harajaon" [Younger by Birth Order, Elder in Ritual Perquisites]. *Dalihan na Tolu* I (2): 31.

Appadurai, Arjun

1986 "Is Homo Hierarchicus?" *American Ethnologist* 13 (4): 745-761.

Banfield, E. C. with L. F. Banfield

1958 *The Moral Basis of a Backward Society.* New York: Free Press.

Bartlett, Harley H.

1934 "The Sacred Edifices of the Batak of Sumatra." *Occasional Contributions from the Museum of Anthropology of the University of Michigan,* 4: 1-31 (reprinted in *The Labors of the Datoe and Other Essays on the Bataks of Asahan (North Sumatra)*, Michigan Papers on South and Southeast Asia 5: 209-303).

1955 "Fire in Relation to Primitive Agriculture and Grazing in the Tropics: Annotated Bibliography," (mimeo). Ann Arbor: University of Michigan Botanical Gardens.

1956 "Fire, Primitive Agriculture, and Grazing in the Tropics." In *Man's Role in Changing the Face of the Earth*, W. L. Thomas, Jr., ed., pp. 692-720. Chicago: University of Chicago Press.

1957 "Fire in Relation to Primitive Agriculture and Grazing in the Tropics: Annotated Bibliography," Vol. II (A-G Tropics in General; H-J South Asia and Oceania) (mimeo). Ann Arbor: University of Michigan Botanical Gardens.

1961 "Fire in Relation to Primitive Agriculture and Grazing in the Tropics: Annotated Bibliography," Vol. III (mimeo). Ann Arbor: University of Michigan Botanical Gardens.

Barton, Roy F.

1919 *Ifugao Law.* University of California Publications in American Archaeology and Ethnology 15 (1).

1922 *Ifugao Economics*. University of California Publications in American Archaeology and Ethnology 15 (5).

Belshaw, Cyril S.

1954 *Changing Melanesia: The Social Economics of Culture Contact*. London: Oxford University Press (repr. 1968).

1965 *Traditional Exchange and Modern Markets*. Englewood Cliffs, N.J.: Prentice-Hall.

Biro Pusat Statistik [Central Bureau of Statistics].

1957 *Penduduk Indonesia II. Luar Djawa dan Madura 1957* [Population of Indonesia Outside Java and Madura, 1957]. Jakarta.

1971 *Sensus Penduduk 1971, Penduduk Menurut Ketjamatan diluar Djawa-Madura* [Census of Population, 1971, by Subdistrict Outside Java and Madura]. Jakarta.

1974 *Statistik Indonesia, 1972-1973* [Statistical Pocketbook of Indonesia]. Jakarta.

Bloch, Maurice

1975 "Property and the End of Affinity." In *Marxist Analyses and Social Anthropology*, M. Bloch, ed., pp. 203-228. New York: Wiley.

Boeke, J. H.,

1966 "Village Reconstruction." In *Indonesian Economics: The Concept of Dualism in Theory and Practice*, pp. 301-316. The Hague: W. van Hoeve (as cited in Keyes 1983).

Bohannan, Paul

1955 "Some Principles of Exchange and Investment among the Tiv." *American Anthropologist* 57: 60-70.

1960 "Africa's Land." *The Centennial Review* 4: 439-449.

1963 *Social Anthropology*, New York: Holt, Rinehart and Winston.

1967 "The Impact of Money on an African Subsistence Economy." In *Tribal and Peasant Economies: Readings in Economic Anthropology*, G. Dalton, ed., pp. 123-135. Austin: University of Texas Press (orig. publ. 1959).

Bohannan, Paul, and Laura Bohannan

1968 *Tiv Economy*. Evanston, Ill.: Northwestern University Press.

Bray, F. A., and A. F. Robertson

1980 "Sharecropping in Kelantan, Malaysia." In *Research in Economic Anthropology: A Research Annual*, Vol. 3, G. Dalton, ed., pp. 209-244. Greenwich, Conn.: JAI Press.

Brookfield, H. C., and P. Brown

1963 *Struggle for Land: Agriculture and Group Territories among the Chimbu of the New Guinea Highlands*. Melbourne: Oxford University Press.

Brosius, J. Peter

1983 "Significance and Social Being in Ifugao Agricultural Production" (mimeo). In the HITE Collection, East-West Center, Honolulu.

Bruner, Edward M.

1961 "Urbanization and Ethnic Identity in North Sumatra." *American Anthropologist* 63: 508-521.

Burridge, K. O. L.

1975 "The Melanesian Manager." In *Social Anthropology: Essays in Memory of E. E. Evans Pritchard*, J. Beattie and G. Lienhardt, eds., pp. 86-104. London: Oxford University Press.

Burton, R., and N. M. Ward

1827 "Report of a Journey into the Batak Country, in the Interior of Sumatra, in the Year 1824." *Transactions of the Royal Asiatic Society of Great Britain and Ireland* I: 485-513.

Cancian, Frank

1965 *Economics and Prestige in a Maya Community: The Religious Cargo System in Zinacantan.* Stanford, Calif.: Stanford University Press.

Castles, Lance

1972 "The Political Life of a Sumatran Regency: Tapanuli 1915-1940." Ph.D. thesis, Department of History, Yale University.

1974 "Internecine Conflict in Tapanuli." *Review of Indonesian and Malayan Affairs* 8 (1): 73-80.

1975 "Statelessness and Stateforming Tendencies among the Batak Before Colonial Rule." In *Pre-Colonial State Systems in Southeast Asia*, L. Castles and A. Reid, eds., pp. 67-76. Kuala Lumpur: Malaysian Branch of the Royal Asiatic Society.

Chayanov, A. V.

1964 "Peasant Farm Organization." In *The Theory of Peasant Economy*, D. Thorner, B. Kerblay, and R. E. F. Smith, eds. Homewood, Ill.: Richard Irwin (orig. publ. 1925).

Clark, Colin, and Margaret Haswell

1964 *The Economics of Subsistence Agriculture.* New York, St. Martin's Press.

Clarke, W. C.

1966 "From Extensive to Intensive Shifting Cultivation: A Succession from New Guinea." *Ethnology* V (4): 347-359.

Clauss, Wolfgang

n.d. "Subsistence and Commodity Production in the Simalungun Highlands of North Sumatra" (typescript in the author's possession, April 1981).

Codere, Helen

1968 "Money Exchange Systems and a Theory of Money." *Man* N.S. 3: 557-577.

Condominas, Georges

1980 "Agricultural Ecology in the Southeast Asian Savanna Region: The Mnong Gar of Vietnam and their Social Space." In *Human Ecology in Savanna Environments*, David R. Harris, ed., New York: Academic Press.

Conklin, Harold C.

1954 "An Ethnoecological Approach to Shifting Agriculture." *Transactions of the New York Academy of Sciences*, Series II, XVII (2): 133-142.

1957 *Hanunóo Agriculture: A Report on an Integral System of Shifting Cultivation in the Philippines*. Rome: Food and Agriculture Organization of the United Nations, FAO Forestry Development Paper No. 12.

1963 *The Study of Shifting Cultivation*. Washington, D.C.: Department of Social Affairs, Pan American Union (Studies and Monographs III, Technical Publications and Documents).

Cook, Scott

1966 "The Obsolete Anti-Market Mentality," *American Anthropologist* 68: 323-345.

Cortesão, A. (ed. and tr.)

1944 *The Suma Oriental of Tomé Pires: An Account of the East from the Red Sea to Japan, Written in Malacca and India in 1512-1515, and the Book of Francisco Rodrigues*, 2 vols. London: Hakluyt Society.

Crump, Thomas

1981 *The Phenomenon of Money*. London: Routledge & Kegan Paul.

Cunningham, Clark

1958 *The Postwar Migration of the Toba-Bataks to East Sumatra*. New Haven: Yale University, Southeast Asia Studies Monograph Series.

Dalton, George

1961 "Economic Theory and Primitive Society," *American Anthropologist* 63: 1-25.

Danhof, G. N.

1940 "Bijdrage tot oplossingkennis van het alang-alang vraagstuk in het Lampongsche districten" [Contribution to a Solution of the Imperata Question in the Lampong District]. *Tectona* 33: 197-233.

Darling, F. Fraser

1956 "Man's Ecological Dominance through Domesticated Animals on Wild Lands." In *Man's Role in Changing the Face of the Earth*, W. L. Thomas, Jr., ed., pp. 778-787. Chicago: University of Chicago Press.

Daubenmire, R. C.

1974 *Plants and Environment: A Textbook of Autecology*. New York: Wiley.

Davenport, William H.

1961 "When a Primitive and Civilized Money Meet." In *Symposium: Patterns of Land Utilization and Other Papers*, V. Garfield, ed., pp. 64-69. Seattle: American Ethnological Society.

DeWalt, Billie R.

1979 *Modernization in a Mexican Ejido: A Study in Economic Adaptation*. Cambridge: Cambridge University Press.

Dewey, Alice

1962 *Peasant Marketing in Java*. New York: Free Press.

Dixon, John

1982 "Use of Expenditure-Survey Data in Staple-Food Consumption Analysis from Indonesia." In *Food Security: Theory, Policy and Perspectives from Asia and the Pacific Rim*, A. H. Chisolm and R. Tyers, eds., pp. 241-262. Lexington, Mass.: D. C. Heath.

Dobbin, Christine

1977 "Economic Change in Minangkabau as a Factor in the Rise of the Padri Movement, 1784-1830." *Indonesia* 23 (April 1983): 1-38.

1983 *Islamic Revivalism in a Changing Peasant Economy, Central Sumatra 1784-1847*. Malmö and London: Curzon Press, Scandinavian Institute of Asian Studies Monograph Series No. 47.

Donham, Donald

1985 "History at One Point in Time: 'Working Together' in Maale, 1975." *American Ethnologist* 12 (2): 262-284.

Douglas, Mary

1958 "Raffia Cloth Distribution in the Lele Economy." *Africa* 28: 108-122.

Dove, Michael R.

1981 "Symbiotic Relationships between Human Populations and *Imperata cylindrica:* The Question of Ecosystemic Preservation and Succession in South Kalimantan." In *Conservation Inputs from the Life Sciences*, M. Nordin et al., eds., pp. 187-200. Bangi, Malaysia: Universiti Kebangsaan.

1983 "Theories of Swidden Agriculture and the Political Economy of Ignorance." *Agroforestry Systems* I (1): 85-99.

1985a "The Agroecological Mythology of the Javanese and the Political Economy of Indonesia." *Indonesia* 39: 1-30.

1985b *Swidden Agriculture in Indonesia: The Subsistence Strategies of the Kalimantan Kantu'*. Berlin: Mouton.

Drake, R. Allen

1982 "The Material Provisioning of Mualang Society in Hinterland Kalimantan Barat, Indonesia." Ph.D. thesis, Department of Anthropology, Michigan State University.

Echols, John M., and Hasan Shadily

1961 *An Indonesian-English Dictionary*. Ithaca, N.Y.: Cornell University Press.

Evans-Pritchard, Edward E.

1940 *The Nuer: A Description of the Modes of Livelihood and Political Institutions of a Nilotic People*. New York: Oxford University Press.

Firth, Raymond

1929 *Primitive Economics of the New Zealand Maori*. London: Routledge.

1963a *We, the Tikopia: A Sociological Study of Kinship in Primitive Polynesia* (second edition 1957; first edition 1936). Boston: Beacon Press.

1963b "Offering and Sacrifice: Problems of Organization." *Journal of the Royal Anthropological Institute* 93: 12-24.

1964a "Capital, Saving and Credit in Peasant Societies: A Viewpoint from Anthropology." In *Capital, Saving and Credit in Peasant Societies: Studies from Asia, Oceania, the Caribbean and Mid-America*, R. Firth and B. Yamey, eds., pp. 15-34. Chicago: Aldine Press.

1964b *Social Organization and Values*. London: Athlone Press.

1965 *Primitive Polynesian Economy*. New York: W. W. Norton (orig. publ. 1939).

1966 *Elements of Social Organization*. Boston: Beacon Press (orig. publ. 1951).

1967 "Themes in Economic Anthropology: A General Comment." In *Themes in Economic Anthropology*, R. Firth, ed., pp. 1-28. London: Tavistock.

1971 "Economic Aspects of Modernization in Tikopia." In *Anthropology in Oceania: Essays in Honor of Ian Hogbin*, L. Hiatt and C. Jayawardena, eds., pp. 47-75. Sydney: Angus and Robertson.

1972 "Methodological Issues in Economic Anthropology." *Man* N.S. 7 (3): 467-475.

1979 "Work and Value: Reflections on the Work of Karl Marx." In *The Social Anthropology of Work*, S. Wallman, ed., pp. 177-206. London: Academic Press.

Force, Ronald W., and Brenda Bishop (eds.)

1981 *Persistence and Exchange: A Symposium*. Honolulu: The Pacific Science Association.

Foster, George

1967 "Peasant Society and the Image of the Limited Good." In *Peasant Society: A Reader*, J. Potter, G. Foster, and M. Diaz, eds., pp. 300-323. Boston: Little, Brown.

Frake, Charles O.

1955 "Social Organization and Shifting Cultivation among the Sidangan Subanun." Ph.D. thesis, Department of Anthropology, Yale University.

Fraser, Lindley M.

1937 *Economic Thought and Language: A Critique of Some Fundamental Economic Concepts*. London: A. & C. Black.

Freeman, J. Derek

1958 "The Family System of the Iban of Borneo." In *The Developmental Cycle in Domestic Groups*, J. Goody, ed., pp. 15-52. Cambridge: Cambridge University Press.

1970 *Report on the Iban*. London: The Athlone Press (orig. publ., 1955 as *Iban Agriculture: A Report on the Shifting Cultivation of Hill Rice by the Iban of Sarawak*).

Fried, Morton

1975 *The Notion of Tribe*. Menlo Park, Calif.: Benjamin Cummings.

Friedman, Jonathan

1975 "Tribes, States and Transformations." In *Marxist Analyses and Social Anthropology*, M. Bloch, ed., pp. 161-202. New York: Wiley.

Geertz, Clifford

1963 *Agricultural Involution: The Processes of Ecological Change in Indonesia*. Berkeley and Los Angeles: University of California Press.

Gerlach, J. C.

1938 "Bevolkingsmethoden van ontginning van alang-alang-terreinen in de Zuider- en Oosterafdeeling van Borneo" [Folk methods of Bringing Imperata Lands under Cultivation in the South and East Districts of Borneo]. *Landbouw* 14 (7): 446-450.

Godelier, Maurice

1977 *Perspectives in Marxist Anthropology.* Cambridge: Cambridge University Press (partial translation of *Horizon, trajets marxistes en anthropologie,* Robert Brain, tr.).

Gonda, J.

1952 *Sanskrit in Indonesia.* Nagpur, India: International Academy of Indian Culture.

Greenwood, Davydd J.

1976 *Unrewarding Wealth: The Commercialization and Collapse of Agriculture in a Spanish Basque Town.* Cambridge: Cambridge University Press.

1980 *Community-Level Research, Local-Regional-Governmental Interactions and Development Planning: A Strategy for Baseline Studies.* Ithaca, N.Y.: Cornell Center for International Studies, Rural Development Occasional Paper No. 10.

Gudeman, Stephen

1978 *The Demise of a Rural Economy: From Subsistence to Capitalism in a Latin American Village.* London: Routledge and Kegan Paul.

1986 *Economics as Culture: Models and Metaphors of Livelihood.* London: Routledge & Kegan Paul.

Gudeman, Stephen, and Mischa Penn

1982 "Models, Meanings, and Reflexivity." In *Semantic Anthropology,* D. Parkin, ed., pp. 89-106 London: Academic Press.

Hagreis, B. J.

1930-1 "Ladangbouw" [Swidden agriculture]. *Landbouw* 6 (1): 43-76.

Hagreis, B. J., and H. Vonk

1927-8 "Beknopte beschrijving van den inhemmschen landbouw in Tapanuli" [Brief Description of the Indigenous Agriculture in Tapanuli]. *Landbouw* 3: 681-706.

Haibach, W. G.

1927 "Vervolgmemorie van de onderafdeeling Samosir, Pangururan, Mei 1927" [End-of-term report on the subdistrict Samosir] (typescript). SWO Library of the Royal Tropical Institute, Amsterdam.

Hamilton, Lawrence

1983 "Removing Some of the Myths and Mis-es (Misinterpretation, Misinformation and Misunderstanding) about the Soil and Water Impacts of Tropical Forestland Uses." Paper delivered at the International Conference on Soil Erosion and Conservation, January 16-22, 1983, Honolulu.

Hanks, Lucien M.

1966 "The Corporation and the Entourage: A Comparison of Thai and American Social Organization." *Catalyst* 2: 55-63 (cited in Van Roy 1971).

1972 *Rice and Man: Agricultural Ecology in Southeast Asia.* Chicago: Aldine Press.

Harris, Marvin

1968 *The Rise of Anthropological Theory.* New York: Crowell.

Hill, Polly

1963 *The Migrant Cocoa Farmers of Southern Ghana: A Study in Rural Capitalism.* Cambridge: Cambridge University Press.

1986 *Development Economics on Trial: The Anthropological Case for a Prosecution.* Cambridge: Cambridge University Press.

Hoebel, E. A.

1968 *The Law of Primitive Man.* New York: Atheneum.

Holt, Claire

1967 *Art in Indonesia.* Ithaca, N.Y.: Cornell University Press.

Hutagalung, Wasinton

1961 *Tarombo-Marga ni Suku Batak* [Genealogy of Clans of the Batak People]. Medan, Indonesia: Bin Harun.

Jasin, H., and Allan W. Smith

1978 "Distribusi daripada Pengusaha Pribumi dan non-Pribumi di Kotamadya Medan" [Distribution of Indigenous and Non-Indigenous Business in the Capital City of Medan]. *Ekonomi dan Keuanggan Indonesia* 26 (2): 165-173.

Joustra, M.

1910 *Batakspiegel* [Batak Mirror], 1st ed. Leiden: S. C. van Doesburgh.

Junghuhn, F.

1847 *Die Battaländer auf Sumatra*: Vol. 2, *Völkerkunde.* Berlin: Reiner.

Kahn, Joel S.

1976 "Tradition, Matriliny and Change among the Minangkabau of Indonesia." *Bijdragen tot de Taal-, Land- en Volkenkunde* 132: 65-95.

1980 *Minangkabau Social Formations: Indonesian Peasants and the World Economy.* Cambridge: Cambridge University Press.

Kellman, M. C.

1969 "Some Environmental Components of Shifting Cultivation in Upland Mindanao." *Journal of Tropical Geography* 28: 40-56.

Keuning, J.

1958 *The Toba Batak, Formerly and Now.* (C. Holt, transl.) Ithaca, N.Y.: Cornell Modern Indonesia Project, Translation Series.

Keyes, Charles

1977 *The Golden Peninsula.* New York: Macmillan.

1983 "Peasant Strategies in Asian Societies: Moral and Rational Economic Approaches—A Symposium." *Journal of Asian Studies* 42 (4).

Kipp, Richard D.

1978 "Adaptive Strategy in a Migrant Community: The Extension of Karo Batak Kinship Networks." In *Cultural Ecological Perspectives in Southeast Asia*, W. Wood, ed., pp. 165-173. Athens, Ohio: Ohio University Center for International Studies.

Kipp, Rita S.

1976 "The Ideology of Kinship in Karo Batak Ritual." Ph.D. thesis, Department of Anthropology, University of Pittsburgh.

1983 "A Political System of Highland Sumatra, or Rethinking Edmund Leach." In *Beyond Samosir: Recent Studies of the Batak Peoples of Sumatra*, R. S. Kipp and R. D. Kipp, eds., pp. 125-138. Athens, Ohio: Ohio University Center for International Studies.

Kirsch, A. Thomas

1973 *Feasting and Social Oscillation: A Working Paper on Religion and Society in Upland Southeast Asia.* Ithaca, N.Y.: Cornell Southeast Asia Program Data Paper No. 92.

Korn, V. E.

1953 "Batakse Offerande" [Batak Sacrifice]. *Bijdragen tot de Taal-, Land- en Volkenkunde* 109 (1 & 2): 32-51; 97-127.

Kunstadter, Peter

1978 "Subsistence Agricultural Economies of Lua' and Karen Hill Farmers, Mae Sariang District, Northwest Thailand." In *Farmers in the Forest: Economic Development and Marginal Agriculture in Northern Thailand*, P. Kunstadter, E. C. Chapman, and S. Sabhasri, eds., pp. 74-133. Honolulu: University Press of Hawaii.

Lando, Richard P.

1979 "The Gift of Land: Irrigation and Social Structure in a Toba Batak Village." Ph.D. thesis, Department of Anthropology, University of California at Riverside.

Leach, Edmund R.

1949 "Some Aspects of Dry Rice Cultivation in North Burma and British Borneo." *Advancement of Science* 6 (2): 26-28.

1965 *Political Systems of Highland Burma: A Study of Kachin Social Structure.* Boston: Beacon Press (orig. publ. 1954).

1966a "The Structural Implications of Matrilateral Cross-Cousin Marriage." In *Rethinking Anthropology*, pp. 54-104. London: Athlone Press (orig. publ. in *Journal of the Royal Anthropological Institute* LXXXI [1951]: 23-55).

1966b "Rethinking Anthropology." In *Rethinking Anthropology*, pp. 1-27. London: Athlone Press.

Lehman, Frederic K.

1963 *The Structure of Chin Society.* Urbana: University of Illnois Press.

Lévi-Strauss, Claude

1969 *The Elementary Structures of Kinship* (translated from *Les Structures Élémentaires de la Parenté*, 1949, by J. H. Bell, J.R. von Sturmer, and R. Needham, Editor). Boston: Beacon Press.

Lewis, Oscar

1951 *Life in a Mexican Village: Tepoztlan Restudied.* Urbana: University of Illinois Press.

Liddle, R. William

1970 *Ethnicity, Party and National Integration: An Indonesian Case Study.* New Haven, Conn.: Yale University Press.

1972 "Ethnicity and National Integration: Three East Sumatran Cases." In *Culture and Politics in Indonesia,* C. Holt et al., eds., pp. 126-178. Ithaca, N.Y.: Cornell University Press.

Lingat, Robert

1949 "Les Origines du prêt à l'intérêt au Siam" [The Origins of Interest-Bearing Loans in Thailand]. *Revue historique de droit français et étranger,* ive série 27: 212-235.

Loeb, Edwin M.

1935 *Sumatra: Its History and People.* Vienna: Institut für Völkerkunde der Universität Wien.

Malinowski, Bronislaw

1935 *Coral Gardens and Their Magic: A Study of the Methods of Tilling the Soil and of Agricultural Rites in the Trobriand Islands,* Vol. 1. London: Allen and Unwin.

Marsden, William

1811 *The History of Sumatra,* 3rd ed. London: J. McCreery.

Mayer, Enrique J.

1974 "Reciprocity, Self-Sufficiency and Market Relations in a Contemporary Community in the Central Andes of Peru." Ph.D. thesis, Department of Anthropology, Cornell University.

Mauss, Marcel

1967 *The Gift: Forms and Functions of Exchange in Archaic Societies,* I. Cunnison, transl. (orig., 1925). New York: Norton.

Mears, Leon A.

1981 *The New Rice Economy of Indonesia.* Jogjakarta, Indonesia: Gadjah Mada University Press.

Meeker, Michael, Kathleen Barlow, and David M. Lipset

1986 "Culture, Exchange, and Gender: Lessons from the Murik." *Cultural Anthropology* 1 (1): 6-73.

Meggitt, Mervyn J.

1971 "From Tribesmen to Peasants: The Case of the Mae Enga of New Guinea." In *Anthropology in Oceania: Essays in Honor of Ian Hogbin,* L. Hiatt and C. Jayawardena, eds., pp. 191-209. Sydney: Angus and Robertson.

1974 "'Pigs are our Hearts!': The Te Exchange Cycle among the Mae Enga of New Guinea." *Oceania* 44: 165-203.

Meillassoux, Claude

1981 *Maidens, Meal and Money: Capitalism and the Domestic Community* (tr.

of *Femmes, greniers et capitaux*). Cambridge: Cambridge University Press.

Melitz, Jacques

1974 *Primitive and Modern Money: An Interdisciplinary Approach.* Reading, Mass.: Addison-Wesley.

Middendorp, W.

1913 "Memorie van Overgave van de onderafdeeling Samosir, afdeeling Bataklanden" [End-of-term report on the subdistrict of Samosir . . .] (typescript). In the possession of D. van der Meulen.

Mills, J.

1922 *The Lhota Nagas.* London: Macmillan.

1937 *The Rengma Nagas.* London: Macmillan.

Mitchell, William E.

1988 "The Defeat of Hierarchy: Gambling as Exchange in a Sepik Society," *American Ethnologist* 15:638-657.

Mohr, E. J. C.

1944 *The Soils of Equatorial Regions with Special Reference to the Netherlands East-Indies* (transl. R. L. Pendleton). Ann Arbor, Mich.: Edwards.

Moore, Sally Falk

1986 *Social Facts and Fabrications: "Customary" Law on Kilimanjaro: 1880-1980.* Cambridge: Cambridge University Press.

Murphy, Robert F.

1970 "Basin Ethnography and Ecological Theory." In *Languages and Cultures of Western North America: Essays in Honor of Sven S. Liljeblad*, E. H. Swanson, ed., pp. 151-171. Pocatello: Idaho State University Press.

Mus, Paul

1933 "Cultes Indiens et Indigènes au Champa" [Indian and Indigenous Cults in Champa]. *Bulletin de l'École Française d'Extrême-Orient* 33: 367-410.

Netting, Robert M.

1968 *Hill Farmers of Nigeria: Cultural Ecology of the Kofyar of the Jos Plateau.* Seattle: University of Washington Press.

Nugent, David

1982 "Closed Systems and Contradiction: The Kachin in and out of History," *Man* N.S. 17:508-527.

Oboler, Regina S.

1985 *Women, Power, and Economic Change: The Nandi of Kenya.* Stanford, Calif.: Stanford University Press.

Oerlemans, L. J.

1937 "Memorie van Overgave betreffende de onderafdeeling Samosir" [End-of-term report on the subdistrict of Samosir] (typescript). SWO Library of the Royal Tropical Institute, Amsterdam.

Oki, Akira

1977 "Social Change in the West Sumatran Village: 1908-1945." Ph.D. thesis, Australian National University, Canberra.

1984 *An Indonesian Socio-Economic Study (Indonesia Shakai-Keizai Kenkyu): Minangkabau Economic Process and Social Change during the Colonial Period (Shokominchiki to Shakai-nenka).* Tokyo: Keiso Shobo.

O'Malley, William

1977 "Indonesia in the Great Depression: A Study of East Sumatra and Jogjakarta in the 1930s." Ph.D. thesis, Department of History, Cornell University.

Panoff, Michel

1977 "Énergie et Vertu: Le Travail et ses Représentations en Nouvelle-Bretagne." *L'Homme* 17 (2-3): 7-21.

Parkin, Harry

1978 *Batak Fruit of Hindu Thought.* Madras, India: Christian Literature Society.

Paynter, Robert, and John W. Cole

1980 "Ethnographic Overproduction, Tribal Political Economy and the Kapauku of Irian Jaya." In *Beyond the Myths of Culture: Essays in Cultural Materialism*, E. Ross, ed., pp. 61-99. New York: Academic Press.

Pederson, Paul B.

1970 *Batak Blood and Protestant Soul: The Development of National Batak Churches in North Sumatra.* Grand Rapids, Mich.: W. Eerdmans.

Pelzer, Karl J.

1948 *Pioneer Settlement in the Asiatic Tropics.* New York: American Geographical Society (orig. pub. 1945).

Pendleton, Robert L.

1939-40 "Some Interrelations between Agriculture and Forestry, Particularly in Thailand." *Thailand Research Society Journal (Natural History Supplement)* 12 (1): 33-52.

Penny, David H.

1964 "The Transition from Subsistence to Commercial Family Farming in North Sumatra." Ph.D. thesis, Department of Agricultural Economics, Cornell University.

Peters, Emrys

1960 "The Proliferation of Segments in the Lineage of the Bedouin of Cyrenaica." *Journal of the Royal Anthropological Institute* 90 (1): 29-53.

1967 "Some Structural Aspects of the Feud among the Camel-Herding Bedouin of Cyrenaica." *Africa* 37 (3): 261- 282.

Pires, Tomé

1944 (see A. Cortesão)

Polanyi, Karl

1957 *The Great Transformation: The Political and Economic Origins of Our Time.* Boston: Beacon Press (orig., 1944).

Popkin, Samuel

1979 *The Rational Peasant: The Political Economy of Rural Society in Vietnam.* Berkeley and Los Angeles: University of California Press.

Pospisil, Leopold

1963a *The Kapauku Papuans of West New Guinea.* New York: Holt, Rinehart and Winston.

1963b *Kapauku Papuan Economy.* New Haven, Conn.: Yale University Publications in Anthropology (cited in Paynter and Cole 1980).

Richards, Audrey

1939 *Land, Labour and Diet in Northern Rhodesia: An Economic Study of the Bemba Tribe.* London: Oxford University Press for the International African Institute.

Sadgopal, Anil

1981 "Between Question and Clarity." *Science Today* (October): 22-31.

Sahlins, Marshall

1960 "Political Power and the Economy in Primitive Society." In *Essays in the Science of Culture in Honor of Leslie H. White*, G. Dole and R. Carneiro, eds., pp. 390-415. New York: Crowell.

1963 "Poor Man, Rich Man, Big-Man, Chief: Political Types in Melanesia and Polynesia" *Comparative Studies in Society and History* 5: 283-303.

1965 "On the Sociology of Primitive Exchange." In *The Relevance of Models for Social Anthropology*, M. Banton, ed. London: Tavistock (reprinted in Sahlins 1972).

1972 *Stone Age Economics.* Chicago: Aldine Press.

1985 *Islands of History.* Chicago: University of Chicago Press.

Salisbury, Richard F.

1962 *From Stone to Steel: The Consequences of a Technological Change in New Guinea.* Melbourne and London: Oxford University Press.

1965 "The Siane of the Eastern Highlands." In *Gods, Ghosts and Men in Melanesia*, P. Lawrence and M. J. Meggitt, eds., pp. 50-77. London: Oxford University Press (cited in Strathern 1973).

1970 *Vunamami: Economic Transformation in a Traditional Society.* Berkeley and Los Angeles: University of California Press.

Sanchez, Pedro A.

1977 *Properties and Management of Soils in the Tropics.* New York: Wiley-Interscience.

Sarumpaet, J. P.

1986 "The Samosir Dialect of Toba-Batak." In *Pacific Linguistics*, C-94, Paul Geraghty, et al., eds., pp. 73-86.

Schneider, Harold K.

1968 "Economics in East African Aboriginal Societies." In *Economic Anthropology: Readings in Theory and Analysis*, E. LeClair and H. K. Schneider, eds., pp. 426-445. New York: Holt, Rinehart and Winston.

Schneider, Jane

1980 "Trousseau as Treasure: Some Contradictions of Late Nineteenth Century Change in Sicily." In *Beyond the Myths of Culture*, E. Ross, ed. New York: Academic Press.

Schrieke, B.

1966 *Indonesian Sociological Studies: Selected Writings of B. Schrieke*, Part I. The Hague: W. van Hoeve.

Schwimmer, Eric

1979 "The Self and the Product: Concepts of Work in Comparative Perspectives." In *Social Anthropology of Work*, S. Wallman, ed., pp. 287-315. New York: Academic Press.

Scott, James

1976 *The Moral Economy of the Peasant: Rebellion and Subsistence in Southeast Asia.* New Haven, Conn.: Yale University Press.

Sherman, D. George

1980 "*What* 'Green Desert'? The Ecology of Batak Grassland Farming." *Indonesia* 29 (April): 112-148.

1981 "The Culture-Bound Notion of 'Soil Fertility': On Interpreting Non-Western Criteria of Selecting Land for Cultivation." *Studies in Third World Societies*: Publication No. 14, *"Blowing in the Wind": Deforestation and Long-Range Implications*, pp. 485-511.

1982 "Social Organization of Samosir Batak Livelihood in Relation to their System of Beliefs and Values." Ph.D. thesis, Department of Anthropology, Cornell University.

1987 "Men Who Are Called 'Women' in Toba-Batak: Marriage, Fundamental Sex-Role Differences, and the Suitability of the Gloss 'Wife-Receiver.'" *American Anthropologist* 89: 867-878.

Siegel, James T.

1969 *The Rope of God.* Berkeley and Los Angeles: University of California Press.

1986 *Solo in the New Order: Language and Hierarchy in an Indonesian City.* Princeton, N.J.: Princeton University Press.

Singarimbun, Masri

1975 *Kinship, Descent and Alliance among the Karo Batak.* Berkeley and Los Angeles: University of California Press.

Siregar, Susan Rodgers

1979 "A Modern Batak Horja: Innovation in Sipirok Adat Ceremonial." *Indonesia* 27: 103-128.

1981 *Adat, Islam, and Christianity in a Batak Homeland.* Athens, Ohio: Ohio University Center for International Studies.

Skinner, G. William

1964 "Marketing and Social Structure in Rural China (Part I)." *Journal of Asian Studies* 24 (1).

Soemarwoto, Otto

1983 "Constancy and Change in Agro-Ecosystems." Paper presented at the HITE/EAPI Conference on Cultural Values and Tropical Ecology at the East-West Center, Honolulu, June 1983.

Soewardi, B., D. Sastradipradja, A. H. Nasoetion, and J. H. Hutasoit

1974 *Studies on Alang-alang (Imperata cylindrica* (L.) *Beauv.) for Cattle Feeding.* Bogor, Indonesia: BIOTROP Bulletin (SEAMEO) 8.

Stevenson, H. N. C.

1943 *The Economics of the Central Chin Tribes.* Bombay: The Times of India Press (repr. 1968).

Steward, Julian

1955 *Theory of Culture Change.* Urbana: University of Illinois Press.

Strathern, Andrew

1973 "Kinship, Descent and Locality: Some New Guinea Examples." In *The Character of Kinship*, J. Goody, ed., pp. 20-33. Cambridge: Cambridge University Press.

1977 *The Rope of Moka: Big Men and Ceremonial Exchange in Mt. Hagen, New Guinea.* Cambridge: Cambridge University Press.

Suryatna, E., and J. L. McIntosh

1976 "Food Crops Production and Control of *Imperata cylindrica* on Small Farms" (mimeo). Workshop on Alang-alang, *Imperata cylindrica*, Seminar BIOTROP, July 26-29, 1976, Bogor, Indonesia.

Tichelman, G. L.

1942 "Bataksche Sarcofagen" [Batak Sarcofaguses]. *Cultureel Indie* IV: 246-262.

Tideman, J.

1922 *Simeloengoen: het Land der Timoer-Bataks in zijn vroegere Isolatie en zijn Ontwikkeling tot een Deel van het Cultuurgebied van de Oostkust van Sumatra* [Simalungun: The Land of the Eastern Batak in their former Isolation and Its Development as a Portion of the Culture Area of the East Coast of Sumatra]. Leiden: Becherer (cited in Bartlett 1955).

Timmer, C. Peter

1975 "The Political Economy of Rice in Asia: Indonesia." *Food Research Institute Studies* (Stanford University) 14 (3): 197-231.

van Bemmelen, L.

1931 "Vervolgmemorie van Overgave van de onderafdeeling Samosir" [End-of-term report for the subdistrict of Samosir] (typescript). SWO Library of the Royal Tropical Institute, Amsterdam.

van Beukering, J. A.

1947 *Het Ladangvraagstuk: Een Bedrijfs- en Sociaal-Ekonomisch Probleem.* Batavia: Mededeelingen van het Department van Ekonomische Zaken in Nederlandsche Indie, No. 9.

van Breda de Haan, J.

1898 *Regenval en Reboisatie in Deli* [Rainfall and Reforestation in Deli], *Mededeelingen uit s'Lands Plantetuin* XXIII. Batavia: G. Kolff (cited in Bartlett 1957).

van der Meulen, David

1977 *Hoort gij de Donder niet? Het Begin van het Einde onzer Gezagvoering in Indie—een Persoonlijke Terugblijk* [Didn't You Hear the Thunder? The Beginning of the End of our Authority in the Indies—A Personal Retrospect]. Franeker, Netherlands: T. Wever.

van Leur, J. C.

1955 *Indonesian Trade and Society*. The Hague: W. C. van Hoeve.

van Roy, E.

1971 *Economic Systems of Northern Thailand: Structure and Change*. Ithaca, N.Y.: Cornell University Press.

Vergouwen, J. C.

1964 *Social Organization and Customary Law of the Toba-Batak of North Sumatra*. The Hague: Martinus Nijhoff (transl. from *Het Rechtsleven der Toba-Bataks*, 1933, by J. Scott-Kemball).

Villaverde, J.

1909 "The Ifugaos of Quiangan and Vicinity." *Philippine Journal of Science* 4(4): 237-262 (cited in Brosius, 1983).

Volkman, Toby Alice

1985 *Feasts of Honor: Ritual and Change in the Toraja Highlands*. Urbana: University of Illinois Press.

Warneck, J.

1912 "The Growth of the Church in the Mission Field." *International Review of Missions* I (1) (cited in Pederson 1970).

1977 *Toba-Bataksch-Deutsch Wörterbuch* [Toba-Batak-German Dictionary]. The Hague: Martinus Nijhoff (orig. publ. 1906).

Weiner, Annette

1976 *Women of Value, Men of Renown: New Perspectives in Trobriand Exchange*. Austin: University of Texas Press.

1985 "Inalienable Wealth." *American Ethnologist* 12 (2): 210-227.

Welter, C. F. H.

1935 "Memorie van Overgave betreffende de onderafdeeling Samosir" [End-of-term report on the subdistrict of Samosir] (typescript). SWO Library of the Royal Tropical Institute, Amsterdam.

Wittfogel, Karl

1956 "The Hydraulic Civilizations." In *Man's Role in Changing the Face of the Earth*, W. L. Thomas, Jr., ed., pp. 152-164. Chicago: University of Chicago Press.

Wolf, Eric

1960 *Peasants*. Englewood Cliffs, N.J.: Prentice-Hall.

Wolters, Oliver W.

1967 *Early Indonesian Commerce: A Study of the Origins of Śrivijaya*. Ithaca, N.Y.: Cornell University Press.

Ypes, W. K.

1932 *Bijdrage tot de Kennis van de Stamverwantschap, de Inheemsche Rechtsgemeenschappen en het Grondenrecht der Toba- en Dairibataks* [Contribution to the Knowledge of the Lineage-Relations, the Indigenous Legal Communities, and the Land Law of the Toba and Dairi Bataks]. Leiden: Adatrechtstichting.

Zinke, P., S. Sabhasri, and P. Kunstadter

1978 "Soil Fertility Aspects of the Lua' Forest Fallow System of Shifting Cultivation." In *Farmers in the Forest: Economic Development and Marginal Agriculture in Northern Thailand*, P. Kunstadter, E. C. Chapman, and S. Sabhasri, eds., pp. 134-159. Honolulu: University Press of Hawaii.

Index

Library of Congress Cataloging-in-Publication Data

Sherman, D. George, 1947-
Rice, rupees, and ritual: economy and society among the Samosir Batak of Sumatra / D. George Sherman, with the assistance of Hedy Bruyns Sherman.
p. cm.
Bibliography: p.
Includes index.
ISBN 0-8047-1666-8 (alk. paper):
1. Toba-Batak (Indonesian people)—Economic conditions. 2. Samosir Island (Indonesia)—Economic conditions. 3. Toba-Batak (Indonesian people)—Social life and customs. I. Sherman, Hedy Bruyns. II. Title.
DS632.T62S44 1990
305.8'9922—dc19 89-4408
CIP